# On the Fifth Day

# On the Fifth Day
## Animal Rights & Human Ethics

Edited by Richard Knowles Morris
and Michael W. Fox

ACROPOLIS BOOKS LTD
Washington, D.C. 20009

**ACROPOLIS BOOKS LTD.**
*Colortone Building, 2400 17th St., N.W., Washington, D.C. 20009*

*Printed in the United States of America by*
COLORTONE PRESS Creative Graphics, Inc.
*Washington, D.C. 20009*


**Library of Congress Cataloging in Publication Data**
Main entry under title:

On the fifth day.

1. Animals, Treatment of—Addresses, essays, lectures. I. Morris, Richard Knowles.
II. Fox, Michael W., 1937-
HV4711.05      179'.3      77-12983
ISBN 0-87491-196-6

# To Oliver M. Evans

*Industrialist, a Founder, Director and Past President of The Humane Society of the United States; Vice President of the World Federation for the Protection of Animals; a humanitarian, whose vision made possible this collection of essays.*

*Then God commanded, "Let the waters be filled with many kinds of living beings, and let the air be filled with birds."... Evening passed and morning came—that was the fifth day.*

*Then God commanded, "Let the earth produce all kinds of animal life: domestic and wild, large and small—and it was done. So God made them all, and he was pleased with what he saw.*

Genesis 1:20, 23 - 25

*On the Fifth Day*
*Creation of Beings began*
*Their fate determined by Man*
*For either good or ill*
*And so it continues still.*

Anonymous

# Contents

# Acknowledgments

To ACKNOWLEDGE HERE ALL THOSE INDIVIDUALS who in one way or another contributed to this project would be an impossible task. The man to whom this volume is dedicated and without whom it would not have come into being is the late Oliver M. Evans. Several years ago, Mr. Evans discussed with the Reverend Charles N. Herrick, formerly of the staff of The Humane Society of the United States (HSUS), the possibility of asking scientists, philosophers and theologians to submit formal statements of the latest findings in their fields where such findings might have bearing on questions of concern to those active in animal welfare work. Mr. Evans encouraged Professor Morris to edit the manuscripts, and early in the planning stages, these three men consulted Professor Robert S. Brumbaugh of Yale University, whose constructive suggestions proved most helpful.

Also deserving of gratitude is Patrick B. Parkes, Executive Vice President of HSUS, who carried out the many central tasks required for an undertaking of this kind, and the HSUS headquarters staff for bearing up under the added duties which the project entailed. Special thanks go to Mary M. Juliano of Rocky Hill, Connecticut, who typed the original manuscript.

COLEMAN BURKE
*Chairman of the Board*
*The Humane Society of the United States*

v

# Preface

THIS BOOK SETS FORTH THE MAJOR scientific, philosophical, and theological foundations for a humane ethics and humane attitudes. It grew out of the belief that a significant reduction in animal suffering will take place when the relationships between human beings and other animals are more fully understood.

The collection attempts to deepen and broaden this understanding, by bringing together the work of world renowned scholars in the fields of science, philosophy, and theology, and making it available to a wide audience. The contributors to this volume hold a special distinction in that each of them has taken a serious interest in the rights of animals as they relate to his or her particular discipline. A measure of the extent of the reputation of these individuals may be found in the biographical sketches at the end of the book. In the nature and depth of their commitment, they may be compared to Albert Schweitzer, Joseph Wood Krutch, and Rachel Carson.

The Humane Society of the United States continually seeks new ways to broadcast its central message and describe its activities to the millions of potential humanitarians who have yet to engage actively in the prevention of cruelty to animals. The national society and its regional offices annually publish a considerable volume of literature on such matters as animal shelters, humane education centers, the proceedings of leadership conferences, and legislative campaigns for laws to protect both wild and domesticated animals from the cruelties of man.

As an extension of our education effort, this book reaches out to students, scientists, educators, and theologians. It also speaks to the many aware citizens who are interested in ethology and ecology, and who have gained a sensitivity to the complexity of animal life and behavior, and the interrelationships among various life forms on this planet.

I hope that this book will receive the attention it deserves, not only in the colleges and universities, but among those thinking, sensitive, civilized citizens of the world who are as concerned as we are with the problem of how to reduce the suffering of all sentient beings.

JOHN A. HOYT, *President*
*The Humane Society of the United States*

Washington, D.C.

# Introduction

Now IS THE TIME TO SEEK THE FOUNDATIONS of a more humane ethics than we have. It is a time when humanitarians everywhere need common ground on which to build a united cause. It is a time when young people are increasingly aware of the total environment and exhibit a growing sensitivity for all forms of life. Yet, paradoxically, it is a time of violence, of indifference, of powerful lobbies bent on destroying what we once believed to be endlessly renewable resources. It is a time when physical and psychological cruelties to both man and beast abound, and the message of humanitarians is needed now more than ever before. This book was composed to help cope with these problems by contributing toward the development of humane ethics and humane attitudes.

The magnitude of animal research in today's universities and laboratories raises serious questions about man's relation and responsibilities toward other forms of life. Man's use and abuse of literally billions of animals for food, entertainment, companionship, work and clothing also call for an appraisal of these responsibilities. And we seem only recently to have become aware that man's insatiable consumption of the organic and inorganic resources of the biosphere cannot go on forever.

Man's debt to animals has been so enormous that it long ago generated a need for a humane ethics that would free itself of the human-centered concerns of the past and incorporate in the human duty the kinds of behavior dictated by man's interdependence with other sentient beings. Though the statistics on animal

1

consumption and abuse are staggering, no such ethics has yet appeared in the West.

The empirical findings of the physicist, biologist, evolutionist, ethologist, neurophysiologist and ecologist are forcing contemporary thinkers to reappraise traditional patterns of thought. Some of these findings are contained in the essays in this book. These new and emerging understandings of the inter-relatedness of all life should assist the humanitarian to forge a comprehensive ethics that could establish a more adequate conceptual scheme for interaction with other living things.

Until the conception of this book, the humane movement and animal welfare societies have done very little to probe and analyze systematically our present state of knowledge for guidelines with which to build a philosophy of life that would both explain and justify their concern. We have been content to rely upon individual sensitivity, emotion and insights. No one has seriously attempted to formulate a public rationale for what many have held to be a correct visceral reaction to the unnecessary suffering of infra-human beings at the hands of man. The problem is that this approach is open to charges of sentimentality, and it can keep people who are concerned about animals from effectively communicating their message to the general public, and to the university, scientific and theological communities.

The humane movement has, in the past, tried to educate the public, usually with an approach of exhortation: "Be kind to animals." To the callous or greedy, to the scientist with his cultivated indifference, to the utilitarian farm-animal producer, to the Western theologian for whom man is the only soul-bearer, to the philosopher obsessed with self, the named imperative is something easily ignored. The need for a humane ethics grounded in public, communicable knowledge has never been more urgent.

Why should anyone be humane to animals? Are humane attitudes the mark of a civilized person? Do people have obligations toward other living things? Do animals, who know pain, suffer anxieties, express loyalty to and dependence on people, have rights that deserve consideration? What are these rights? Are people debased by being unkind or cruel to other sentient creatures, or are they spiritually and psychologically unaffected by such actions? Can Western man survive without a radical modification of his values in

2

the direction of greater compassion, benevolence and service toward his fellow man and animals alike? What do various systems of philosophy and religion offer us in a search for a new ethics toward other living things?

These are the kinds of questions this book asks and attempts to answer. And they are the kinds of questions and answers that we hope will lead to a humane ethics which has been so long absent from Western thought.

*There are many recent developments in science, philosophy and theology in this book which embody elements required in any consideration of an ethics that adequately treats the relationships between man and other life forms.*

Our society will become more humane to the extent that the new understandings of science, philosophy and theology are incorporated in and made compatible with the humane ethics sought.

R. S. Brumbaugh provides a historical over-view of mankind's past attitudes and relationships with animals. Against this necessary background of how the past may have shaped our present view, R. K. Morris assays today's view of animals in religion, science and philosophy. Subsequent chapters by J. Feinberg and C. Dallery explore the question of animal consciousness and the related issues of animal rights and human obligations, both ethical and legal, towards nonhuman beings. The biology of humans may help us understand how we think and act, and likewise, understanding the biology of other animals may change the ways in which we regard and treat them. Contributions by A. Montagu and M. W. Fox deal with these biological parameters and help lay bare many myths and misconceptions about the nature of human and nonhuman animals which have hitherto contaminated our thinking. Objective scientific knowledge of the psychology, emotions, social behavior and ecology of animals add credence to the more intuitive, but no less valid, sense of fellow-feeling towards animals. Emotional concern over the well-being of animalkind does not have to be based exclusively upon anthropomorphic projections: it can, as these chapters reveal, be based instead upon a sound scientific and philosophical rationale. R. Caras makes a strong emotional appeal to reason in demanding an end to the countless abuses of animals in society today. Many of these abuses are based upon anthropocentrism, and such cultural blindspots in our code of ethics and religious beliefs are dissected by J. B. Cobb, Jr. On the other side of this essentially egocentric or human-centered world view lies the future fulfillment of humanity: fulfillment being possible only through a radical change in human values, attitudes, perceptions, and actions. With a firm foundation of humane ethics and responsible compassion, as elaborated upon in the chapters by C. Hartshorne and A. Freeman Lee, such a change is possible. Mankind has the power and potential to attain fulfillment in co-creative harmony with all life.

*The attitude and behavior of man toward other forms of life arise from the concepts we hold of the nature of living beings.* F. S. C. Northrop observed that our behavior is a function of the concepts we hold. It follows, then, that to change behavior requires a change in the concepts we are willing to entertain. How did we get the concepts we hold? This, Northrop insists, is the moral question of our time. To act benevolently, that is, humanely, would seem to require a hard look at attitude formation. This same view is expressed and explored by M. W. Fox, who develops a "biospiritual" ethics as an essential fulcrum to turn human attitudes and actions from egocentricity to ecoconsciousness: a world view where mankind assumes the role of humane stewardship.

The essays in this collection, we hope, contribute to a new humane ethics. They analyze humane values and attitudes toward animals as reflected in past and present schools of philosophy. They set forth empirical, logical, or authoritative bases for a new humane ethics. And they also explore the psychological, spiritual, and emotional benefits to be derived from conceptual schemes that adequately assess man's relation to other living creatures. These original contributions by a distinguished group of scientists, philosophers and theologians should provide the tools humanitarians and educators have lacked in their efforts to foster a genuine reverence for life.

This volume leads the reader through history, the intricate arguments, and the basic doctrines of the humane point of view. While the papers are as varied as the contributors themselves, the reader is certain to find common elements among the collected essays.

If this volume becomes part of the prologue to a new era of concern for the sentient life which cannot speak for itself, then it will have served its purpose. It can provide us with the necessary insight to help foster a reverence for all life and, by so changing mankind's relationship with the rest of creation, bring about a radical transformation in our ways of thinking, doing and relating. This book may help us therefore to become more fully human in our relationships with our fellows and our fellow creatures, that is, more aware, empathetic, compassionate and responsible: humane stewards with dominion over ourselves, working in creative harmony with all life.

Washington, D.C.                                    Richard Knowles Morris
                                                    Michael W. Fox

# Of Man, Animals, and Morals: A Brief History

# 1

*Robert S. Brumbaugh*

FOR 2,500 YEARS, WESTERN PHILOSOPHERS have been discussing the nature of animals, their likenesses to and differences from human beings, and the relations that should hold between other animals and ourselves. From the beginning of philosophy, some thinkers have held that animals were very much like persons, that their likeness to us created some ethical obligations toward them, and that they had some value in their own right. But an almost equal number have defended the opposite view, that animals are mere machines toward which we have no ethical responsibility, but which we are free to use for food, work, or entertainment. Until our own century, the debate remained undecided. The present essay is an account of major periods and positions in the continuing discussion. In a final section, I will suggest that we in the twentieth century—thanks to new findings in science and new techniques in philosophy—are finally in a position to decide the question, though it remained unsolvable until now.

## THE CLASSICAL PERIOD: FOUR ANCIENT GREEK VIEWS

At the beginning of Western science and philosophy, of which indeed they were the inventors, the ancient Greeks could not decide between the alternative notions about animals suggested by their religious, medical, and technological traditions. They explored four options: animism, mechanism, vitalism, and teleological anthropocentrism. This classical range includes the central ideas of later discussion, except that it omits evolution.

**Robert S. Brumbaugh** is Professor of Philosophy, Yale University.

6

Animism, the view held by Greek religious members of the Orphic group and by philosophers of the Pythagorean School, holds that animals and persons have souls that are the same in kind. These souls are indestructible and change the bodies they animate, moving for example from animal to human or human to animal bodies in successive incarnations. Some laws of cosmic justice regulate the succession of lives. One of the earliest jokes at the expense of an advocate of kindness to animals is a story invented about Pythagoras in the sixth century B.C. When a neighbor was beating a dog, the story goes, Pythagoras asked him to stop, for "it is the soul of my late friend: I can tell from his voice!"

A second Greek view, mechanism, holds that men and animals are mere machines. It is therefore like animism in considering animals and human beings to be alike but exactly opposed to it in holding that there is no "vital force" or "soul" differentiating living organisms from inert matter. The Greek mechanists held to a version of the atomic theory, according to which all of reality could be explained by the behavior of material particles moving through empty space. The "soul" in Greek religion would, in this view, be nothing but some complicated physical organ, which would dissipate at death. Somewhere in the background here may have been a technological tradition of building "wind-up toys"—animals and dancing puppets—with their mechanical imitations of "vital" behavior. At any rate, the mechanists argued that one can explain both physiology and behavior by a close analysis of the physical parts of organisms.

Vitalism, on the other hand, recognized a difference between organic and inorganic substances and a continuity—but not an identity—between the "vital principles" or organisms of differing kinds. Epitomized by Aristotle, this philosophic view was more influenced by the medical traditions of ancient Greece than by the religious or technological tradition. The vitalists stressed the interdependence of soul and body (this in opposition to the animists) and the difference between them (this in opposition to the mechanists). Aristotle saw a kind of scale or ladder of nature, in which higher forms of life shared simple functions with lower forms, but added more complex behavior. This scheme of continuity could have been combined with a theory of evolution, but in fact it was interpreted in terms of a timeless Order of Nature in which the set of types was always the same.

The fourth Greek view I have called by the rather clumsy name of teleological anthropocentrism because it is so nonintellectual that we have no technical philosophic label for it. It is not so much a position of professional philosophers as a "common-sense" philosophic standpoint, which seems to appear first in the eminently common-sensical writing of Xenophon. Xenophon defended the notion that everything in the world has been created for *human* pleasure, use, profit, and benefit. This is a splendid piece of wishful thinking, still repeated by some American business interests; it would justify anything we did to our environment and its content that was pleasant or profitable, in however short a run. Somewhere behind Xenophon's view lies a dim notion on his part that since God has built the system for our exploitation, we can count on Him to keep it exploitable and in repair. That notion is no doubt shared by a good many later Western thinkers who agree with Xenophon; but none of them takes the trouble to examine the assumption critically.

Among the Romans, the popular attitude toward animals is rather along Xenophon's line: they are best treated as things humans can use for banquets or amusements. The Roman schools of philosophy carried on the Greek debate in abstract analyses: the Epicureans, for example, were mechanists; the Neoplatonists tended to be animists; and so on. But those intellectual debates seem to have been far removed from the operative "philosophy" that dictated the way of life of the circus and the Forum. That was much more like Xenophon.

## ROME: SCHOOLS AND CIRCUSES

The historical phenomena of the Roman period are more difficult to understand. On one hand, animal training reached a new high point, with dancing bears and similar acts. On the other hand, the wholesale slaughter of animals—particularly exotic ones, such as giraffes and ostriches—became a popular spectacle for public entertainment, reaching, at its high point, a massacre of some thousands in one afternoon of the circus. At the same time, for entertainment, wild animals were loosed on unarmed opponents. The Christians were, for a time, considered criminals

8

deserving of this treatment. Some strange ambivalence is certainly involved here, for unless one recognizes *some* similarity between himself and an animal, there is no pity, fear, or victory in the slaughter of the latter. But such a recognized identity cannot bring sympathy—it must be in some suppressed hostile part of ourselves that we can feel this empathy. And perhaps the war of animals and people, with its shifting outcomes depending on the afternoon's program of entertainment, also reflected both a perceived identity and a desired superiority.

The following description gives a more detailed account of the games:

> *Venationes:* The contests of beasts with one another or of men with beasts, formed part of the shows of which the Romans were passionately fond. They were first introduced at the games of Marcus Fulvius Nobilior, 116 B.C. Those who took part in these contests were called *bestiarii.* They were either criminals and prisoners of war, who were poorly armed or completely unarmed, pitted against wild beasts which had previously been made furious by hunger, branding, and goading; or else hired men who, like gladiators, were trained in special schools and fully armed. Even in the last century of the Republic, and still more under the Empire, incredible expenses were incurred in the collection of the rarest animals from the remotest quarters of the globe, and in the other arrangements for their baiting. Thus Pompey provided a show of 500 lions, 18 elephants, and 410 other African animals; and Caligula caused 400 bears and the same number of animals from Africa to tear each other to pieces. Occasionally at these combats with wild beasts the man condemned to death was attired in an appropriate costume so as to represent a sanguinary scene from mythology or history, as, for example, Orpheus being torn to pieces by bears. Down to the end of the Republic these shows took place in the Circus, and the greater exhibitions were held there even after that time, until the amphitheaters became the usual places of performance; and indeed, when they were combined with the gladiatorial exhibitions, they took place in the early morning before them. [The repugnance of some of the more cultivated Romans for these exhibitions is shown in a letter of Cicero's, *Ad. Fam.* vii 1 sec 3.] They were continued down to the 6th century.[1]

Among the *philosophers* of Rome there were four schools, two inclined to stress the *continuity* of the lower animals and man, the other two producing treatises on the total *discontinuity* between beings with "reason" and "beasts."

But a polarization existed between these philosophers, with their abstract, intellectual convictions, and the Roman public, with its very concrete ways of seeking excitement and its keen sense of existence. While the philosophers—some of them—would repeat Plato's myth that the human soul is a charioteer, Reason, with two steeds, Spirit and Desire, the public would go to quite nonmythical chariot races, so designed that a 75 per cent casualty rate of gear and participants was about par for the course. Whether it was the risk to chariot, horses, or driver that gave this sport its great appeal seems never to have been analyzed by the Roman philosophers.

A final extreme of intellectualism in Roman philosophy was Neoplatonism, developed in the third century A.D. Neoplatonism had a doctrine of the unreality of the whole world of individuality, space, and time. For its proponents, no important ethical issue could arise concerning the way to regard other beings that were merely appearances in a rich ocean of unreality; and yet their belief in reincarnation underscored the kinship of living creatures, all fallen from an ultimate source of being. In fact, in moments of relaxation from his quest to escape, the Neoplatonic philosopher could revel in the richness of the forms of life his world contained and might feel a common bond with all living creatures in the shared desire for immortality.

## THE CHRISTIAN VIEW

Until the thirteenth century, Christianity was largely Neoplatonic in its philosophic structure. More than the other imported religions in Rome, it stressed community, love, and concern among believers; and one might think that these traits could easily have been extended from concern for persons to a concern for all created beings. Christianity prevented such an extension, however, and also asserted a doctrine of personal immortality, which implied an infinite gulf between the human soul and that of any lower animal. Perhaps the most accurate statement about the official Christian position from the fifth century to the thirteenth is that it was ambivalent in the matter of man's relation to other animals. Ordinary practice, however, with cockfights and bear-baiting, seems to have continued more in the tradition of the Roman theater than of the universal sympathy of a St. Francis. So, on occasion, did the Christians' treatment of pagans, or of one another; the fact that it was the *soul* that mattered, and that this soul was not physical but independent of the body, sometimes suggested that one might, with no disrespect to the soul, still mistreat or destroy the body in which it happened to be residing. Indeed, such threatened harm to the body could be seen as morally desirable, as a deterrent to wicked behavior that would affect the soul.

Some tension accompanied the thirteenth-century revival of Aristotelian philosophy and science, which brought with them a vitalism that was not compatible with the supposed discontinuity between men and the other animals. One particularly disturbing feature of Aristotle's thought was his distinction between two kinds of *purposes* or *final causes.* On the one hand, human beings might think "practically," looking for the value of things *for us;* but in nature each individual thing, viewed "theoretically," could be seen to have a kind of purpose and value *for itself.* From its own point of view, the young pig did not desire or regard as its destiny becoming someone's garnished roast of pork. From Xenophon through Aristotle through the Stoic school, the preposterous idea of a world designed for human exploitation diffused quite thoroughly into Western common sense. If God had not meant pigs to be roast pork, why did He make them so delicious? So ran the common-sense, teleological mind set.

Something a bit more subtle was needed, however, after the recovery of Aristotle and the translation of his science, along with Arabic medical and biological works, in the thirteenth century. For it began to look as though the pig had a soul, though a mortal one, of his own, with "faculties" of nutrition, locomotion, reproduction, sensation, and imagination—and even some dim "instinctive" desire for immortality of the species. All this comes naturally to a scientist who, as Aristotelians do, stresses

11

*observation of the external world* as the starting point of knowledge, as opposed to the Augustinian stress on *insight and introspection*. And it comes vividly to any medical man or zoologist who notices how elegantly the individual type-specimen contains its "final causes" in itself as a homeostatic organism. Yet in thirteenth-century Christian philosophy, the total gulf between an "active" and a "passive" mind, a "rational" and an "appetitive" or "vegetative" soul, had to be maintained.

Later, in the Scholastic tradition, the idea that animals might undergo unjustifiable suffering was rejected. Human suffering could be accepted; it was believed to be part of a divine plan in which, in the long run, virtue would be rewarded and in which suffering might be a necessary educational device for testing or teaching. Animal suffering, which had seemed irrelevant except to a few mystics and poets during earlier periods, required explanation when the older idea of an animal as an end in itself reappeared. For a nonhuman mortal creature had no future immortality in which God could balance and rectify its sufferings. Either, then, God would not be perfectly just, or mortal animals could not suffer. The final outcome was a late Scholastic doctrine according to which animals lower than man could experience instantaneous pain without fear and anticipation of its future continuation—but such a state was not to count as "suffering." (If Arabic or medieval philosophers had known of the class of anesthetics that produces "twilight sleep," under which the patient is conscious during surgery but fear and memory and anticipation of pain are suspended, they might have cited twilight sleep as an analogy. But I know of no evidence that there were any anesthetic drugs other than opiates known at that time in the West.)

Animals as characters in allegory and romance inhabit the medieval encyclopedias—such as that of Vincent of Beauvais—and the oft-copied bestiaries, descendants of the older physiognomic treatises and still older Aesop fables. Predatory animals took on new colors and properties in heraldry, with a style that we still use in athletics today: we see falcons and wolverines, but neither asses, cows, nor pigeons in the major leagues.

MODERN PHILOSOPHY: DESCARTES

Modern philosophy, after an explosive opening, was divided into the rationalists of the European continent and the empiricists

12

of Great Britain. The Continental Rationalists (Descartes, Spinoza, Leibniz, Kant, Fichte, Hegel) had unbounded confidence in systematic logic, pure reason, and the new science of physics. The British thinkers (at least Locke, Berkeley, and Hume) were inclined to put more trust in their firsthand experience than in the architectural skyscrapers of pure intelligence. Under the joint influence of Christianity and a new mechanistic physics, Descartes argued that all animals—other than man, who has an immortal soul—are simply machines.

Descartes, who began modern philosophy by rejecting Aristotelianism in both psychology and physics, saw a world divided very neatly into two parts. On the side of religion and psychology lay the (human) mind—with freedom of choice, the ability to use language, and a will. On the side of physics and physiology lay the body—a material machine, caught in the laws of conservation of momentum and matter, its nerves running "like bell-pulls" to receptive levers and counterweights in the brain. The behavior of animals was simply a result of the complex laws of mechanics. Medicine could best be developed, not as a separate art nor as a vitalistic enterprise, but simply as a branch of applied physics—a kind of carpentry.

Even by the seventeenth century, this idea probably had not penetrated very far into Western popular belief, which was in large part based on the small town and small farm experience of the ancient and medieval periods. Yet as early as the fourth century B.C. the Greek philosopher Democritus had suggested on theoretical grounds that animals are simply material machines. He had gone on to suggest that human beings are only machines, too. His ideas were taken over by Epicurus and the Roman Epicureans, but such ideas could, of course, not be defended during the early Christian and medieval periods. The idea has a special attraction, for inventors have always liked to build mechanical actors and animals. We would, it appears, like not only to communicate with other orders of living things (the myth of the golden age), have power to train them to respect our will (the dancing bears of Rome and medieval fairs), but also to create them (the dream of Faust's prize student, Wagner, and some others).

Yet the mechanistic theory in Descartes is quite different from ancient atomism. For Descartes, the human ability to use

13

language—which even the most stupid men have, yet the most intelligent animals lack—proved a qualitative difference so great that we can be assured that human beings have immortal souls, whereas all other animals are only machines. Descartes tried to imagine various mechanical devices programmed to respond verbally to different situations, but he concluded that *in principle* none could be built with the adaptive versatility of even the most backward French-speaking peasant. To drive this wedge between the status of man and that of the rest of nature, it became important to deny and disprove any analogies that might imply that animals have an intelligence like our own. It was also important to deny that our behavior is capable of explanation without reference to intelligence (or, as we might be tempted to say today, to human dignity and freedom).

In Descartes's most popular and justly famous work, the *Discourse on Method,* he asks his reader to convince himself that animals are in fact machines by buying and dissecting a beef heart, noting the valves, ventricles, and so on, that make it a thermal engine. Today this advice has lost most of the overtones it had in 1637; we no longer think of the heart as the seat of the passions, as a symbol of "great-hearted" or "lion-hearted" valor, and so on. But the intended ice-water effect on anyone inclined toward such sentimentalities, physiognomy, heraldry, Aristotelian zoology, or empathy with animals, is still quite clear.

It is hard to know just what to make of Descartes's insistence that respect for human dignity requires us to show no respect toward animals. He does not mean hostility, though as far as I can see he would find nothing *ethically wrong* with hostility, except that its motive might be irrational. Whatever we make of it, Cartesian thought reinforces tendencies that have militated against morality, sensitivity, and realistic observation.

With the prestige of Cartesian science behind the thesis that animals are mere mechanisms and the inherited misinterpretation of Greek philosophy that makes animals tools created for human benefit, we are ready for such views to disappear from Western European philosophic thought and be replaced by the theory of evolution by the end of the nineteenth century. Animals also tend to disappear from 1637 to about 1859. Less efficient than tractors, more ornamental

14

dead than alive (as hat plumes or shoe leather), and edible, they became dispensable.

But before the animal-machine view disappeared, it occasioned one of the most spectacular pieces of encyclopedic virtuosity ever written, the article on "Rorarius" in Bayle's *Philosophical Dictionary*.[2] With extravagant erudition, Bayle collected opinions as to the status of the souls of animals—and a contemporary reader will still find the collection interesting and illuminating. The title of the article reflects the thesis of one J. Rorarius that man is the least intelligent of all animals—a thought inspired when he heard some courtiers criticizing his great hero, Charles V.

In Bayle's article, two different themes are combined. The first is the soul-body or mind-body relation in general, the second is the rational-irrational distinction that separates animals from men. Bayle takes up the Cartesian view, which he thinks would be very useful to Christianity if it were only more plausible. He summarizes the Scholastic view of a soul with stratified "faculties." He analyzes the view of Leibniz, who resolved the mind-body problem by hypothesizing that reality was built out of small mental or organic elements, the "monads." The Leibnizian monads do not act directly on one another—indeed, since they are like souls rather than physical particles, they are unextended and "have no windows through which anything can go in or out." But they "represent" one another by way of a "pre-established harmony," which also correlates the laws of physics with laws of thought.

The Leibnizian influence on contemporary philosophy has been very marked; both Russell and Whitehead follow his lead in different directions. And Bayle, in the second edition of his *Dictionary*, believed that Leibniz had solved the question of the relation of the physical to the mental in principle, though not in detail. Souls are indestructible, but they change in the clarity with which they "represent" what goes on. Death is a sort of dimming of consciousness, a temporary confusion of awareness. Attractive as this view is, if one reads it as an anticipation of Whitehead's philosophy of organism, in which the final element is an "actual occasion" that is organic rather than inertly mechanistic, Leibniz himself would not hold such a view. His theological convictions led him to draw a sharp line between the "kingdoms" of Nature and Grace. In the former, God stands related to all souls and animals "as an inventor is causally related to machines"; in the latter (a kingdom of souls that have become brilliant by a special illumination), God stands "in the relation of a monarch to his subjects." And the Kingdom of Nature is ordered to further the Kingdom of Grace.

If, then, Bayle correctly saw an important principle in the view of Leibniz, he was equally right in seeing that Leibniz's detailed exposition was quite as inadequate as its application. Here are some sections of the *Monadology,* in which Leibniz falls back to a position close to Descartes.

> The passing condition, which involves and represents a multiplicity in the unit [*unité*] or in the simple substance, is nothing but what is called *Perception.* . . .

> [By sec. 82 the monads get totally transformed] . . . but when those souls which are chosen [*élus*], so to speak, attain to human nature through an actual conception, their sensuous souls are raised to the ranks of reason and to the prerogative of minds [*esprits*].

> It is this that enables spirits [or minds—*esprits*] to enter into a kind of fellowship with God, and brings it about that in relation to them He is not only what an inventor is to his machine (which is the relation of God to other created things), but also what a prince is to his subjects, and, indeed, what a father is to his children.[3]

If we have no idea of ecological balance, or of nature as having some aesthetic value in its own right—apart from its usefulness to *us* for lumbering or strip-mining—we simply extend the dualism that separated Descartes's human self from the rest of reality—mineral, vegetable, or animal.

### MODERN PHILOSOPHY: LOCKE

While the rationalists of Europe were insisting that animals *had to be* machines in order to make the overall systems of concepts work, philosophers in England and Scotland took another point of view. They argued that—no matter what abstract conceptual systems suggested about the matter—direct observation

16

was the final test of the truth of hypotheses. And on this basis it seemed to them that direct observation showed that animals were *not* mechanical and that the supposed infinite differences between human and animal "reasoning" could be interpreted as a matter of degree as easily as one kind. Perhaps not everyone would have accepted Locke's personal belief that causing pain or destroying life needlessly was morally wrong. But Locke set the tone for an empirical rather than a rationalistic temper in British philosophy. He was convinced that attitudes toward animals transfer to attitudes toward other human beings, hence that as part of a sound educational program, children must be taught to be considerate of animals as well as of each other.

Current American common sense in politics, education, and atittudes toward animals comes from Locke, whereas the part of it that deals with science, matter, causality, and mathematics is still dominated by the ideas of Descartes and his followers down through Kant. *(This historical split explains certain current inconsistencies. The attitude of a medical experimenter is going to be Cartesian, while that of a bird-watcher or pet owner will be Lockean, and the two just do not coincide.)*

Locke wrote:

> One thing I have frequently observed in Children, that when they have got possession of any poor Creature, they are apt to use it ill: They often *torment*, and treat very roughly, young Birds, Butterflies, and such other poor Animals, which fall into their Hands, and that with a seeming kind of Pleasure. This I think should be watched in them, and if they incline to any such *Cruelty*, they should be taught the contrary Usage. For the Custom of Tormenting and Killing of Beasts, will, by Degrees, harden their Minds even towards Men; and they who delight in the Suffering and Destruction of Inferiour Creatures, will not be apt to be very compassionate, or benign to those of their own kind. . . .
>
> I cannot but commend both the Kindness and Prudence of a Mother I knew, who was wont always to indulge her daughters, when any of them desired Dogs, Squirils, Birds, or any such things, as young Girls use to be delighted with: But then, when they had them, they must be sure to keep them well and look diligently after them, that they wanted nothing, or were not ill used. . . .[4]

17

In England, psychology was explored in a much more medical, or in some ways more mechanistic, spirit than it had been on the Continent after the seventeenth century, and the result was the discovery of new analogies between the connections of experience and behavior for both animal and human subjects. Hume's work constituted a final challenge to his opponents to show any significant way in which human thinking, operating by the laws of association of ideas, differed from the reasoning of animals, except in subtlety.

Anthropology later added its contribution, inspired by such voyages as those of Columbus and the discovery of primitive peoples in the New World. It turned out that the line between nonhuman and human animals was not easy to draw, and it was partly through the good luck of having Father Las Casas as its observer that the Spanish Colonial Office finally officially put the Indians barely across the line on the human side.

Rousseau and Voltaire, with their myth of the Noble Savage, put primitive natives firmly on the human side, only to find civilized man a more problematic case.

## MODERN PHILOSOPHY: KANT AND THE UTILITARIANS

The different philosophic attitudes of England and the Continent continued to be reflected in the later Continental ethical systems of Kant—a rationalistic ethics resting on dignity and duty—and of English Utilitarianism—an ethics resting on utility and pleasure.

In Kant's ethics, man alone has a free and responsible "self" that deserves respect. Pleasure, pain, and practical advantage are *ethically irrelevant* in his view; and indeed, they are regarded with some suspicion, since they tempt us to give up our freedom. This is not a comfortable position, since Kant's free human selves are at the same time caught in the mechanism of a deterministic physical universe. The dilemma is the result of taking Newtonian physics absolutely literally and seriously and then trying to find a mechanical account of human responsibility. The Kantian position includes the view that all the lower animals are mere machines toward which we have no *ethical* responsibility. Thus the Cartesian

18

split between human selves and everything else in creation is perpetuated.

In England, there is a tendency to take physical science less seriously than on the Continent. (Part of the reason may be that English philosophers were historians, diplomats, or psychologists rather than scientists.) Ethics is based in sentiments or feelings rather than in an absolute rationality and dignity. This tradition culminated in Utilitarianism, an ethics of consequences and of the pursuit of maximum pleasure—the latter concept given somewhat different formulations by Bentham and Mill. Where Kant ruled pain and pleasure to be ethically irrelevant, Bentham defined the ethical action as that course which leads to a "maximum excess of pleasure over pain." In calculating the outcome of an action, one must regard each person as equal to any other—an excellent technical or rhetorical device on Bentham's part for pointing out that even peasants and factory workers have feelings of pain and pleasure. But the position, extended beyond its political application, involves technical difficulties in its assumption that one moment of pleasure or pain is equal to any other. The first difficulty is where to draw the line between the moments of pain of adults, children, infants, higher animals, and other animals. (An Englishman using his common sense will be inconsistent here rather than accept the position that *all* living things must be respected and never killed—he will probably feel, for example, that mosquitoes should be wiped out.)

Bentham might have protested that he had only meant to discuss the consequences of legislation for citizens, not to wander off into such remote speculation. But, whether or not they were influenced by his notion that every pain or pleasure counts, British and American legislatures within half a century were passing laws to protect animals and children from cruel treatment—this had already been done for criminals.

## EVOLUTION

What finally changed the whole discussion of animals and our relation to them was the theory of evolution and its impact on science and philosophy. The idea that nature is ordered on a scale from higher to lower had existed in the West ever since the Greeks; but the evidence establishing the historical reason for this—that "higher" forms on the scale had, historically, developed from "lower" ones—was pieced together conclusively only in the nineteenth century. The indirect effects were multiple. For one thing, the theory suggested a kind of time that was different from the repeating cycles proposed in earlier cosmological theory or the wholly predictable collisions and separations between the unchangeable particles of a classical mechanistic model. The time in which evolution can occur must be radically one-directional and linear, with an element of creativity in its advance. Even if one could reduce the process of evolution to a mechanical screening by natural selection, still the qualitative changes that emerge with time suggest advancing process as the final nature of things.

The continuity of forms of life implied by this theory seemed to justify an attempt to understand lower forms as qualitatively similar to the higher ones, though with less differentiation and intensity. Something like an "appetite" for value, a "mental pole," seemed to run all the way through nature. Considerable resistance to any such idea occurred among religious thinkers eager to stress the *discontinuity* of man and the rest of creation, but by and large the new scientific ideas have found religious acceptance—if somewhat gradually.

Perhaps the most interesting impact of the evolutionary view was its suggestion that the ultimate units of process might not be hard material particles but might themselves be processes, more like elementary organisms. The advent of the theory of relativity in physics, which forced natural science to give up its simpler mechanistic models and its total self-assurance, helped pave the way for this new reading of nature as "alive." Some of the most interesting extensions of these changes in views have been in the development of "process theology."

The discovery of continuity explains two things. First, it gives a clear causal (or at least sequential) account of why the results of experiments with animals also apply to human beings, so far as they do. Second, it suggests why human beings are able to recognize the feelings and behavior patterns of other animals. But these two implications are not easy to adjust in practice. For if "lower" animals have feelings and experiences analogous to our own, we have a certain ethical, or at least aesthetic, responsibility toward them. But insofar as we want to use animals for efficient,

20

objective experimental or educational purposes, any such consideration of their interests will interfere. In fact, teachers today often deliberately set about desensitizing students to the animals they study.

Some current developments suggest that the recognition of resemblances between other animals and ourselves will play a more important role in the next decade. Ethology, for example, has redirected attention to group behavior of animals in their native habitats, and elementary social structure has been found. Physical anthropology even finds that social structure among great apes is not all that elementary. Observers are trying to isolate and study animal traits such as aggression and territoriality that seem to persist up the evolutionary scale and that may give us needed insights into human social behavior.

### CONTEMPORARY WORK: IN SIGHT OF A RESOLUTION

Given the theory of evolution, the advances of twentieth-century philosophy seem, finally, to be on the point of offering new insights and techniques that can resolve the long deadlock we have been tracing through Western philosophic thought.

The first relevant advance is a clarification, by way of formal logical and philosophical analysis, of just what is meant by "ethical responsibility." Modern deontic logic offers two particularly important insights here. The first is simply a sharpening of an idea often accepted in modern thought, that "things identical in kind are identical in value, and can be substituted for one another in ethical or legal formulas." F. S. C. Northrop, in his *Complexity of Legal and Ethical Experience,* points out that Western concepts of person and the law correspond to some of the postulational techniques of scientific thought.[5] The general formula for this rule is that if $x$ is a variable standing for any person, and if $a$ is one person and $b$ is another, then whatever holds for every $x$ holds for $a$ and for $b$. In talking about relations between persons, rather than the relation between individuals and the law, we find a logical relation between rights and obligations: whenever $a$ has a right, $b$ has an obligation to respect it. Rights and obligations thus mutually imply each other.

It is important to notice that when we are talking in this very formal, precise way about the equal rights of $a$ and $b$, for example,

21

we do so on the assumption that both share a common characteristic, $P$. That is, since both are citizens, or adult human beings, or whatever, the formula applies. While there have been many arguments and quibbles about which characteristics should count, the general formula leads to the important implication that insofar as we and other animals are alike, they have certain rights in their relations to us, and we have correlative obligations toward them as a result of this likeness. For example, if it is wrong to inflict pain pointlessly on any $x$ that has the characteristic of being capable of feeling pain, then even if $a$ is an admiral and $b$ is a flatworm, it is wrong to inflict pain pointlessly on either one. If the admiral does not see it that way, we must try to get him to put himself, if only for a brief moment, in the place of the flatworm. (Only a few of the animists discussed earlier would think that the flatworm might be able to put himself in the place of the admiral.) If we use modern logical notation, we can write out a pattern of relations in the form "for every $x$, if $x$ is a $P$, then $x$ is a $Q$," in this way: $(x) P (x) \supset Q (x)$. And we can indicate that $a$ and $b$ both are instances of $x$ by a special way of writing "for $x$, $a$ can be substituted," and "for $x$, $b$ can be substituted": $x/a$, $x/b$. The statement that for every $x$, if $x$ has a sense of pain, then $x$ has a right not to be hurt needlessly is a case of the general pattern. The logical rule that we have been arguing for is that in such a case, if $x/a$ and $x/b$, then $P(a) \supset Q (a)$ and $P(b) \supset Q(b)$.

This is a neat formal clarification, yet the reader may feel that it leaves the *substantive* issues just as undecided as before. For example, *if* all animals were mere machines and so could not suffer, any argument claiming that we are ethically responsible for preventing their pointless suffering would of course be absurd. Yet how does one tell whether only some pathetic fallacy or a genuine objective similarity justifies the comparison of an admiral to a flatworm? At this juncture, a new philosophical method, that of *phenomenology*, is extremely relevant and promising.

As our look at past history has shown, philosophers have tended to approach such particular questions as the nature of animals in the context of a whole system of commitments and preconceptions. Each believes he already knows the way the world is "supposed to be," whether his model is animistic, mechanistic, vitalistic, or teleological. As a consequence, each observation is adjusted to fit the rules and concepts that are supposed to determine what can possibly exist to be observed and what is going to count as an "observation."

Phenomenologists are now developing a technique of making and reporting observations without first running them through a screen of assumptions to decide whether what we actually saw or felt was or was not possible. A medieval Christian abbot, committed firmly to the notion that dogs are mortal mechanisms, might pass a pleasant afternoon playing ball with the abbey's pet St. Bernard. He might have more fun and use more strategy in the game than he would have had he played with one of the less adroit brothers in the monastery; yet he not only *would not* but *could not* have seen the dog's behavior as vital, goal-oriented, radically nonmechanical. A philosopher who has read Descartes and is preoccupied with some mind-body problem knows before the question is posed that the baseball bat of a professional player cannot be a part of his body. It is really only a tool, the motions and momentums of which are calculated inferentially. But no ballplayer ever felt that the bat was related to him in that way; the philosopher is so concerned to be consistent with the presuppositions of his description that he quite misses the concrete situation.

The first step toward applying this new technique to the question of the nature of living things has been taken by Hans Jonas, in his pioneering book, *The Phenomenon of Life*. A considerably greater tolerance for what *is there*, as opposed to what we have *assumed* must be there, has found its way into recent work on animals in such areas as studies of aggression, territory, ape society, and ethology generally. And, unless I am completely mistaken, continuation of this approach will finally establish, beyond doubt and without elaborate hypothetical superstructure, enough basic resemblance between human beings and other animals to make our ethical responsibility toward them clear.

The development of ecology and the popular interest in it suggest that there will be increasing recognition of the aesthetic experience and the physical interdependence of the total balanced order of nature. This is an order in which we are parts, not masters; disastrous experience has by now proven (to anyone who might have doubted it) that the old view of nature as intended for

23

human exploitation leads to the suicide of man. The other animals are parts of this order as well: they can be interesting, educational, aesthetically satisfying. In future philosophies animals will probably be recognized for themselves and not considered designed solely for human satisfaction. They will be looked upon as parts of a much larger order; and they will be considered to have a right to be there.

I think this current intersection of ethics, phenomenology, and ecology can lead to a new understanding of the questions whose history we have been tracing. Interestingly, we seem to have followed a long circuit and come back to the world of the ancient Greeks, a world of nature alive—but we have come back with a new sense of individual human dignity and ethical compassion.

Yet as Locke realized, it is still very easy to educate people to think of any living thing different from themselves as an unfeeling (or less sensitive) machine—whether the difference from oneself is in the number of legs, or in the sex, or in the skin color. To allow this assumption is a stupid bit of miseducation, wrong in every way. But it is a natural transfer from the sadistic fun of the Roman amphitheater, or the Cartesian reduction of animals to machines, or the narrow attitude that pervades the modern experimental laboratory, or the style of the hunter who can only be superior by destroying.

A look at the history of philosophy, a survey of the present findings of science, and a consultation of the world's religions suggest that we must take sides in this matter—and they suggest which side we must take.

CONCLUSION

In conclusion, we might look again at the suggestions in the first section of this brief history. There I predicted that current work in philosophy and science would facilitate a decision between alternative views that have been in competition through 2,500 years of Western intellectual history.

Work in formal logic (particularly deontic logic) and the analysis of legal concepts will, I believe, clarify the notion of ethical obligation in such a way that as soon as the facts of our likeness to or remoteness from other animals are established, the legal and ethical implications of those facts will at once be clear.

Further development of phenomenology promises to be decisive in establishing the fact that animals are like us.

The implications of ecology for philosophy clearly rule out the evasive assertion, often used in the past, that all we need to be concerned with are the human pleasure and profit that can be gained by exploiting the environment. Continuing *that* mind set, it is now clear, will result not only in the destruction of the environment but in the disappearance of human profit and pleasure altogether as the human race vanishes.

Perhaps it was not until the nineteenth century that decisions could be made among the alternative views that were proposed. But by the twentieth century, Western science and philosophy have agreed on a theory of evolution, which involves a continuity among lower and higher forms of life and rules out any theories postulating an *infinite* gap between human beings and living things of any other kind. On the other hand, better observation and study have long since confirmed the significant differences between men and other animals, differences that led some of the ancient Greeks to reject the idea of a fixed number of transmigrating souls that stay essentially alike and the same regardless of what bodies they may animate at any given time.

The conclusion is that we can learn from animals, appreciate them, share projects with them—and that we are ethically responsible to them just insofar as each species is or is not like ourselves. We may or may not care for sentimentality, but we can hardly fail to agree with Locke that there is no excuse for needless and arbitrary cruelty and that it is morally perverse to enjoy paining or destroying any living creature.

## NOTES

1. "Venationes," in O. Seyffert, *A Dictionary of Classical Antiquities,* trans. and rev. H. Nettleship and J. E. Sandys (London: S. Sonnenschein & Co., 1891).
2. "Rorarius," in Pierre Bayle, *Dictionnaire Historique et Critique,* 3rd ed., revised, (Rotterdam: M. Bohm, 1720) 4 vols.
3. G. W. Leibniz, *The Monadology,* trans. G. Montgomery (Chicago: Open Court Publishing Co., 1902), sec. 14, 82, 84.
4. John Locke, *Some Thoughts Concerning Education,* 5th ed. (London: printed for A. and J. Churchill, 1705). See James Axtell, ed., *The Educational Writings of John Locke* (Cambridge: Cambridge University Press, 1968), sec. 116, pp. 225-226.
5. F. S. C. Northrop, *The Complexity of Legal and Ethical Experience* (Boston: Little Brown & Co., 1959).

# Man and Animals: Some Contemporary Problems

2

*Richard Knowles Morris*

I T IS THE PURPOSE OF THIS ESSAY (1) to unmask some of the conditioning agents still operative in our culture that program modern man to ignore what he may directly intuit—namely, the unitary relationship between himself and all other forms of life; (2) to demonstrate as far as possible how these constraints contribute to our inability to devise a communicable explanation of this relationship that would bring it into the realm of public knowledge for consideration and debate; and (3) to sketch in brief outline some of the principal elements in a world view that recognizes the aforementioned relationship and calls for a thorough reconsideration of human conduct toward other living things.

Each of the three stated purposes is modified by the word "some" or the phrase "as far as possible." Therefore, this essay makes no pretense at being exhaustive of the areas chosen for discussion, or definitive in any sense whatsoever. It does claim to speak to the theme of this volume and to consider the religious, scientific, educational, and philosophical problems as each speaks, or fails to speak, to the better treatment by man of other sentient beings.

## THE RELIGIOUS PROBLEM

The Judeo-Christian tradition that largely provides the foundations for the ethical character of Western culture has left us with the heavy legacy of a man-centered view of the universe, whether one speaks of the universe in physical or metaphysical terms. The ambivalence of the Bible in deciding the true

**Richard Knowles Morris** is Professor of Education and Anthropology, *Emeritus*, Trinity College (Hartford, Connecticut).

relationship between man and the animals often puts its arguments beyond the pale of reasonable discussion. In Genesis the Lord begins creation by making both man and the animals vegetarians (Gen. 1:29-30),[1] but not before He had given man "dominion over the fish of the sea, and over the fowl of the air, and over the cattle, and over all the earth, and over every creeping thing that creepeth upon the earth" (Gen. 1:26). So either by the time of the Fall, or in the first tragic expression of the Fall when Cain slew Abel because the Lord valued Cain's offering of grain less than Abel's sacrifice of the first of his flock, man became omnivorous. Even so, man was to observe certain rites, and by the time of Noah and Leviticus principles of cleanliness defined what was kosher, for: "But flesh with the life thereof, which is the blood thereof, shall yet not eat" (Gen. 9:4; Lev. 17:10-16). As God was to man, so man was to the lower beasts and fowl and fish, and they were to fear man even as he was to fear God in this early hierarchy of being (Gen. 9:1-3; Deut. 12:15; see also Gen. 9:6 and Exod. 21:28-29).

Here and there in the Old Testament are hints that man's concern for the sometimes painful lot of other beings, especially his beasts of burden, might flower into a tender and all-embracing compassion. Even cattle were to rest on the Sabbath (Exod. 20:10; 23:12), and man was not unequally to yoke the ox and the ass together (Deut. 22:10). In Proverbs it was recognized that the righteous man regarded well the life of his beast, but not so the wicked man. In the words of the "preacher" (Ecclesiastes), Judaism came within a hair's breadth of accepting the Eastern insight that man and beast share the same fate on earth. Chapter 3 opens with the beautiful passage: "To everything there is a season, and a time to every purpose under heaven: A time to be born, and a time to die; a time to plant and a time to reap; A time to kill and a time to heal." The chapter closes (3:19-21):

> For that which befalleth the
> sons of men befalleth beasts;
> even one thing befalleth them;
> as one dieth, so dieth the other;
> Yea, they have all one breath;
> so that a man hath no preeminence
> above a beast: for all is vanity.

27

> All unto one place; all are
> of dust, and all turn to dust again.
> Who knoweth the spirit of man
> that goes upward, and the spirit
> of the beast that goeth downward
> to the earth?

The closing but telling question is left unanswered. The poetry of the Song of Solomon about the "Rose of Sharon" and the "voice of the turtle [dove] heard in the land" appears for the moment to countenance the preacher's concept of the unity of life until one comes to the lines: "Take us the foxes, the little foxes, that spoil the vines: for our vines have tender grapes" (Song of Sol. 2:1-15).

Whatever symbolism one cares to read into these biblical passages, it is clear that man emerges with the flattering mandate to hold dominion over all life forms on earth. He even sits in judgment on the ox that goads a stranger, for in the Torah itself he is given the right to stone to death the offending animal (Exod. 21:28-29). The same verses make the human master liable for his animal's behavior.

The New Testament which offered such hope for men everywhere, regardless of station, did little to improve the lot of God's lesser creatures. Mention of animals in the metaphors and parables of the Galilean consist almost exclusively of unfavorable comparisons with man as, for example, the admonition not to give "that which is holy unto dogs, neither cast ye your pearls before swine" (Matt. 7:6 and cf. Matt. 7:16-20).

"Man's best friend" is depicted over and over again as a cur. That the dog is especially singled out for verbal abuse undoubtedly reflects its plight in the Middle East in the centuries immediately preceding and following the birth of Christ. Even under Hebrew law the dog was considered unclean and not to be eaten and was held in contempt (1 Sam. 24:14; 2 Sam. 9:8; Isa. 56:10-11). A dog licks the sores of Lazarus, whereupon Lazarus dies (Luke: 16:20-22). A dog heads the list of such objectionables as "sorcerers, and whoremongers, and murderers and idolators" (Rev. 22:15). In the *Apocryphal New Testament*[2] even Satan runs off in the body of a dog (I Inf. 14:6).

Birds are divided into the "clean and unclean" and the biblical illustrator Calmet listed twenty unclean birds mentioned

28

in the Bible, ranging from "bat" to "vulture." Swine and fish without scales were also considered unclean. Only sheep seem to fare well at the hands of the authors of the New Testament, but how much of this is allegory tied to the pastoral traditions of the region and how much is the symbolism of Jesus in passages saying that he was "moved by compassion toward them [people] because they were sheep not having a shepherd" (Mark 6:34), is very difficult to assess. In any case, the lamb, famed for meekness and as a "banisher of sin" (John 1:29) moves stage center in Revelation's account of heaven and becomes equated with the Son of God (Rev. 5:6-8; 15:3). And in the millennia not yet reached, the lamb lies down with the lion. Perhaps the most heartening advance for the cause of animals is found in Hebrews in the declaration that animal sacrifice on the altars of God do not help assure priest or layman a place in heaven, though the reasons given for this decision have to do with man's salvation and not with any conclusion that animal sacrifice is inhumane.

The books of the Apocrypha are considered outside the canon of the Scriptures by a decision made at Nicea in 325 A.D., but these books were acceptable and available to the literate world before that date. They make even clearer the late Hebrew and early Christian deprecation of animal life. Books I and II of the Infancy in the *Apocryphal New Testament* give us a particularly grotesque and puerile account of the boy Jesus and the miracles that he wrought by molding clay birds and beasts into which he breathed life. If there is a quantum of truth to these "apocryphal" accounts in which Jesus stoned birds, struck one playmate dead and another blind, then Christianity was not to be any fountainhead for a new humane doctrine.

The horrors of the Roman persecutions of the Christians did nothing to increase Christian empathy for animals. Exceptions occur largely in fiction and painting echoing a morality of a later age. Those Christians who forgave lions for their man-generated hunger and anger and their subsequent behavior must have been saints indeed. It took the genius and kindness of a Francis of Assisi, many centuries later, to make some impact on the naive Christian ethic that had successfully precluded animals from the grand design.

Christianity did, indeed, give the West much of its decisive character, yet all the attempts of Western philosophers and theologians, from the thirteenth century on, to build "the naive ethical world-view of Jesus" into a system of religious or philosophical import have come to naught.[3] In the first few centuries of its history, Christianity was intent on other-worldly goals, convinced that the end of the world was imminent. The Christian *Weltanschauung* therefore virtually ignored the possibilities of improving temporal conditions on earth. This development drove ethical concerns inward and the quality of a moral life on earth was seldom argued, much less realized. As Albert Schweitzer remarked, the world did not come to an end, and the "optimistic element" in the world view—namely that the ethical force always triumphs over the natural force—found new application in modern times in acts that have added to man's worldly progress. The old hostility toward secular affairs has vanished, and today a Christian acts in the belief that the ethical force alone can make a difference in the affairs of men. The new morality of the young, awkward and confused as it is, shares this new Christian commitment. The movement has an evangelistic urgency: it must work this time—or else.

The chance for a strong "optimistic-ethical world-view" to emerge from Christianity, especially one that would link the natural and the ethical worlds together into a monistic whole, seems frightfully remote. The reason lies in the fundamental dualism of the Christian position between a natural world and a perfected supernatural world that stand at opposite poles, a dualism not unlike those found in the early history of the perennial mind-body problem: nature versus nurture (Plato), form versus matter (Aristotle), soul versus body (rationalized Christianity), and spirit or *Geist* versus body (Continental Rationalists). In all such dualisms, the natural world is to be superseded, transcended, and certainly conquered. The categorical imperative belongs to the realm of the spirit and therefore is something to be contemplated only, since moral man in the Kantian view cannot make a difference in the natural world, which, though described by the *Geist*, is in itself unknowable. Animals have had little place in any of these grandiose schemes except to entertain, feed, and work for man while man struggles for supposedly higher things. Animals are part of nature and must therefore obey mechanical laws, but religious and philosophical man has declared himself apart from and above nature while at the same time pronouncing his mastery over it.

Until an ethics is reached in the Western world that puts moral man back in nature and makes him responsible for his behavior toward all other forms of life; until an ethics like Stoicism once again proclaims that the good and educated man is one who deals "wisely with the phenomena of existence,"[4] where plants and animals are part of those phenomena; until an ethics includes the directly inspected, immediately felt cosmological unity of all things, expecially living things, then and only then will the individual's life view deserve to take precedence over a communicable world view, since, epistemologically speaking, a total reconciliation of the two is probably impossible. Here is the road to new and fresh insights, mystical as the approach undoubtedly seems.

The path alluded to here does not call for the demise of reason and the substitution of emotion as some philosophers and theologians might insist. Indeed, the contrary is true, for it is reason that led us to the significance of the nonrational in the first place, and it is reason that will enable us to communicate the nonrational that the exercise of reason revealed. This done, the so-called "gut reaction" (a Buddhist-type empathy recognizing that other beings suffer, that they share with us a determination to live, that they therefore have rights against us such that man has a duty not to injure them intentionally or unnecessarily) would bring animals within the moral purview of man where they should be and (if one will forgive a brief sentiment) where by heaven they should remain.

Whether the inheritors of the great Judeo-Christian tradition can make so dramatic a shift in their point of view, whether they should, and how they might accomplish the change are subjects of the utmost importance. For where a reverence for all life is missing in doctrine, it is difficult to see how man-feeling and man-thinking can call such a deficient doctrine a religion. A basic principle is needed to unite the universe into one ethical whole. Law and morality collapse where an ethics fails to prevail, and this is a social fact that we overlook at our peril.

One might expect to find in this section reference to certain other world religions that treat animals and plants in a more realistic way than is the case with Christianity. In Jainism,

31

Hinduism, and Buddhism, as well as in Taoism and Confucianism, religion is never really divorced from philosophy and neither discipline enjoys the isolation and independence so peculiar in the West. Hinduism, for example, is not only religio-philosophical, but it is psycho-socio-cultural as well, as the Code of Manu makes abundantly clear.[5] Its doctrines do not permit us to include it under the Western category of religion. Also, to call it philosophy suggests something more externally oriented than what we regard as religion and removes it even further from Eastern thought. Rene Guenon, one of the best Western authorities on the Vedanta, has stated the problem clearly. He writes of Western thought " . . . when we consider what philosophy has become in modern times, we cannot help but think that its absence from a civilization is hardly a matter of regret."[6] This criticism notwithstanding, it appears reasonable to undertake a discussion of Eastern insights into the relation between man and the animals under a concluding heading that is not confined to the categories of religion, science, or philosophy (see pages 39ff.)

## THE SCIENTIFIC AND EDUCATIONAL PROBLEM

If the Christian religion has failed to provide man with the motives and the rationale for a human kindness that would extend the protective wings of compassion to other sentient forms of life, then modern science, pure and applied, has compiled an even worse record in a much shorter period of time. Science became the sacred cow of the West in the post-Galilean-Newtonian era, leading men to boast about predicting the future of the universe. But by the advent of the twentieth century, modesty was more appropriate for the scientist who knew that "man had not yet contacted physical reality," and that his methods could not give him certainty of knowledge.[7]

Perhaps it was inevitable that nineteenth-century optimism should have so conditioned man that those who never got beyond the Newtonian period in their understanding of the sciences would keep the sacred cow alive into the twentieth century. Many teachers of science in the lower schools, and some in the colleges, still manifest this syndrome. It has no doubt been a contributing factor in the suffering of animals on a mass scale at the hands of man. This problem has increased quantitatively and depreciated

32

qualitatively with the innovative madness that has struck education. Science teachers in the lower grades have gone almost unchecked in their use and abuse of animals in their desire to let students apply the do-it-yourself methods of "discovery" and "inquiry," which are neither innovative nor, strictly speaking, methods. A few science teachers openly confess that they feel part of their task is to condition children to be indifferent to the flow of blood and insensitive to the convulsions of animals who become the victims of school science experiments.

Recent science fairs in one state stimulated secondary school students to perpetrate on animals the following "experiments": producing alcoholism, neurosis, cancer, rickets, skin defects, blindness, deafness and the loss of smell; killing animals by acceleration and impact in toy rocket flights; bringing on convulsions, lung collapse, and air-bloated intestines in "high altitude" tests; administering electric shock; attempting castration and surgical parabiosis. The last case involved a Siamese union of rats performed by a high school student. Investigation revealed that castration and surgical attempts required forty-four pairs of rats before the union was accomplished in order to test the flow of injected hormones across the parabiotic barrier. The entire experiment, with a full summation of the results, was found in a report made twenty years earlier by a medical team.[8]

One can only hope that the quantity of animals required for statistically significant experiments is not readily available to elementary and high school students. From a scientific point of view, plants are far superior in assuring the quantitative measures needed, and their use would spare many animals pain, fear, and anxiety. Equal success could be achieved by other substitutes for live animal experiments. A single demonstration that inflicts suffering on other beings to demonstrate *what is already known* raises ethical questions of no small import.

"Learning by doing" is a sound pedagogical principle that Aristotle recognized long ago. It was revived by Comenius, Rousseau, and John Dewey, each in his own time. But by what strange distortion of reason has it become popular to maintain that reading and thinking are not doing? If we were to base a philosophy of education on the thesis that each individual must repeat the entire experience of mankind (the discredited cultural

33

epoch theory), then civilization itself would disappear. If we were to believe that the great laws and theories of advanced inquiry can be rediscovered in empirical experience, then we would soon find ourselves back in the time of Thales, the Miletian, and all technology would disappear. "Doing" must have a broader base than overt action. Learning must change behavior, not simply repeat it. Education must honor vicarious experience as authority (however tentative), or the next generation may boast of its ability to manipulate the technology that others have provided but will be ill-prepared to add one iota to its future development or extend human knowledge and understanding.

After the Oppenheimer affair, the debates surrounding the fates of Hiroshima and Nagasaki, the controversy stimulated by the late Rachel Carson's *Silent Spring*, the first heart transplant by Christiaan Barnard, and recent controversies over gene splicing (recombinant gene engineering), it is not likely that the scientist, theoretical or applied, can any longer escape into a valueless world. The scientist's moral responsibilities will henceforth include closing the gap between himself and John Q. Public—not by presuming to teach John the abstract intricacies of his science, but by reporting honestly and fearlessly the implications of his findings for the sphere of technology. Each generation needs men like Sir James Jeans, George Gamow, Isaac Asimov, Loren Eiseley, and others to interpret the advances of science. This effort will call for an integrity not yet apparent on the contemporary scene, as witness the pretensions of some of the social sciences. And in the melee of change, the same scientist must correctly assess his moral obligations to animals and even to plants, on which animals and man depend for the conversion of the energy of the sun into life-sustaining food.

There are of course related problems. Technology feeds on itself. Paradoxically, we may require technology to solve the very problems it creates. Ecology, ethology, conservation, and wildlife management are muddy subjects, because, though they may appear morally high-sounding to some, they are ill-defined and their appeal generally boils down to man's self-interest. In ecology, who rightly distinguishes between a Stewart Udall and a Rachel Carson; in ethology, between a Konrad Lorenz and a Peter Kropotkin; in conservation, between the U.S. Army Corps of

34

Engineers and a John Muir; in wildlife management, between an Aldo Leopold and a Joseph Wood Krutch? The very recital of a variety of points of view demonstrates how far the sciences and their related disciplines have still to go to give us hope that scientific man will join in solving the problem of achieving the kind of morality that will not only contribute to man's survival, but promise us at the same time that man can be humane, compassionate, and, in short, civilized.

## THE PHILOSOPHICAL PROBLEM

At times in history philosophers have constructively influenced the affairs of men. The present is not one of those times. Moral and social philosophers, along with theologians, have always been a primary source of values—the objectives for human societies, the ideals, the goals, the "oughts," and the "impossible dream" that human beings aspire to but never attain. These values become the criteria by which we judge the right from the wrong, the good from the evil, the just from the unjust, the humane from the cruel. But we find that as the human condition changes, values change. They may be modified slowly, altered dramatically, or displaced altogether, creating a vacuum that calls for new guidelines for the human endeavor. In turbulent times such as our own, philosophers themselves appear as uncertain of reality and their own identities as anyone else, the chief difference being that they are likely to communicate their dilemma in more sophisticated language.

It is really not surprising that many intellectuals, including philosophers, have encouraged the current epidemic of cultism, communes, the occult, the importation of Eastern gurus, the revival of meditation, and, joining the psychologists, have participated in sensitivity sessions, love encounters, "skiing and being," and other experiments purporting to release the full measure of a person's potentiality as a human being. Yet all these activities are symptomatic of deeper disturbances—of alienation, the breakdown of values, and moral bankruptcy. Imitation of certain Oriental practices, such as Yoga (in its various forms), vegetarianism, Zen (popular as a Western cult since the 1950s) and other exercises, now occurs independently of the larger framework in which they were originally conceived and in which alone they

35

are meaningful. Most of these popular excursions into the unknown, when indiscriminately blended with Western existentialist absurdities, consist of turning inward in search of the self, leaving the individual even more sadly isolated and alienated than before.

The Protestant infatuation with existentialism is probably the culmination of forces set in motion, however innocently, by Martin Luther himself as far back as 1517. (Let us not argue the claim of some that Jesus was the first existentialist.) Any authority external to the individual was thereafter to be the fair game of Everyman, who slowly but inexorably became persuaded by Western pundits to believe that he was and should be his own priest. But this only scratches the surface of the difficulties with the position.

Many disciples of existentialism insist that it is not a philosophy, that it cannot be systematized, and that its premises cannot be argued. It is extremely ironical, therefore, that by using rational argument a substantial segment of an entire generation has been taught to hold as infallible insights the basic principles of the position: existence precedes essence; existence is contingent; existence is fundamentally absurd; we basically live alone; morality is an individual matter that may be reduced or expanded to the degree that one feels urged to be committed or involved. On the basis of such premises it has been held that, since human existence consists in choosing, even though the world may be absurd, man is not. But in the Sartre version, choosing is purely arbitrary at best, and therefore one cannot be blamed for his choices. So we should expect to endure all manner of defiance, for, in this view, as Richard Pratte points out, "hell is other people."[9] In such a philosophy of the absurd, or such an absurd philosophy, animals—vertebrate and invertebrate—and even plants must likewise impinge on the existentialist's tender consciousness and get in the way of the free expression of the individual's full subjectivity. Thus another dimension is added to hell.

In the now vast literature of existentialism, one does not find an ethics that recognizes that man has any obligation to sentient beings other than himself, and even for the human situation the case is not impressive. Martin Buber is almost alone in attempting to comment on the problem of man *vis-à-vis* other living things.

But, using his language, one must presume that animals and plants are Its in an I-It relationship and can never achieve an I-Thou relationship, which apparently is reserved exclusively for man-to-man and man-to-God transactions. Hans Jonas, in his remarkable work *The Phenomenon of Life*, while supporting many of the insights of the existentialists, criticizes them for being "obsessed with man alone." He declares later in the same volume that no philosophy, contemporary as it may be, shows less concern for nature than existentialism, since "it leaves nature no dignity at all."[10]

Philosophy in the West is as anthropocentric as we found science and religion to be. The pragmatism of Peirce and James said almost nothing about animals and man's relation to them except insofar as the use or observation of animals enlightens man's view of himself. For a student of the latter-day version of pragmatism, John Dewey's experimentalism, to recall a passage that reveals man's intelligent coexistence with other forms of life would require a strenuous exercise in memory.

Other philosophers who might be called the "degree-of-difference boys" argue that an obvious hierarchy exists among living beings, and man, of course, is not only at the top but is so different in degree as to be different in kind. The argument is about as old as the Tree of Porphyry, and about as convincing. These persons, caught in the inescapable predicament of Protagoras, classify themselves and declare with impunity that their interests, wants, and desires must take precedence over the needs of all other beings. The hunter, male or female, who kills for sport and not for necessary food, the toreador or torero who tortures the bull in an artistic ritual to demonstrate personal skill, the rodeo cowboy who tightens the flank or bucking strap on a horse or bull until the animal bolts forth from its chute to relieve its agony—these are the men and women who practice what the "degree-of-difference boys" preach as a right of man because of his favored position in the hierarchy of being. The deeper ethical questions remain unanswered.

Issues concerning human freedom arise in connection with any discussion surrounding man's superiority over all other of God's creatures. Though the definitions of freedom are legion,

37

none seems to have the subtlety and profundity of Kant's "a thing is free when it is not caused," or Spinoza's declaration that "I am most free when I am a slave." But the majority of definitions in vogue today are epitomized by arguments for simple choice. Certainly from Descartes to the present most men have denied animals and plants any freedom, since they are conceived of as objects obeying mechanical laws. The Watsons and the Skinners would include man within the mechanistic view. But there seem to be few proponents of the reverse position to maintain that animal acts may also be expressions of choice (and hence of freedom) even as in the classical example of the donkey who must choose between two mounds of hay or die.[11]

Some thinkers insist, perhaps rightly, that man's ability to manipulate symbols, particularly through language, multiplies his choices or options, thus increasing the number of actions available to him. Herbart has said that ideas are the father of action. But on this and previous assertions, the cause of human freedom and its presumed exclusiveness attract new supporters for the dogma of anthropocentrism.

One possible Western antidote to the conclusions in the preceding two paragraphs might well be the "philosophy of process" (not to be associated with a metaphysically naive phenomenology) as found in the works of Alfred North Whitehead. Here, whatever may be the events of cosmic process, animals and plants share in the reality and are significant elements in the total scheme of things. Events are the concretions—whether man, animal, plant, or mineral—that exist. To paraphrase Spinoza, each is a link in a chain of events that none can replace or destroy, and each shall remain so for all eternity. Whitehead wrote, "Everything that in any sense exists has two sides, namely its individual self and its signification in the universe."[12] It is no accident that Whitehead is one of the rare modern philosophers to devote space to animals.

Contemporary Western philosophy holds with Western religion, science, and education the dubious distinction of being enchanted, like Narcissus, with man alone. It is part of man's overpowering weakness to clothe himself in his own egotism. The trouble is that the emperor needs new clothes.

38

CONCLUSION

It may take a fifth Copernican revolution to shift the center of Occidental thought from a concentration on the Many to a genuine exploration of a more Oriental One.[13]. The evidence contained in the preceding pages demonstrates the need for some sort of revolution to neutralize Western man's egotism, nullify his atomistic analysis of things social and physical, improve his conduct toward all living things, and put man back in nature where he belongs. (In deference to the women's liberation movement, "man" in this context includes women and "he" is editorial shorthand for any individual member of the human race, male or female. The usage condones no bias as to sex but rather betrays a culturally devised linguistic trap that not even a Noam Chomsky has been able to spring.)

The barriers to the advent of a thought revolution that could help us lay the foundations for a more humane and encompassing ethics are sketched in the foregoing sections of this paper. We saw some of the factors in our culture that have conditioned us to look upon animals and plants as placed on the earth for the sole use, pleasure, and service of man. We saw man programmed in the past few years to turn inward on himself to declare that "hell is other people" and that if nature is something external to man, it is without redeeming qualities of its own, unless man makes it so. We saw the blundering social sciences confound the problems of methodology and we saw the humane and civilized approaches to ecology, ethology, conservation, and wildlife management become fragmented in purpose and confused in meaning. So what form the fifth Copernican revolution might take is still debatable and what follows in this conclusion is only suggestive.

Nearly a decade ago, I wrote:

> Those of us who are concerned with education, and for a humane education in particular, need to strike out boldly in a direction only vaguely familiar to the West. It is found in the concept of compassion developed by Joseph Wood Krutch and in the phrase "the reverence for life" as enunciated by Albert Schweitzer. On this road we may find a new moral conscience for mankind. It embraces a way of life found in the ancient Upanishads of India and in the commandments of the Buddha and in the doctrine of "ahimsa" in the religion of the Jains. It

39

is derived from or assumes the even more fundamental premise of the Oneness of all life, not the equality of life forms, but the similarity of life's processes. We find it summarized in the Brihadaranyaka (Upanishad) "The inorganic is life that sleeps, the plant is life that feels, the animal is life that knows, and man is life that knows that it knows." . . . Furthermore, life so defined is good physics, good chemistry, good biology.[14]

The important point to understand about the idea of cosmic unity is that it recommends itself for the reason that it can be grasped not only by the intellect but by any honest inspection of one's own experience. In Hinduism, Brahman, Atman, atman, maya, moksha, and similar notions were certainly not originally postulated in any Western manner, but intuited, felt, revealed in process, or directly inferred from experience in the Northropian sense of "concepts by inspection."[15] However, the Unqualified One (Nirguna Brahman) and the Qualified One (Saguna Brahman), the oversoul, the empirical self, the cosmic illusion of materiality, and deliverance from phenomenal existence (respectively) can be equally metaphysical considerations in an intellectual world, and they were that for the great philosopher and nondualist teacher of the Vedanta, Sankaracharya (788-820 A.D.)[16]

Clearly, therefore, cosmic unity that embraces minerals, plants, and animals is a reality whether reached by empirical perception or by a Kantian mental construct indirectly inferred from experience. Since oneness on these grounds is no mere eidolon, our previously mentioned friend, John Q. Public, can share emotionally what the theologian, scientist, and philosopher may conclude intellectually to be the oneness of all life. Therefore, it is difficult to imagine carrying out any command-ment that prohibits killing or injuring any living creature unless the commandment is tied to the ethical significance of the larger world view represented by the notion of oneness.

The prohibition against killing or harming any living creature, the doctrine of *ahimsa* attributed to the Jains, is not a positive doctrine of compassion, but the negation of any will to kill or injure. This is the very etymology of the word: it means to be free from violence. It is a live-and-let-live policy not dissimilar to the indifference of many Westerners to the general plight and suffering of their fellow men. However, allegations that people reserve their

40

indifference for minorities or out-groups is simply an overreaction to current social problems, since it is not only minorities or out-groups who suffer.

Suppose, however, that *ahimsa* is brought under the Hindu view of the homogeneity of all creation, or the Buddha's view that suffering is the price of all life. Then a positive ethical meaning seems to emerge for the concept of *ahimsa* or nonviolence. Those who maintain that the monism of the Brahmanic tradition belongs to the theoretical world of discourse and so does not mandate sympathy for the animal world overlook a fundamental difference in the ways of knowing between the East and the West. Western followers of Fichte, Hegel, and Kant, once they can get an idea to resemble a propositional construct of the human mind, deprecate the possibility of real knowledge or wisdom being acquired by directly intuited, immediately sensed experience. "Ontological knowledge is impossible," they insist; therefore, morality does not refer to things in sensed experience but is an order created and contemplated only within. This certainly is more devastating for animal welfare than a world view that conceives of animals as participants in the same kind of existence as man, for on the latter view "one need only add a little love."

The doctrine of nonviolence for the Jains and for Hindu followers of the monistic Vedanta was intended as an expression of an effort to keep clear and clean of this world by abstaining from *himsa* (violence), which is an inescapable property of earthly reality. It was part of the genius of Gandhi to change the principle from a negative, nonworldly one to a positive one in the form of his famous passive resistance. Adding to *ahimsa* an aura of worldly activity was an important event not only "in the thought of India but in that of humanity."[17] But there is a sense in which the force of the nonviolent passive resistance of Gandhi and Martin Luther King became "nonviolent violence" because their impatience could not abide the time it takes for "the spiritual operation of an idea." We have witnessed the parallel impatience of youthful demonstrators who protested the Vietnam war with violent nonviolence. Attempts to convert the Jain-Hindu principle from a mere abstinence from violence to a passive but forceful resistance to violence that would result in compassionate behavior have never quite succeeded, unless Buddhism proves the exception.

41

"I have come to see," wrote Gandhi, "what I did not so clearly before, that there is non-violence in violence. . . . I had not fully realized the duty of restraining a drunkard from doing evil, of killing a dog in agony or one infected with rabies. In all these instances violence is in fact non-violence."[18] Further, he pointed out to the world the shameful state of animals in his beloved India. So he considerably modified his view from the one he had held in his "experiments in the science of Satyagraha" (his autobiography), in which he insisted that duty consisted of refraining from the destruction of any of earth's creatures as the only path by which one could throw off "the deadly coil of *himsa*."[19] In his later years, he did not abandon the doctrine altogether but redefined it not only to refuse to do physical injury but never to violate the essence—that is, the truth—of a living thing.[20]

It is clear that many have faltered in the search for an ethics that is not exclusively confined to a discussion of human relationships. What we seek and what we should believe is possible is an ethics that looks at the entire biosphere of the planet earth—and beyond—and defines man's obligations and duties toward the inorganic, the plant, the animal, and fellow humans, and then bravely sets forth the rights that sentient living things most certainly have over and against man. How such an ethics can be achieved without the ingredients of a world view that acknowledges the Oriental notion of cosmic unity, and the incessant drive to free oneself from violence, is hard to comprehend. We would do well to listen to the Eastern notion of freedom. It is not a freedom to do as one pleases, but the higher freedom of the spirit attained only when the self is free from ignorance, free from greed, free from illusions, and free from violence. What is encouraging is the growing leadership in education, religion, science, and philosophy that willingly devotes its attention to the full dimensions of this ethical problem and man's moral behavior. Further, there is a groundswell of popular concern for the need to build a more moral, humane, and civilized world, accompanied by a feeling that time in which to meet the need may be running out. The contemporary problems of anthropocentrism, solipsism, cultism, and scientism, as sketched in the preceding pages, threaten a fair hearing for those theologians, philosophers, and scientists who speak to the moral issues involved in man's conduct toward other living things. Each side will have its season and somewhere out of the Babel of tongues will emerge a workable truth to spare sentient beings intentional pain or injury at the hands of man.

> There are, it may be, so many kinds of voices in the world, and none of them is without signification. Therefore, if I know not the meaning of the voice, I shall be unto him that speaketh a barbarian, and he that speaketh *shall be* a barbarian unto me.[21]

## NOTES

1. All biblical citations are from the King James Version of *The Holy Bible*.
2. *The Apocryphal New Testament*, 2nd ed. (Boston: Bazin and Ellsworth, 1821).
3. Albert Schweitzer, *The Philosophy of Civilization* (New York: Macmillan, 1953), pp. 110-112.
4. Epictetus, *The Works of Epictetus*, trans. T. W. Higginson (New York: Thomas Nelson, n.d.), p. 33. See also pp. 72, 74-75.
5. Kemal Motwani, *Manu: A Study in Hindu Social Theory* (Madras: Ganesh, 1937).
6. René Guénon, *Man and His Becoming According to the Vedanta* (New York: Noonday Press, 1958), p. 12.
7. Sir James Jeans, *The Mysterious Universe* (New York: Macmillan, 1930), p. 50.
8. This paragraph is based on a statement prepared by the writer and researched by the staff of The Humane Society of the United States, Conn. Branch, Inc., 1969. Cf. Richard K. Morris, "The Misuse of Animals in the Science Classroom," *Proceedings*, National Leadership Conference, HSUS, Hershey, Pa., 1969.
9. Richard Pratte, *Contemporary Theories of Education* (Scranton, Pa.: Intext Educational Publishers, 1971), p. 266.
10. Hans Jonas, *The Phenomenon of Life* (New York: Harper & Row, 1966), foreword and ninth essay, p. 232.
11. It is entirely possible that freedom is a by-product of mechanisms (negative feedback that changes behavior, etc.) and if this should prove to be the case, man could no longer claim that he was the only free agent in the animal kingdom.
12. Quoted by Iver LeClere in *Whitehead's Metaphysics* (New York: Humanities Press, 1965), p. 188.
13. The first occurred when Copernicus shifted to a heliocentric view of the solar system; the second, when Immanuel Kant proposed that if the senses would not give us veridical knowledge, then we must shift to the mind as the informer; the third, when Oswald Spengler insisted that history and not biological evolution could alone explain the development of man; the fourth, when John Dewey, with an immodesty rivaling that of Kant, declared a Copernican revolution by shifting the center of gravity in education from the teacher to the student.
14. Richard K. Morris, "A Philosophy of Humane Education for Our Schools," *Teacher Education Quarterly* 23, no. 3 (Spring 1966): 1-5.
15. F. S. C. Northrop, *The Logic of the Sciences and the Humanities* (New York: Macmillan, 1947).
16. Swami Nikilananda, *The Upanishads*, 4 vols. (New York: Harper and Brothers, 1949) for the commentaries of Sri Sankaracharya, and René Guénon, *Man and His Becoming*.
17. Albert Schweitzer, *Indian Thought and Its Development* (Boston: Beacon Press, 1957), pp. 229-235, and specifically, p. 234.
18. Quoted in Erik H. Erikson, *Gandhi's Truth* (New York: Norton, 1969), p. 374.
19. M. K. Gandhi, *An Autobiography or The Story of My Experiments with Truth*, 2nd ed. (Ahmedabad: Navajwain, 1959), p. 257.
20. Erikson, *Gandhi's Truth*, p. 412.
21. *1 Cor.* 14:10-11.

# SUGGESTED READING

Eiseley, Loren. *The Invisible Pyramid.* New York: Scribner, 1970.

Erikson, Erik H. *Gandhi's Truth.* New York: Norton, 1969.

Gandhi, M. K. *An Autobiography.* Ahmedabad: Navajwain, 1927 (2nd ed. reprint, 1959).

Guénon, René. *Man and His Becoming According to the Vedanta.* New York: Noonday Press, 1958.

Jonas, Hans. *The Phenomenon of Life.* New York: Harper & Row, 1966.

Krutch, Joseph Wood. *The Great Chain of Being.* Boston: Houghton Mifflin, 1957.

Leopold, Aldo. *A Sand County Almanac.* London: Oxford University Press, 1968.

Lorenz, Konrad. *On Aggression.* New York: Harcourt, Brace, 1963.

Montagu, Ashley, ed. *Man and Aggression.* New York: Oxford University Press, 1968.

Morris, R. K. "A Philosophy of Humane Education for Our Schools." *Teacher Education Quarterly* 23, no. 3 (Spring 1966): 1-5.

Motwani, Kemal. *Manu: A Study in Hindu Social Theory.* Madras: Ganesh, 1937.

Nikilananda, Swami. *The Upanishads.* 4 vols. New York: Harper and Brothers, 1949.

Northrop, F. S. C. *The Meeting of East and West.* New York: Macmillan, 1946.

——————————. *The Logic of the Sciences and the Humanities.* New York: Macmillan, 1947.

Schweitzer, Albert. *Indian Thought and Its Development.* Boston: Beacon Press, 1957.

——————————. *Out of My Life and Thought.* New York: Henry Holt, 1949.

——————————. *The Philosophy of Civilization.* New York: Macmillan, 1953.

Whitehead, Alfred North. *Modes of Thought.* New York: Free Press, 1968.

——————————. *Process and Reality.* New York: Social Science Publishers, 1929.

——————————. *Science and the Modern World.* New York: Pelican Mentor Books, 1948.

# Human Duties and Animal Rights 3

*Joel Feinberg*

Hardly anyone these days believes that morality permits us simply to have our way with animals and treat them in whatever manner suits our fancy or promotes our profit. That we do have duties of action and omission concerning animals is widely granted, but confusion over the ground and scope of those requirements, even when the duties are incorporated into law, is rife. Disagreements on these matters sometimes are derived from radically opposed basic attitudes toward animals or are rooted in clashing beliefs about such inaccessible facts as the nature of animal mental states, capacities, and vulnerabilities. (Some people disagree about whether fish feel much pain when hooks are stuck in their mouths, and among those who agree that fish *do* feel severe pain, some do, and some do not, care.) Other disagreements, however, are no doubt caused by misunderstandings of our moral vocabulary, which can be perplexing even in its application to all-human contexts, and becomes utterly bewildering in its extended applications to the nonhuman world. These conceptual confusions, while difficult, are somewhat more tractable than disagreements in basic attitude and in beliefs about animal psychology, and I shall attempt in this essay to dissipate some of them.

Insofar as a moral or legal system is rational there will be grounds for the various duties it imposes on those who are subject to its rules. Grounds for duties can be divided into two types. First, duties to treat other parties in certain ways may be derived from the prior claim of the other parties against us to be treated in those ways. Thus if *A* borrows ten dollars from *B* and promises to

**Joel Feinberg** is Professor of Philosophy, University of Arizona, Tucson.

repay it by a certain date, then when that date arrives, *A* has a duty to pay *B* ten dollars, because *B* at that time has a valid claim against *A*, derived from *A's* promise, for ten dollars. The original transaction between the two parties gave *B* a right (valid claim) to repayment, and *in virtue of that right, A* has a duty to pay. If *B* were to waive his right, he would by that gesture destroy the ground for *A's* duty, and the duty would cease to exist. Similarly, human beings have valid claims conferred by moral principles and/or legal rules to noninterference in certain respects, and in virtue of these rights, other parties have a duty to respect their privacy, their property, and their persons.

Some of our duties, however, are based on a second type of ground. We have general moral duties—to be charitable and friendly, for example—that are not derived from the prior claims of any particular needy supplicant against us. Similarly, in some circumstances we have duties to obey the law even when no specific persons can claim our obedience as their own due. Moreover, our consciences can impose exacting moral requirements to act in heroic and self-sacrificing ways that could not plausibly be demanded or claimed from us as their due by those who benefit from them. The rule of *noblesse oblige* imposed duties on the nobility toward even those members of the lower classes thought to be undeserving of good treatment and thus in no position to claim it as their right.

There is then a variety of grounds for moral and legal duties other than the rights of those to whom the duty may be owed. We may have a duty to treat another in a certain way simply because he has a right or valid claim against us to that treatment, *or* simply because God, or conscience, or law, or self-ideal, or social role demands it of us, or because for some other reason it seems the decent or fitting thing to do, even in the absence of claims against us by our likely beneficiaries. Our duties to animals, I believe, are of both kinds. Some are correlated with valid moral claims of the animals themselves against us and thus require that we respect animal *rights;* others do not have that kind of support but are based on other reasons that are no less stringent.

I

According to a great many philosophers[1] and jurisprudents,[2] animals *do not* have rights for the simple reason that they are not

46

the kinds of beings who *can* have rights. We can have duties *concerning* animals, these writers are often quick to add, but those duties are not owed to the animals as their due, and thus cannot be claimed against us as rights. Animals in this respect are like trees and rocks, automobiles and buildings, which are not the sorts of things of which it even makes sense to say they could have rights of their own. In respect to having rights, animals are more like pebbles and sunbeams than they are like full-fledged human beings. I believe that this view of the moral status of animals is radically mistaken, not because its distinguished proponents are somehow misinformed about the facts or insensitive in their attitudes, but rather because they misunderstand the basic terms of their own moral vocabulary even as applied to human beings.

To have a right is to have a claim against others to their action or omission in one's behalf and perhaps also against the state for enforcement of the claim against others. A claim is a right, properly speaking, when it is *valid*—that is, when it is recognized by legal or institutional rules or, in the case of moral rights, by the moral principles that inform an enlightened and sensitive conscience. Some claims, although based on good and relevant reasons, are in principle vulnerable to counterclaims. A valid claim, on the other hand, is a decisive case, invulnerable or conclusive. As such it is a morally sufficient title and an extremely valuable possession, neither dependent on nor derivative from the compassionate feelings, propriety, conscientiousness, or sense of *noblesse oblige* of others. It is a claim against another party in no way dependent for its incumbency on the love of the other party or the lovableness of its possessor. Hence, wicked, wretched, and odious human beings maintain certain rights against others, and the duties of others based on those rights are incumbent even on those who hate the claimants, and hate with good reason. A right is a matter of justice, and justice, while perhaps no more valuable than love, sympathy, and compassion, is nevertheless a moral notion distinct from them.

Because a right is a claim, it falls in neatly with a complex of claim-connected responses and attitudes. A claim-right, I have written elsewhere,[3] "can be urged, pressed, or rightly demanded against other persons. In appropriate circumstances the right-holder can urgently, peremptorily, or insistently call for his rights, or assert them authoritatively, confidently, unabashedly. Rights are not mere gifts or favors, motivated by love or pity, for which gratitude is the sole fitting response. A right is something a person can *stand* upon, something that can be demanded or insisted upon without embarrassment or shame. When that to which one has a right is not forthcoming, the appropriate reaction is indignation; when it is duly given there is no reason for gratitude, since it is simply one's own or one's due that one received."

When we think of others as claimants or right-holders against us, then, we think of them with a certain kind of *respect,* not merely with a feeling of duty or sympathy. The truest test of the existence of this respect is its steadfast persistence as an attitude of mind even toward the unlovable, the incapable, and the morally deficient, when these are otherwise qualified for it.

One would think that the conceptual suitability of animals for rights had been established once and for all by "cruelty to animals" statutes that seem to confer on animals at least legal rights to humane treatment. Still, it is always possible to say on the other side that such statutes were designed merely to protect public or private property or to protect human beings from corruption, or to protect the sensibilities of a minority of animal lovers who, as human beings, certainly do have rights. And there is little doubt that such reasons were the primary motives of the English legislators who originally passed animal protection bills. Edward Westermarck reports, for example, that "the bill for the abolition of bearbaiting and other cruel practices was expressly propounded on the ground that nothing was more conducive to crime than such sports, that they led the lower orders to gambling, that they educated them for thieves, that they gradually trained them up to bloodshed and murder."[4] Not a word about the pain and anguish of the animals! "Indifference to animal suffering," as Westermarck comments, "has been a characteristic of public opinion in European countries up to quite modern times."[5]

Whatever the motives of the original legislators, however, there can be little doubt now, in this final quarter of the twentieth century, that the directly intended beneficiaries of animal protection statutes are the protected animals themselves. Indeed, it is difficult even to invent plausible alternative rationales for the statutes. They cannot be designed wholly to protect property, for

48

example, because mistreatment even of one's own chattels is forbidden. They cannot be designed exclusively to protect tender human sensibilities, because wholly private and unobserved mistreatment of animals is also prohibited. They could be intended to prevent the development of cruel habits that could eventually lead to violence against other human beings, I suppose, but why then are there so few statutes prohibiting the portrayal in literature and films of violence aimed *directly* at human victims? The simplest and least factitious account of the rationale of these laws is that they are intended, in the words of John Chipman Gray, "to preserve the dumb creatures from suffering."[6]

The fact that animals are the intended beneficiaries of protective legislation, however, does not yet prove that they have legal rights; and indeed the prevailing view of Anglo-American jurisprudence has been that animals do not, indeed cannot, have rights. Several reasons have been offered for this conclusion, but none can survive careful scrutiny. In the first place, it is commonly said that animals cannot have rights because they are not "moral agents."[7] Since they are incapable of having duties and responsibilities, they are not capable of being full-fledged members of our moral community, and thus they lack the moral "standing" to be right-holders. Since they cannot bear duties, they are not genuine moral subjects, and since they cannot be moral subjects, the argument concludes, they cannot be moral objects either. There are two possible replies to this argument. One is to deny the premise that animals are incapable of duties; the other is to deny the logic that deduces "no rights" from "no duties." To reply in the former way, I think, is to walk into a trap.

So far as we can know, no animals other than man have the intellectual equipment necessary for the reliable performance of duty and the discharge of responsibility. They cannot make promises or enter into contractual agreements. Nor can they even grasp the concept of a duty or a commitment. These failures of intellect and volition, I think, disqualify animals as genuine moral agents eligible for our trust and answerable for their failures.

One counterargument to these commonplace observations is that dogs and horses can be trained through instruction and discipline to bring their behavior up to a rather exacting standard. Dogs in particular are said even to manifest

49

unmistakable signs of guilty conscience when they depart from the humanly assigned standard.[8] Here, again, the discussion of the moral status of animals can be snarled by an inadequate understanding or careless application of our ordinary moral concepts. Well-trained dogs sometimes let their masters down; they anticipate punishment or other manifestations of displeasure; they grovel and whimper, and they even make crude efforts at redress and reconciliation. But do they feel remorse and bad conscience? They have been conditioned to associate manifestations of displeasure with departures from a norm, and this is a useful way of keeping them in line, but they haven't the slightest inkling of the *reasons* for the norm. They don't *understand* why departures from the norm are wrong, or why their masters become angry or disappointed. They have a concept perhaps of the *mala prohibita*—the act that is wrong because it is prohibited, but they have no notion of the *mala in se*—the act that is prohibited because it is wrong. Even in respect to the *mala prohibita* their understanding is grossly deficient, for they have no conception of rightful authority. For dogs, the only basis of their master's "right" to be obeyed is his *de facto* power over them. Even when one master steals a beast from another, or when an original owner deprives it of its natural freedom in the wild, the animal will feel no moralized emotion, such as outraged propriety or indignation. These complex feelings involve cognitive elements beyond an animal's ken. Similarly, to suffer a guilty conscience is to be more than merely unhappy or anxious; it is to be in such a state because one has violated an "internalized standard," a principle of one's own, the rationale of which one can fully appreciate and the correctness of which one can, but in fact does not, doubt.

Punishment can be inflicted on animals to good effect. But unlike the genuine punishments inflicted on human criminals, it is not understood by a symbolic convention to express moral judgments on the offender or his past conduct. No animal could understand a moral judgment made about him in any language, natural or contrived. No animal could appreciate the morally blameworthy quality of his deviant act any more than it could appreciate the rational grounding of the violated rule. And no animal could be reasoned with by an appeal to commonly held ideals and convictions. That is why the full-fledged legal punishment of animals would be ludicrous, and that is why animals are not assigned legal duties and made legally answerable for their discharge.

Still another familiar way of describing this animal deficiency is to say that animals are not *persons*. As a friend and respecter of animals, I have no objection to this way of speaking, provided what is meant by a "person" is a being who is a conceptually appropriate subject of both rights and duties, for in that case one can deny that animals are persons on the grounds that they cannot have duties, while still keeping open the question whether they can have rights. On the other hand, if we follow John Chipman Gray[9] and take "person" to mean any being who can be a subject of *either* duties *or* rights, then we cannot deny that animals are persons without foreclosing analytically (to the animals' disadvantage) the question whether they can have rights. That is a good reason for rejecting Gray's usage, and it is reinforced by a consideration mentioned by Gray himself—namely, that in another very familiar, nontechnical sense, the word "person" is often used as a synonym for "human being," so it might seem unnecessarily paradoxical to assert that animals are persons. If we reject Gray's disjunctive criteria of personhood, however, then as respecters of animal rights, we have no reason to assert that animals *are* persons, and the appearance of paradox can be avoided.

Some friends of animals may be tempted to speak of them as persons for another reason. They overreact to the traditional practice of the common law of lumping animals in the same category as "mere things," with inanimate objects, plants, artifacts, and all the various objects that can be human property. (No one can deny, of course, that domesticated animals *are* property, but it *can* be denied that they *ought* to be property or that they are *merely* property.) These people then hastily assume that any being is either a person or a thing and opt for animal personhood. But in fact *animals are neither persons nor "mere things."* To treat them as mere things is to withhold from them even the possibility of right-ownership, but to treat them as persons, at least minimally on the same moral footing as human beings, may be to treat them even worse. We can have too high a regard for animals for the animals' own good, as evidenced by the bizarre practice of holding animals criminally responsible for the

51

harms they cause to human beings, a custom that survived in Europe well into modern times.[10]

Overregard for beasts, oddly enough, is not so much a product of modern sophistication gone erratic as it is an essential ingredient of the primitive mind. The same habits of mind that inclined our prehistoric ancestors (and our primitive contemporaries) to ascribe humanlike minds to trees, winds, and mountains, led them to think of animals as humanlike spirits in eccentric guises, beings fully capable of honorable transactions as well as resentment, vindictiveness, and conspiracy:

> The savage, not only momentarily, while in a rage, but permanently and in cold blood, obliterates the boundaries between man and beast. He regards all animals as practically on a footing of equality with men. He believes that they are endowed with feelings and intelligence like men, that they are united into families and tribes like men, that they have various languages like human tribes, that they possess souls that survive the death of the bodies ... He tells of animals that have been the ancestors of men, of men that have become animals, of marriages that take place between men and beasts. He also believes that he who slays an animal will be exposed to the vengeance either of its disembodied spirit, or of all the other animals of the same species which, quite after human fashion, are bound to resent the injury done to one of their number. Is it not natural, then, that the savage should give like for like? If it is the duty of animals to take vengeance upon men, is it not equally the duty of men to take vengeance upon animals?[11]

When one considers the way men treat the other men who *are* their equals, when one ponders the sad chronicle of murders, vendettas, savage punishments, and holy wars, all accompanied by the swaggering self-righteousness that only human "persons" can achieve, and when one considers also the motives we have for treasuring our possessions, one is tempted to suggest that treating animals as mere things might on the whole be to treat them better than to treat them as the persons they are not. In any case, if it is the "friends" of animals who insist on their personhood, animals have little need for enemies.

The first argument against the possibility of animal rights then does employ a correct premise: animals *are* rendered by their intellectual deficiencies incapable of having duties or of being morally responsible agents or "persons." It simply does not follow, however, that the intellectual shortcomings that disqualify animals for duties automatically disqualify them for rights as well. Both law and common sense present numerous examples of the rights of the incompetent. Infants not yet able to walk or talk (much less make promises, sign contracts, appreciate the wrongfulness of their conduct, and so on) most assuredly have moral claims against us as well as enforceable legal rights. So do insane, feebleminded, and senile persons. Even incorrigibly brain-damaged persons are commonly held to have a right to be treated humanely. So the first argument provides no persuasive reason for denying that animals are the kinds of beings that can have rights.

The second argument does no better. Animals may have claims against us, but they cannot *know* that they do, nor can they even grasp the concept of a right or another's duty to them. Hence, they cannot *make* claim, on their own, to something as their due or initiate legal proceedings, on their own, for their own protection. These reasons were held sufficient by Gray[12] for denying that animals can have legal rights, and no doubt a parallel claim could be made for animal disqualification for moral rights. The immediate reply to this argument, of course, is that one need not *know* that one has a right in order to have it, and that animals no less than infants and insane persons can make claims in law courts through proxies speaking in their behalf. (The very word *attorney* derives from a Norman term that meant any kind of stand-in or substitute.)

An advocate of the second argument against the possibility of animal rights, however, often anticipates the point about proxy representation and has a counterrejoinder. Human beings can be represented by proxy, he acknowledges, because they are capable, at least potentially, of willing or consenting to such representation. On the other hand, "The persons calling upon the State for enforcement of the statutes [protecting animals] are regarded by the Law as exercising their own wills, or the will of the State or of some other organized body of human beings."[13] They cannot claim to be speaking as representatives of the animals' own wills unless the animals consent, and on this matter the animals remain forever mute. Similarly, it is urged that animals cannot hire proxies on their own, contract with them, instruct, direct, or approve their procedures, or cancel, release, or waive their services. In these respects, then, the relation between an attorney or a trustee and his animal client would be radically different from the typical relations between representatives and their human clients. It must be conceded that the possibility of hiring, agreeing, approving, canceling, and the like is present in the typical (all human) case of proxy representation, but I can discover no logical or conceptual reason why that *must* be so, and indeed in some special examples involving human principals and their agents it is not in fact so. Legal rules, for example, require that a criminal defendant be represented at his trial by an attorney and impose a state-appointed attorney on reluctant defendants, whether they like it or not. Whatever the wisdom of this policy, it appears perfectly coherent and intelligible.

Not all relations called "representation" are alike. John Doe may be unable to attend a business meeting at which an important vote is to be held, so he appoints Richard Roe as his delegate and empowers Roe to vote for him, carefully instructing Roe how he is to vote. The agreement between the two parties makes Roe the representative of Doe in a very limited sense: he is merely a "mouthpiece," a kind of human instrument through which Doe registers his own will. Roe, as a stand-in, has no discretion of his own. Other cases of representation, however, are entirely different in this regard. Sometimes, for example, John Doe hires an expert to solve his problems and grants him discretion within wide limits to exercise his own professional judgment. A buyer, trustee, guardian, or lawyer is often a representative in this sense—he is not a mere instrument of his client's *will,* simply registering decisions made independently by the client, but he is a representative of his client's *interests.* A creature need have no will or choice of his own, nor even any clear awareness of his predicament, to be represented in this second way. Mere possession of interests is quite sufficient.

At this point in the dialectic, the person arguing against the possibility of animal rights is driven to his final position. If he has accepted the argument up to now, his only remaining move is to deny that any animals but man can have interests. The possession of interests can be seen at this point to be the crucial mark of conceptual suitability for right-ownership. Not only are interests necessary for a being to be represented in the relevant sense; they are also essential to its being the sort of thing that can have a *good* of its own, for to act in a creature's interest is to act for its good. It may seem at first as though even plants and "mere things," which assuredly do not have interests of their own, might yet have a good or welfare that we can promote or retard. Certain kinds of fertilizer are "good for" lawns (as we say), and certain kinds of gasoline and oil are "good for" automobiles. But clearly all we can mean by these useful idioms is that the fertilizer or the gasoline and oil promote *our* interest in the lawn or the automobile. Particularly in the case of the mere thing, where the absence of an interest of its own is certain, it is clear that the object, though it can be good or bad in a great variety of respects, can *have* no good of its own.[14] "An automobile needs gasoline and oil to function, but it is no tragedy for *it* if it runs out—an empty tank does not hinder or retard its interests."[15]

Now we are in a position to see the relevance of the question with which we began this section—whether animals are the directly intended beneficiaries of protective legislation. To concede that animals can be beneficiaries (as the deniers of the possibility of animal rights were reluctant to do) is to acknowledge that they are the sorts of beings who can have interests and therefore a good of their own that can be represented by proxies and protected by guardians. Possession of interests by no means automatically confers any particular right or even any right at all upon a being. What it does is show that the being in question is the kind of being to whom moral or legal rights can be ascribed without conceptual absurdity. To have a right, after all, is to have a claim, and to have a claim is to be in a legitimate position to make certain demands against others. A mute creature can make claims only by means of a vicarious representative speaking for it, but if it has no interests of its own, it cannot be represented in this way, having no "behalf" in which another can speak. Moreover, if a creature has no interests of its own, it has no good or welfare of its own and cannot be helped or hindered, benefited or aided, in which case it has no "sake" for which one could act. In that event there could be no coherent reason for regarding any conduct of others as

55

its due, and thus the concept of a right would simply not apply to it.

It is not true, however, that animals do not have interests (in the relevant sense) of their own. However the concept of an interest is ultimately analyzed, the materials out of which interests are compounded must surely be wants and aims. These in turn presuppose at least certain rudimentary cognitive equipment—the ability to recognize and distinguish, to expect and believe, and to adopt means to ends. The higher animals, at least, do seem to have conative lives of their own. Most of us (whatever our philosophical disagreements) agree in recognizing the behavioral manifestations of their wants and the objectives of their pursuits. The trustee for funds set aside for the care of animals can easily know what it is to act in the interests of the animal he cares for, and if he should abscond with the funds, another party can speak up indignantly in the mute animal's behalf, demanding for it its due. Unlike mere artifacts and plants, moreover, animals can experience suffering and frustration, states that are surely not in their interests. Compared to those of human beings, animals' interests are few and simple, but such as they are, they are sufficient to make talk of their rights coherent and meaningful.

## II

Granted then that animals are the kinds of beings that *can* have rights, do they in fact have any, and if so, what rights do they have? Beginning with the relatively trivial, claims can be made on behalf of specific animals to goods that belong to them as a result of agreements made between human beings. Because of the intellectual incompetence of animals, it is impossible for a human being to make a promise to an animal or for the animal to reply with the promised *quid pro quo* required for a legal contract. But human beings can and do make promises to one another of which animals are the intended beneficiaries. I see no difference in principle between these arrangements and contractual agreements that confer rights on third-party human beneficiaries—for example, an agreement between a policyholder and an insurance company to pay a given sum to the policyholder's children in the event of his death. Upon the death of the insured, the children have a valid claim that can be pressed in their behalf against the

56

insurance company in a court of law. This claim is valid even if the children had no knowledge or understanding of the contract that created it.

Similarly, human beings commonly make wills leaving money to trustees for the care of animals. Is it not natural to speak of the animal's *right* to his inheritance in such cases? If a trustee embezzles money from the animal's account,[16] and a proxy speaking in the mute beast's behalf presses the animal's claim, can the proxy not be described as asserting the animal's *rights*? Our legal tradition says not, but its reasons embody the confusions about the concept of a right that I have tried to dispel.

More important, there is no reason to deny that animals have general legal rights to noncruel treatment derived from statutes designed to protect them. These statutes are sometimes notoriously vague and, because of their escape clauses, very weak. In at least one case, however, a British act confers quite definite rights on animals—for example, the right to "complete anaesthesia" before being used in any "experiment calculated to give pain."[17] A proxy representative speaking for a rat might well seek an injunction on the animal's behalf to prevent a planned surgical operation without anaesthesia, or if such an operation is performed, criminal prosecution might be initiated for the violation of the rat's legal rights.

An even more fundamental right, one that is equally undeniable and is possessed by all creatures capable of suffering, is a general *moral right* not to be treated cruelly. What I mean by a moral right is a claim whose validity derives not (necessarily) from a legal or institutional rule, or a convention or agreement, but rather from a moral principle binding on the consciences of all moral agents. The underlying principle here is extremely simple. We condemn and conscientiously avoid inflicting unnecessary pain and suffering on other human beings simply because we regard pain and suffering as an *intrinsic evil*. That is, we judge pain and suffering to be evil simply because they *are* pain and suffering. In the case of human beings, at least, we never ask for any further reason that a given condition is evil and therefore to be avoided or corrected after we learn that it is a painful condition. The question "What's wrong with pain anyway?" is never allowed to arise.

We understand that some pain does more good than harm on balance, but what follows is that justifiable pain is a necessary evil, not that some pain is good in itself. If the essential character of pain and suffering themselves makes them evil—evil not for their consequences but in their intrinsic natures—then it follows that given magnitudes of pain and suffering are equally evil in themselves whenever and wherever they occur. An intense toothache is an evil in a young person or an old person, a man or a woman, a Caucasian or a Negro, a human being or a lion. A skeptic might deny that a toothache hurts a lion as much as it does a human being, but once one concedes that lion pain and human pain are equally pain—in the same sense and the same degree—then one cannot deny that they are equally evils in themselves. All this follows necessarily from the view that pain as such is an intrinsic evil, and not evil only because it tends to produce bad effects of other kinds.

The leading alternative to this argument for animal rights to humane treatment is the view that we owe our duties only to other human beings, not because human beings have some essential characteristic that animals lack, not because animals possess invulnerabilities to pain that humans lack, but only because the members of one species can have moral ties only to their own kind. This view holds that moral rules apply only to members of the human community, that animals are simply not in our club, and that the matter ends there. In this view, the chain of moral reasoning comes to an end at a different place, not at the self-evidence of the evil of pain as such, but rather at the exclusive loyalty of humans to their own kind. In the one view the only answer to the question "Why is pain evil?" is that it is pain. In the alternative view the only answer to the question "Why treat humans humanely but not animals?" is that they are humans.

It may therefore seem that the two views are on an equal footing morally, with nothing to choose between them, but that is not so. To be sure, all chains of reasoning must come to an end someplace, but it does not follow that all proposed stopping places are equally valid. The claim that all pain is evil in itself is a plausible candidate for a self-evident moral proposition, if only because no one can sincerely bring himself to doubt it in his own case. On the other hand, thousands of reflective persons have been led to wonder why the fact of humanity as such qualifies some living things for the right to humane treatment but not others. There is not a trace of self-evidence in the reply "Humans deserve good treatment simply and solely because they are humans and that's the end of reasoning about the matter." Moreover, to make loyalty to humanity the ultimate kind of "reason" in this manner is to make it no reason at all, but rather a piece of self-favoring arbitrariness antithetical to the character of all genuine moral reasoning. About this there is no gainsaying the late C. S. Lewis:

> If loyalty to our own species, preference for man simply because we are men, is not a sentiment, then what is? If mere sentiment justifies cruelty, why stop at sentiment for the whole human race? There is also a sentiment for a white man against the black, for Herrenvolk against the Non-Aryans.[18]

The exclusion of arbitrariness and favoritism is part of what we mean when we characterize judgments as "moral." This explains why we fall naturally into objective modes of speech when we ascribe moral rights. We decide whether or not to grant, recognize, or confer legal rights on classes of persons; as legislators, we discuss whether or not such conferrals would be good policy, useful, or fair. But when we ascribe moral rights, we speak not of deciding, but of discovering and reporting their existence. That is not because we believe they have already been conferred by some cosmic "moral legislature," and ours is not to reason why but simply to report them as discovered fact. Rather, it is because a right is a claim, and the basis of a claim is a reason, and when reasons are sufficiently cogent, they have a coercive effect on our judgments. When this is so, we feel that we have no more choice in making the judgment than we do when we report the findings of our senses about some matter of empirical fact (though surely moral judgments are not *about* some matter of empirical fact). Even in the legislative context, we may decide to create *legal* rights to X because we believe citizens "already have" *moral* rights to X—that is, claims against us to X based on objectively binding, principled reasons.

Among the rights that are often said (in the objective mode) to belong to persons already, prior to and independently of legislative enactment, are those called "human rights." It is interesting to note that the moral right to noncruel treatment

59

satisfies one common definition of a human right—namely, a right held equally by all human beings, unconditionally and unalterably. If we define "cruel treatment" as behavior that inflicts *unnecessary* pain or torment on a creature capable of suffering—that is, pain for which there is no good or sufficient reason—then I should think everyone would agree that cruel treatment (so defined) *always* violates the rights of the being so treated and that those rights rest on no "condition" but the capacity to suffer and cannot ever be justifiably withdrawn or nullified. The one general right that animals most obviously have, then, is a "human right"!

In a narrower sense, of course, a human right is a moral right held unconditionally and unalterably by all and *only* human beings. The right to humane treatment is not peculiarly human in this sense, but there is at least one kind of absolute and unalterable right for which only human beings can qualify, and that is the right not to be degraded and exploited even in painless and humane ways. If we raised human beings for food, or treated them with tranquilizing drugs that rendered them compliant tools for our selfish purposes, or harnessed them like donkeys to carts or rickshaws, we would be violating a right we seldom think to ascribe to animals. We might yet treat them kindly, feed them well, and reward them with pats and sugar cubes instead of blows and angry words. Indeed, it would be good business practice to do so, since we could probably get more labor out of them in the long run for taking good care of them. But to convert humans into mechanical instruments in this way would be to humiliate, degrade, and utterly dehumanize them, even if we did it "humanely." It is difficult for me to conceive of animals being degraded in a similar sense; hence I doubt that the human right to a higher kind of respect, or an inviolate dignity, can properly be ascribed to them. Animals do make some claims against us, and by virtue of their capacity to be claimants and right-holders generally, they do qualify for a certain moral respect. But the higher kind of dignity that precludes even humane use as mere instruments requires a level of rational awareness that animals cannot achieve.

John Locke once wrote of the "natural rights" to "life, liberty, and property." Is it plausible to attribute any of that noble triad to animals? Animals do have claims against us to something like property and liberty, but these claims are clearly derivative from a more basic right to humane treatment. In some modern "animal factories" cattle are crowded so closely together that they have barely room to move their limbs. In mechanized farm buildings the new technology completely destroys the possibility of animal movement. Ruth Harrison writes:

> In some extreme systems the animal spends the major part of its life unable even to turn round in its pen, for example in most veal units, some barley beef units, sow stalls, and sow cubicles. These animals can only stretch their limbs when they are standing, and the bird in the battery cage is unable to stretch its neck fully within the cage or to spread its wings.[19]

These animals are deprived of liberty of movement in precisely the way prison cells deprive human beings of liberty. The rationale for condemning this practice, however, unlike that in the human case, rests on no principle other than that proclaiming the evil of suffering. The more elaborate argument for the value of human liberty as found, for example, in Mill's *On Liberty,* would hardly apply to animals. We need not concern ourselves that a given steer has no choice whether to live in Texas or Montana, or that this lack of ultimate control over the course of his life will stunt his intellectual and moral powers. Inability ever to move out of a narrow stall is another matter. The basis of the conditions in crowded animal factories is as clearly cruelty (actually a kind of "mental cruelty") as it would be in animal-baiting, or vivisection without anesthetic, as Harrison's example vividly shows:

> Lack of movement can lead to boredom, boredom to so-called "vices" such as tail-biting in pigs and featherpecking in birds. Rather than overhaul the system the producer then further deprives the animal, either of light to see its fellows clearly, or by mutilation—the hen of part of her beak or the pig of its tail.

Similarly, animal preserves might be likened to a kind of "property" owned by the various animals that occupy it. Poaching and other violent incursions by humans into the domain reserved for the animals then could be interpreted as a violation of the animal's "property right." But here too the right in question has a derivation different from its human counterpart. Without room to roam wild animals cannot flourish as wild; they become overly dependent on human support and vulnerable to new diseases; eventually they succumb painfully to droughts, famines, and the like. Ultimately, to deprive wild animals of their wilderness sanctuaries is to treat them cruelly, and for that reason, to violate their rights.

Whether or not there is a natural animal right to life is the most difficult and controversial question that can be raised about animal rights, and I can hardly do it justice here. It may be useful, however, to note that ascription of the right even to human beings is not altogether free of confusion and controversy. Those of us who regard human life as something precious in itself insist that all human beings have a claim against their fellows to be rescued when threatened with death and also a claim not to be killed. As a claim, the "right to life" is absolute. But a claim is not quite the same thing as a full-fledged right. Claims can come into conflict with other claims and can be outbalanced or overruled. Claims can differ in degree: some are stronger than others. Rights in a strict and proper sense do not differ in degree and cannot be in conflict with one another. Consider property rights, for example. Jones and Smith might both take to court what they think are valid titles to a given parcel of land. Each has a case to make or a claim to advance to ownership of the land. But ownership is the right to the *exclusive* control of the land. If Smith has a right to the land, then Jones has a duty to stay off it without Smith's consent, and if Jones has the right, then Smith has a duty to stay off. It would thus be contradictory to say that they both have a right and that the rights "conflict." If one has a right, then the other can have no more than an outweighed claim, for a right is a kind of trump card that cannot be outweighed.

Obviously, tragic circumstances may occur in which some can be saved only by killing (or risking death to) others. It cannot be the case, therefore, that all human beings in all circumstances have a right not to be killed or left to die. Indeed, in some circumstances we have the choice between conserving human lives and paying an enormous price in other values. We build roads and tunnels knowing full well that a certain number of workmen will be killed in unavoidable construction accidents, and we leave miners to die in underground cave-ins when the price of their rescue would be millions of dollars. So if our actual practice is an index of our attitudes, we allow even the claim to human life to be outbalanced by claims of other kinds. At most, then, all we can plausibly mean by an absolute human "right to life" is a *claim,* belonging to all human beings as such, to have very serious consideration always given to the value of their lives, not to be killed without cause, and, when endangered, to be rescued whenever this can be done at reasonable cost.

Once more, the cases in which animals most clearly have a claim against us to their lives are instances in which the claim is derivative from the more fundamental right not to be treated cruelly. When we kill a doe we leave her fawns without protection, and that is cruel to *them.* It is for that reason, not respect for animal life as such, that many laws grant a doe special protection against hunters. Even if an animal's life, like a person's, is of some value in itself, it would appear to be considerably less basic a consideration than its claim not to be treated cruelly. The British Cruelty to Animals Act of 1876, for example, seems to respond to a widespread (though not universal) element in the public conscience when it requires that an experimental animal be killed "before recovery from the anaesthetic, if it is in pain or seriously injured."[20] When we contrast this *duty* to kill animals with the great debate over whether there is even a *right* to kill humans deliberately in similar circumstances, it appears that the animal "right to life," if there is such a thing, is generally held to be a much weaker claim than its human counterpart.

The famous argument of Jeremy Bentham for humane treatment of animals, for which he has received much deserved praise from humanitarians over the years, implies or presupposes that there is no independent animal claim to life at all. The basis of all our duties to animals, Bentham thought, is the animal capacity for pain.[21] This imposes a strict duty on us not to cause them to suffer, but leaves us entirely free to kill animals when it is useful to us and not painful to them.

> If the being eaten were all, there is very good reason why we should be suffered to eat such of them as we like to eat: we are the better for it, and they are never the worse. They have none of those long-protracted anticipations of future misery that we have. The death they suffer in our hands commonly is,

and always may be, a speedier, and by that means a less painful one, than that which would await them in the inevitable course of nature. If the being killed were all, there is very good reason why we should be suffered to kill such as molest us: we should be the worse for their living, and they are never the worse for being dead. But is there any reason why we should be suffered to torment them? Not any that I can see.[22]

It should be noted in passing that the Benthamite argument against an animal right to life would make the human right to life itself derivative from a more general right not to suffer pain, a result that could have drastic consequences for lonely but innocent humans who can be killed painlessly to no one's grief.

It is clear, I think, that animals have no general claim against humans to the protection of their lives in the state of nature where they must hunt, kill, and eat one another. Human intervention to save animal lives in the wild, in fact, would itself be a kind of cruelty to the animals whose instincts require them to kill. In short, if we respected animal claims to life as such in the same manner and to the same degree as we respect the human claim to life, our meddlings in nature would become even more officious and counterproductive than they are already.

If animals have any underivative claim to life, it would appear then so weak as to be outbalanced by almost any human purpose of a reasonably respectable sort with which it might come in conflict. We can kill animals for self-protection, for food, for skins, for purposes of sanitation and public health, or to protect still other animals from suffering. One might get carried away by this list, however, and extend it without limit. If an animal's life as such had no value, or if an animal had no claim whatever against us to the preservation of its life, then any human purpose (or even no purpose at all) would be sufficient justification for killing an animal if done in such a way as not to cause suffering. But in fact, to kill a horse, or a dog, or a lion just for one's idle amusement, when no contribution to the well-being of other animals is intended, would be to deny a very real claim without cause and hence to violate the animal's right, weak though it may generally be. Wholly wanton painless killing, even more obviously than killing for sport or amusement, would be an invasion of the rights of the victim.

If the conclusions about the animal "right to life" I have tentatively reached are correct, then at least two things need explaining: (1) why an animal should have any underivative claim to life-as-such at all and (2) why the animal claim to life is such a very weak claim compared with the human "right to life." In the space remaining I can only sketch the outlines of possible answers to these questions.

All animals, like all living things, are disposed by their inherited natures to remain in existence. This "impulse to self-preservation," like any other biological propensity, is something that can be respected and furthered or denied and hindered. One school of moral philosophy, whose chief spokesmen were William James,[23] George Santayana,[24] and Ralph Barton Perry,[25] would make all conative urges, wants, impulses, even unconscious tendencies and directions of growth, worthy objects of moral respect. Any such state or tendency is a kind of "demand" for fulfillment, and other things being equal (which they never are), its satisfaction would be a thing of value. "The essence of value," James said, "is the satisfaction of demand."[26] So long as any demand whatever is frustrated, so long (as James put it somewhere) as "a single cockroach suffers the pangs of unrequited love," the world is not as good a place as it might be. Of course, not every demand for satisfaction is of equal value, and in our actual world it is necessary that many impulses to life be squelched if life itself is to flourish. Nevertheless, it is possible to hold that insofar as anything at all is the object of some "demand," it is, just so far, a thing of value. That would be a way of establishing at least some value for each animal life, however minimal.

An equally difficult question is why animal claims to life should be so much weaker than human claims. I should like to mention one rather quick way with this question, if only in passing. We should remind ourselves that a right is an addressed claim—that is, not only a claim to something, but a claim made against one or more specific persons. Now, an animal right to life could not be a claim against other animals, since animals are incapable of having duties and therefore of respecting the rights of others. Rather, an animal claim to life can be held only against human beings so that the animal claim is logically correlated with the human duty. Human duties to respect animal lives then are simply one part of the larger catalog of human duties of all kinds and must find their proper place in an order of priority. Generally speaking, our duties to persons close to ourselves in space and time, kind and relation, tend to have a greater stringency than our duties to creatures who are more remote in those respects. I have a greater duty to my immediate family than to my remote relatives, to my friends than to strangers, to countrymen than to foreigners. That might explain why the animal claims to life might rank well behind most claims of human beings, even on the assumption that animal life is as valuable a thing in itself as human life.

Our question assumes a more difficult shape, however, when it requires us to justify the assumption that animal life is not as valuable as human life—the assumption most of us in fact make. How is it possible to hold consistently that any human life is a more precious thing in and of itself than any animal life? Recall the earlier argument about cruelty: If pain is an intrinsic evil, then it is an evil wherever and whenever it occurs, and degrees of intensity being equal, it is as great an evil in an animal as in a man. What are we to make of a similar argument applied to life? If human life is a good, intrinsically worth preserving for its own sake, then any life is equally a good, worth preserving for its own sake.

The parallel between the two arguments, I believe, is entirely superficial. Human pain seems self-evidently an evil to those who have known it quite simply because it is pain—because it hurts, and to be hurt is to suffer something evil in itself. Human life, however, seems a supreme good to those who treasure it, not because it is life, but because it is human. It is a truism, but one worth pondering, that one cannot be a human being and manifest whatever is precious in the human condition unless one is alive. Life, then, is a trivially obvious but necessary condition for the existence of any uniquely human properties that may have an intrinsic value. Abstracted from those properties, however, it is far from "self-evident" that life has any value in its own right at all, much less an invariant supreme value "wherever and whenever it occurs." I conclude therefore that it is possible to hold without inconsistency that an individual human life as such is a thing of far greater value than an individual animal life as such. If that judgment of relative worth is to escape the character of a mere sentiment of self-preference, however, it must be grounded in some properties that are present in human nature and missing in animal nature. If we cannot locate such properties and plausibly base the unique worth of human life on them, we may have to fall back ultimately to the Benthamite position that neither human nor animal life as such has an intrinsic value and that human life has a greater claim to protection only because of the greater human vulnerability to suffering from the deaths of others and from "protracted anticipations" of our own.

### III

There is one kind of human duty toward animals that is not derived from any right of animals (or anyone else for that matter) against us, and yet honoring that duty may be even more important, morally speaking, than respecting animal rights. I refer to the duty to preserve *whole species* from extinction—certainly a more important matter morally than preserving the life of any single animal. Yet a species, unlike an individual animal, is not the kind of entity of which it even makes sense to say it can have rights. The name of a species is not that of some superentity distinct and emergent from the individual animals of which it is composed. Rather, it is simply the name of a collection of entities with certain defining characteristics in common. The species of elephant called *Loxodon africanus,* for example, is not an individual superelephant with wants and aims, feelings and beliefs. As a species, therefore, it has no interests of its own and is not even the kind of thing that could have a good of its own. It follows, if my analysis is correct, that a species is not the kind of being that could have a claim or a right.

We often speak of corporate rights and duties. The United States has a right to impose taxes and a duty to enforce laws. The General Motors Corporation has a duty to pay taxes and a right to issue stock. These statements, of course, are perfectly intelligible. A species, however, is quite a different kind of entity from a corporate institution. As a mere unorganized collection, it has no charter, no rules, no offices, no individuals empowered to act or be acted upon in its name.

Our duty to preserve African (not to mention Indian) elephants from extinction could be owed to our own posterity as *their* right. After all, our unborn descendants will have interests that can be represented by proxies now, so it makes good sense to speak of their rights to inherit a world of a certain kind and of our present duties to them to conserve that kind of world. But this can hardly be the whole ground of our duty to save the elephants (or even the major part of it). If the elephants disappear before our great-great-grandchildren arrive, then our descendants will have been deprived of something of value and can rightly complain (over our graves) that we have invaded their interest in inheriting a world that might have contained elephants. But how great a wrong would that be to our descendants? Presumably they would feel about elephants somewhat the way we feel about dinosaurs. It is a shame that there aren't a few survivors, but we don't gnash our teeth over the matter. The enormity of our wrongdoing in permitting the extinction of elephants, however, would be out of all proportion to the minor wrong done to our human descendants.

The duty we have as members of the human species to preserve other species, then, cannot be explained wholly as the consequence of anyone's rights against us. No explanation that a philosopher can dream up will carry nearly the conviction that the statement of the duty itself bears. My inclination is to seek an explanation in terms of the requirements of our unique station as rational custodians of the planet we temporarily occupy. We made no decision individually or collectively to fill the role of superintendents of nature. Like so many of the roles we occupy as individuals, this one was foisted on us by circumstances, and we occupy it as if by default. But while it was not up to us whether to assume responsibility for the care of our planet, it is entirely up to us (as the ancient Stoics said so often) whether we do the job sloppily or well. In the last analysis, our duty to preserve the other species may be largely a matter of very human pride.

### NOTES

1. A leading example is Immanuel Kant, *The Metaphysical Principles of Virtue* (Indianapolis: Bobs-Merrill, 1964), p. 106. See also W. D. Ross, *The Right and the Good* (Oxford: Clarendon Press, 1930), pp. 49ff.

2. For example, C. S. Kenny, *Outlines of the Criminal Law* (Cambridge: Cambridge University Press, 1958), pp. 171-172.

3. Joel Feinberg, *Social Philosophy* (Englewood Cliffs, N.J.: Prentice-Hall, 1972).

4. Edward Westermarck, *The Origin and Development of the Moral Ideas,* vol. 2 (London: Macmillan, 1917), p. 508.

5. *Ibid.,* p. 509.

6. John Chipman Gray, *The Nature and Sources of the Law,* 2nd ed. (Boston: Beacon Press, 1963), p. 43.

7. For example, W. D. Ross, *The Right and the Good.* For a forceful criticism of this view, see W. D. Lamont, *Principles of Moral Judgment* (Oxford: Clarendon Press, 1946), pp. 82-85.

8. See C. Lloyd Morgan, *Animal Life and Intelligence* (London: Arnold, 1890), p. 399.

9. Gray, *The Nature and Sources of the Law,* p. 27.

10. See Edward Evans, *The Criminal Prosecution and Capital Punishment of Animals* (London: Heinemann, 1906).

11. Westermarck, *The Origin and Development,* vol. 1, p. 258.

12. Gray, *The Nature and Sources of the Law,* p. 43.

13. *Ibid.*

14. For a development of this idea, see Joel Feinberg, "The Rights of Animals and Future Generations," in William Blackstone, ed., *Philosophy and the Environmental Crisis* (Athens, Ga.: University of Georgia Press, 1974).

15. *Ibid.*

16. The example is from H. J. McCloskey, "Rights." *Philosophical Quarterly* 15 (1965): 221.

17. British Cruelty to Animals Act of 1876, sections 2 and 3.

18. As quoted without reference to source by Richard Ryder, "Experiments on Animals," in *Animals, Men, and Morals,* ed. S. Godlovitch, R. Godlovitch, and J. Harris (London: Victor Gollancz, 1971), p. 81.

19. Ruth Harrison, "On Factory Farming," in *Animals, Men, and Morals,* ed. S. Godlovitch, R. Godlovitch, and J. Harris (London: Victor Gollancz, 1971), p. 17.

20. British Cruelty to Animals Act of 1876, section 3, part 4.

21. "The question is not Can they *reason?* nor Can they *talk?* but Can they *suffer?*"—Jeremy Bentham, *An Introduction to the Principles of Morals and Legislation* (New York: Hafner, 1948), p. 311n.

22. *Ibid.*

23. William James, "The Moral Philosopher and the Moral Life," in *Essays in Pragmatism* (New York: Hafner, 1948), pp. 65-87.

24. George Santayana, *Reason in Science* (New York: Scribner, 1905), ch. 8-10.

25. Ralph Barton Perry, *The General Theory of Value* (Cambridge, Mass.: Harvard University Press, 1926).

26. William James, "The Moral Philosopher," p. 77.

# Thinking and Being with Beasts 4

*Carleton Dallery*

FOR MOST OF ITS HISTORY, philosophy has been associated with the activities of centers of power, art, science, and wealth. It has been traditionally regarded as one of the "higher" things a man might do in life, and it has until recently been very much in the debt of persons of rank. The very idea of vertical hierarchy underlies much of philosophical literature. For some thinkers, to be "philosophical" means, in part, to be "above" certain things; for others, it means to view things from a higher perspective, from which apparent confusions can be seen as exhibiting law-like patterns; for others, philosophy was a form of *acsesis,* or purifying movement "upward." The great Anaxagoras, when asked why he didn't show more concern about his city, answered that he did indeed, pointing upward to the heavens. Aristophanes, also at the beginning of the Western tradition, showed the archetypical philosopher swinging in a basket above his disciples. To philosophers and critics, philosophy more often than not, and for a variety of reasons, abandoned the earthly realm. For some, the rationale for philosophy was little more than the escape it provided from domesticity, provincialism, women, children, and the hazards of sensual existence.

Today, it might seem as if this tradition is dead, or gasping its last breaths, inasmuch as the main business of its inheritors has been to empty out two thousand years' worth of elevated metaphysical "nonsense" and take up residence in a closet attached to the sciences. Given the tradition and its collapse, it might seem ironic that any philosophers should be asked to put in

**Carleton Dallery** is Assistant Professor of Philosophy, State University of New York at Stony Brook (Long Island).

a word on the side of the earthly—a word for the beasts, for example. Fortunately, a few philosophers are willing to do this.

I mention these two strands in the tangled Western tradition in order to bring out a special characteristic of one movement in contemporary thought, namely phenomenology.[1] Unlike the tradition of elevation, phenomenological philosophy finds sense or meaning in the world—the experienced world and the lived body—which high-flying thought left behind. For phenomenologists, all philosophies are styles of life and express ways of coexisting with the world. Freedom, for a major group of phenomenologists, is not the freedom of *ascesis* or withdrawal or absolute choice, but the freedom of meaningful engagement in and with the world. Thinking, also, is not an attempt to possess the world or inner experience by means of concepts or systems, but rather an unending attempt to express what so far remains unexpressed, produce sense from darkness. Phenomenology is neither a construction "upward" from the world, nor the skeptical purgation of all such constructions in favor of (for example) analyses of concepts or methods in science.

The truth phenomenologists want to express is neither above history, in timeless ideas or notions, nor reducible to history, in the form of facts, material conditions, or Nietzschean "blood knowledge." In describing their enterprise, phenomenologists reject this vertical structure and the options it seems to present: either elevated mastery or skeptical silence. A typical characterization of the phenomenological style emphasizes the philosopher's dialogue with other men, or with humanity, or with nature, or with being, or with all of these.

After condemning American professional philosophy for its withdrawal, the French phenomenologist Maurice Merleau-Ponty (1908-1961), describes his own intention as "facing things head-on." Elsewhere, he says "we are already [immersed] in the true," meaning that we do not need to seek truth beyond our existence or below it (for example, in neurophysiological or unconscious processes). He calls on philosophers to free themselves from modern thought and engage in "prospecting the actual world." It is needless to multiply citations. The point is that phenomenological philosophy is a resolute attempt to "dwell with the world" (borrowing a phrase from Hegel), without assuming an

71

abyssal gap between, say, the experienced and true world, or the contingent and the necessary, or the spiritual and the fleshly, or the ideal and the factual, or the human and the natural, or the higher and the lower.

The intelligibility the phenomenologists seek to put into words comes neither from the mind nor from empirically accessible causal processes. Rather, the intelligibility is already there in the "flesh" of the world and yields gradually but never finally to our efforts of interrogation. In other words, the intelligibility is neither "within us" nor "out there." Rather, it is in the dynamics of the "inter world"—of being-with, not a determinate order of being—because we, as interrogating, speaking beings, express the world and endlessly discover the world expressed through us. To quote the same phenomenologist again: "real philosophy consists in re-learning to see," and "makes us see through words." This world that is prospected philosophically is the same world that is celebrated in poetic song and is imaginatively probed in literature. It is also the world that is presupposed, but taken for granted and rendered mute, by all science. In short, there is only one world; our access to it is multiple in form; and philosophy cannot claim pride of place *over* other modes of access, since the philosopher—knowingly or not—necessarily collaborates with and depends on those other modes.

A fair question at this point is: "Phenomenology for the sake of what?" From a traditional standpoint, the answer must seem bizarre: phenomenological philosophy expresses for the sake of the expressed. Phenomenological philosophy is "for the good of" or "for the being of" even the simplest existence, the least of creatures, too. It is impossible, then, to call phenomenology a humanism in the usual sense. And while it is a certain kind of science or *logos,* it is not a science whose fruit is technology, or increased human power over nonhuman things. The leading pioneer of the phenomenological movement, Edmund Husserl (1859-1938), called the (true) philosopher a "functionary of humanity," but he meant this in the sense that all humanity engages in the effort that the philosopher makes his special calling.

At last we can get to the question of the relevance of phenomenology to the question that unifies this collection of

72

essays. Despite the fact that phenomenological philosophers so far have had very little to say concerning norms for man's relations with his fellow beasts, their aim is to articulate the being of man in such a way as to show the community of flesh, or of being, between mankind and all living things. Through phenomenology, and against the "elevating" tradition, the visible or experienced world is restored to its rightful place as primary. The real animal, for example, is the one I see and interact with, not the one I "possess" through concepts. The real world is not a colorless, mute, closed system of things, hiding beneath "secondary qualities," but the one I meet every day, the one that painters express, the one that wells up in me as I try to understand it.

If the phenomenologists are right, we must revise our notions about which of the sciences are basic or foundational. Ecology, for example, is basic to biology and is, so to speak, the ethical foundation of life science. Earth-keeping, or caring for the real world in its entirety, is basic by comparison to, say, unlocking the secrets of physical nature. Politics is basic in relation to the several "human sciences." Philosophy, as interrogation, is basic to (and may be fused with) other forms of expression, like art and science, since its questions go to the common root shared by those apparently unrelated forms.

To continue in this vein, we might contrast two ways of expressing the much-discussed question of ecology and the environment. One way is to ask how man can survive, and how resources (man's resources) can be preserved. That is not the philosophical way, for it rests on a tacit decision to concern ourselves exclusively with our being as a biological species. Our questions are tied to our survival. If we do not need fish hawks in our network of resources, and if their preservation is not required in order to maintain civil order (assuming conservationists to be dangerous), we might just as well let them perish. In contrast, the philosophical way of getting at this question must reveal, first of all, that it is essential to human beings to transcend our species-boundaries. "Man," says Merleau-Ponty, "is not a natural species, but an historical idea." We are really human to the extent that our active, thoughtful care goes beyond the maintenance of that form of biological existence we call human.

In a book that is remarkably akin in spirit to phenomenological philosophy, *In Defense of Nature,* John Hay says: "In spite of all our pretended substitutions, there is no substitute for a common respect for everything that has reached the distinction of life." And later, "The whole point is that we depend ultimately on an everlasting drive for unity whose wellsprings we did not create but can only draw upon or re-create. The whole point is the human commitment of human experience to universal nature and all its lives."[2] The idea is not new. Other philosophers have expressed it in some form (the Pythagoreans, Empedocles, Charles Peirce, and Paul Weiss, to name a few). Phenomenological philosophy has been concerned to make explicit the ontological grounds of that basic insight. What is it about human beings that gives a basis for saying that human concern is not limited to the welfare and survival of the human species and its resources? Both Husserl and Merleau-Ponty offer the same answer, which is simple to state but not so simple to bring out against all objections.

The answer is *perception.* Merleau-Ponty claims to be carrying forward Husserl's later views on this point, and the claim has lately been contested. But it seems clear enough that both of them recognized the total insertion of humanity in the natural dimension of the world and denied that this insertion is either merely biological or produced by thought. That is to say, we are in and of nature through our multisensory coexistence—or perception.

This is not the place to summarize Merleau-Ponty's magisterial work, *The Phenomenology of Perception* (1946). For our purposes, it is important to note that perception is described as the complex, always open, temporal "access" between world and perceiver. It is neither a causal process nor a process distinct from social relations, speech, or understanding (as it would be if perception were a "thought of seeing"). So in perceiving a snake, for example, I do not simply receive an impression of a sinuous form having a certain mottled pattern; I do not see a cold, indifferent fact, or have a bunch of impressions to which I might or might not endow some value depending on my feelings; I see the *snake,* which is to say that I see its behavior in an environment proper to it and that I "appropriate" the snake's way of being, the snake's perception of certain things around it. But I am free to regard the snake as an object and admire its beauty, or to loathe its slitheriness. I can think about the snake or investigate it as an organism, or kill it for food or fun. The original perception of the snake, though, is richer. Unlike its enemy or its predator, I do not have to respond in a particular way to the snake. The snake is manifest to me in its peculiar way of "having" and moving in an environment. Originally, then, I see it as an analogue to myself, as having certain behaviors like mine (feeding, traveling, threatening, fleeing), as being alive. I could express its being in many ways, and I could also simply enjoy watching it. The owl that captures the snake does not see in this way; the snake, for what it is, is not accessible to the owl. Owls do not investigate snakes, dissect them carefully, bash them with rocks for laughs, or take care to see that they do not perish from the earth.

All of this is to say that my being is in principle open to the being of other things prior to my having an organically determined interest in them as food or as enemies. This point is often emphasized by distinguishing between the world inhabited by humans and the environments inhabited by other organisms. Every other species, meaning every other species in its environment, has a putative place in the human world. But animals are limited to their biologically determined environments; they do not see things that do not relate to food, security, nesting sites, and so on. The animal's environment has a temporal structure, but it *is* always what is present to it. The world for humans has no such limits. It has "horizons" of past and future, and the world is always structured by those horizons. To become just another biological species, then, men would have to forget the past and let the future develop however it might. Indeed, this is not an uncommon style of behavior. Is anything harmed by it? Yes, everything. Man cannot *not* have or inhabit a world; and if other species had the power of voice, they would surely beg that man fully realize the implications of his being *in* and *of* the world (what Merleau-Ponty calls "*être-au-monde*").

Men have recognized the distinction between environment and world since the earliest times, when the dog brought its environment into the human world. These early men, seeing the ways of the dog and nonconceptually appropriating those ways, enrolled the dog as a thing of many qualities. I am not saying that

75

the early men were intellectually clever, any more than I am saying that the early dogs figured out a way to get more meat for less effort. What I am saying is that the domestication of beasts had and still has its origin in perception. A human being can perceive that another living being has an environment peculiar to its species, and a human can perceive what is in that environment.

To clarify the point further, consider the hunting peoples who have rituals of "becoming" other beasts—by wearing their skins and imitating their calls, for example. Far from being primitive foolishness, this behavior is a kind of inquiry. Studying animals is one of the oldest human pursuits, and the cave paintings make it astoundingly clear that early men took an acute interest in things of no organic importance, like the shape and style of animal motion. The rituals and the paintings are developments, concrete elaborations, of the original perceptions of the beasts.

To see the animal moving in its environment is already to "care" about the animal, since in a way I put myself in its place. I say it is foraging, or mating, or fleeing; I know what it is doing because these are analogues of my behavior. Even a small child can do this without recourse to controlling concepts; he can be asked to "think like a fish" or to figure out what he would be doing if he were a deer. The frequency of success in such childish endeavors is not so important as the fact that such approaches to beasts are meaningful. (I remember very clearly learning to "think like a fish" when I was small, and I sometimes have to remind myself now to do that instead of being clever with my fishing tackle.)

But if beasts have no interior being and are automata, as Descartes held, I cannot "think in their place." In fact, I cannot really perceive them. They become real to me only as I add to certain sensations meanings that come from my sentiment or intellect. In outline, this is the tendency of modern thought. Perception is relegated either to blind mechanisms (as in skeptical empiricism and objective psychology) or to operations of the mind (as in Cartesianism and Kantianism). For Husserl and Merleau-Ponty, this amounts to canceling out perception and losing the world (at least losing it in and by means of philosophy). Merleau-Ponty then is not speaking metaphorically when he charges both camps in the modern tradition with blindness; he does not mean blindness to things in the environment (loss of the ability to see), but blindness to the world as lived, the world as open to the environments of other beasts, as providing the ground of our coexistence or being-together.

In modern thought, animals can be regarded as having superficial characteristics in common with humans. Kant acknowledges this by saying that if a child is cruel to a cat, he might grow up to be cruel to humans, which is a consequence to be avoided. In fact, Kant speaks for the entire dual tradition of modern thought when he says " . . . so far as animals are concerned, we have no direct duties. Animals are not self-conscious and are there merely as a means to an end. That end is man."[3]

From the beginning of his career, Merleau-Ponty clearly and stoutly tried to break out of that tradition. The meaning of his attempt becomes clearer for us in a statement he made in some working notes shortly before his death, which I paraphrase here: We can no longer think using the cleavage separating God, man, and creatures such as we find it used by Spinoza, for example. In short, rejecting man as a starting point, and rejecting God as a substance with modifications, Merleau-Ponty's work was moving in the direction of restoring men and beasts to their rightful ontological place in philosophy and in practice. Ironically, the rightful ontological place is the one they already have in perception—though in an alienated, abstract society one has to look to children, painters, poets, "primitives," and other exceptional people to find thought and practice based on concrete perception.

A reader versed in philosophy might suppose that this reversion to concrete or primitive perception is a romantic, irrationalist project. It does, indeed, sound as if knowledge as science, as conceptual grasp, is being compromised if not rejected. A skeptic might object that our perceptions of beasts, even if they are as the phenomenologists describe, do not suffice as a ground for active concern for beasts beyond our self-interests. The simple fact that we see a horse as a horse before we see it as a valuable property, or a status symbol, or an organism, does not mean we must care for the horse in its being or care for the living world in all its complexity.

But the objection presupposes a certain idea of knowledge. Phenomenology does retain a distinction between knowledge and perception even as it grants their inextricable overlapping. A word about knowledge, then, might be in order. To speak simply rather than subtly, in the Stoic tradition resuscitated by Descartes, knowledge is grasping with certainty. Thus Descartes proposed that we will avoid mistakes if only we hold our will in check and avoid both judgment and action until we have achieved knowledge. But knowledge is the special business of the mental substance. For Merleau-Ponty, in contrast (and I think for Husserl too, but less obviously), knowledge is always *incarnated* or *bodily*. A *final* grasp of anything is impossible, since knowledge depends on future activities, confirmations, revision, and qualifications.

There is, in short, knowledge in perception. When we look, we already know in outline what we are about to see. For example, I can visit the nesting places of ospreys and see that the young are not hatching. I see something and know something the birds do not, and I can connect this phenomenon with others. I undertake to find out what the other phenomena are and discover that the accumulated DDT in the birds' diet has adversely affected the formation of the eggshells. In my first perception of "something wrong" I am concerned, like the birds, for the birds' existence and environment, and then I seek knowledge of the scientific kind. I already knew what an environment was and what continuing life meant. To take an older example, prehistoric cave painters already had a kind of knowledge of animal movement. How can we describe this knowledge? It is "knowledge by contact or frequentation," or bodily knowledge. Once I know about such things as musculature, centers of gravity, force, and such, I need not abandon that first knowledge as if it were error; I complete it or add to it. But if I take the abstract knowledge as the only kind of knowledge, I make a momentous mistake, which is to think of my actions as applications of abstract knowledge. Worse, I might postpone practical decisions until I possessed full knowledge. This mistake is manifest daily in arguments about protecting the environment. One such error is to say that we should not act until knowledge is acquired; another is to say that since knowledge will never be acquired, or can never be acquired, we should simply let natural things go their own way, with no intervention from human individuals or institutions.

Elucidating the nature of concrete knowledge, Merleau-Ponty discusses Géricault's paintings of horses. A high-speed, sharp-focus photograph can capture a horse in movement—but the horse seems to be suspended in space, not moving. Yet Géricault's horses "really run on the canvas, in a posture impossible for a real horse at the gallop" because the painting brings me to "see the body's grip upon the soil . . . according to a logic of body and world I know well."[4] This logic of body and world is known to the painter and to everyone through our being as bodies—not conceptually, but not irrationally either. In other places, Merleau-Ponty has characterized this bodily knowledge as "lateral" to distinguish it from the implicitly vertical (mind over body) structure of Cartesian or modern knowledge "about" the working of nature. Lateral or coexistential knowledge is always open; it does not lead to anything like "mastery" over nature. And since coexistential knowledge is primary, we must conclude that the idea of "mastering" nature or setting it right for human uses is chimerical. In fact, the idea as it has determined human activities and human negligence can be seen as a potentially catastrophic event in and for nature; William Leiss has done a brilliant job of showing this, relying in great part on Husserl's work, in *The Domination of Nature* (1972).

Knowledge must be restored to its true nature as a dimension in human existence, as an aspect of human process. It is nonsensical to say that knowledge is "produced and transmitted" and even more absurd to say that it is "stored" in archives or computers. We can believe such notions only if we take for granted some version of the idea of knowledge as grasp or possession; but the idea dissolves as soon as we describe the knowing subject caught in the flesh of the world, engaged in a reciprocal communication that is never finished. In the coexistential sense, then, we know that it is absurd to reduce the world to a concatenation of objects or externally related parts, some of which are disposable and none of which have value except insofar as human needs and human will "give" value to them. In facing the world as if it were valueless objects, or animals as if they were machines, we do so in ignorance of ourselves and in ignorance of the world. More accurately, man dehumanizes himself in accepting the objectivist ontology, because man *is* his relations with the world, and these relations are not limited to mechanical or causal or conceptual ones.

Once again, we can contrast the species-limited worry about the environment with the ontological concern, or knowing practice, with regard to all forms of life (as well as the inorganic base that life requires). The worry stems from fear of death, and I suspect it is consistent with that view to conceive of life as "not being dead" or simply "continuing in existence." The ontological concern is a moment in the larger and complicated process of becoming human—and in the process of the world's being the world. Thus, I might describe "my" concern as responding to the concerns I see about me. While reason might be mine to use, reason in the fuller, ontological sense does not belong to me as my instrument. Reason is "of" the world, and we belong to it. My engagement in rational inquiry and in positive action can be described as my response to an appeal, a solicitation issuing from an other-than-me. How far this is from saying that reason is the slave of the passions! The enlargement of reason in phenomenological philosophy restores the notion of man's having a vocation not of his own choosing. More truly, reason is the maturation of perceptions and passions.

Merleau-Ponty said as much. In our perception, he says, nature is not an object, not something to be manipulated, but "an interlocutor." This is not metaphor. The world I confront does not vociferate; only humans do that. But my attempts at expression "put into words" or express what is undeniably there. The world, that is, has meaning, and "calls" me to my work.

If this is true—and perception reveals it to be true—the human being whose destructive acts are rationalized on the grounds that "the victims are not human, so I don't feel bad" has himself failed to be a human being. He remains somewhat human, and acknowledges a residual value in the victims, by virtue of the fact that he feels called upon to defend such actions. Phenomenologically, the unrestrained destruction of peoples and of nonhuman life is already a destruction of the humanity of the destroyers (including those who condone the actions or those who are negligent). It may also be a dangerous course if what is destroyed is actually needed for the life of the destroyers. But that is quite another point.

It may seem shocking, but the self-destruction of humanity was already an essential possibility latent in the idea of reason as "elevated," noninvolved, abstract, and disembodied. For that idea removed reason from the world, or, to put it another way, expelled the perceived, lived world from reason. We need not claim that philosophical ideas caused certain historical events (that would only throw us back to the notion of a detached reason anyway), but it is essential to the style of modern life that wanton destruction, species-bound practices, competitive individualism, and imperalism express the same loss of world that the dominant trends of science and philosophy have expressed. The American Indians saw this long before phenomenology was a gleam in any white man's mental eye. As Sitting Bull said, " . . . the love of possession is a disease with them. . . . They claim this mother of ours, the earth, for their own and fence their neighbors away; they deface her with buildings and their refuse. That nation is like a spring freshet that overruns its banks and destroys all who are in its path."[5] The phenomenologists, coming late on the scene, argue in another way that the earth is "an other" and that the possessions and mastery promised by modern thought demand the fatal price of losing the world. For those goals, men have blinded themselves.

Evidence suggests that human beings did not begin to act according to a species-limited or individualistic model of behavior until the technological means of "owning" the whole planet and eliminating pests, diseases, and useless things appeared to be at hand. The evidence uncovered by anthropologists amply shows that pretechnological societies—despite their varieties—regarded the entire living world as having (to use Western terms) rights and privileges distinct from human needs. It seems that the idea of our having total power over nature gave birth to our thinking of ourselves as if we were nothing more than clever, homeless organisms looking after our own survival. As Henri Frankfort put it:

> The ancients, like the modern savages, saw man always as part of society, and society as imbedded in nature and dependent upon cosmic forces. For them nature and man did not stand in opposition . . . for modern, scientific man the phenomenal world is primarily an "It"; for ancient—and also for primitive—man it is a "Thou."[6]

81

If the phenomenologists are right, the "primitive" relation to nature as a whole and to natural things is true and concrete, while the Cartesian, rationalistic, and empiricist way of seeing and conceptualizing is abstract and ultimately false to our primary perception. The recent attempts in philosophy, the arts, and anthropology to rediscover and articulate the "primitive" might, then, be a matter of seeking out the truth, as against the self-blinding abstractions of modern thought and society. (Among anthropologists, Paul Radin and Stanley Diamond stand out in this search for emancipatory knowledge.)

The restitution, in phenomenological inquiry, of preintellectual, nontechnological modes of comprehension is rich in consequences for both science and practice. It will be a long time before all these consequences come to light and find their way into general acceptance. A few of them, though, are germane to the present discussion.

Since nature understood concretely or primitively, or nature as perceived, is not the system of objects standing against a disembodied consciousness, consciousness cannot be "above" or outside of nature. Moreover, the course of nature is not indifferent to the perceiver, though it might be for the disembodied knower, the seeker of nature's laws. Nor can we say, with the old and new Darwinians, that natural existence is a sort of mechanical struggle we can observe and eventually conceptualize from above. Such concepts as law, substance, attribute, accident, cause, and adaptation have to be seen as artifices in the unacknowledged service of a consciousness we never experience—that is, a disembodied consciousness. The entire enterprise of human artifices of all kinds can now be evaluated in terms of its complex, ambiguous role in the world of living things. Such evaluation of human culture is, we might say, "called for" by the living things we study and use. The life of other beings enters into our lives as an energizing and guiding principle. The position of our inquiries, then, has to be seen as a mediating one in the midst of all life, rather than as a knowing, possessing one vertically higher than the things studied. This position in-the-midst-of is the reason that all-or-nothing judgments like "man is evil," "nature is innocent," "man is free and not at all determined," or "nature is determined and not at all free" are ruled out. Judgments of

82

that form presuppose that the judge is wholly separated from the judged.

The natural world now comes to be understood as what it truly is in perception—namely, an open text of significances. As Merleau-Ponty once put it, every "corporeity is already a symbolism." To elucidate this point, he cites Adolf Portmann's remark in *Animal Forms and Patterns* (1967) that feathers, fur, colors, and so on are "designed in a very special way to meet the eye of the beholder." That is, the appearances of the animal are not properties of an object or machine, functioning according to laws internal to it, but forms of communication between organisms within given environments. Since the dynamics of this communication are affected in numerous ways, we cannot conceive of "the possible" as what might happen in the future or the "future actuality." Rather, the possible is already an ingredient in the relations between organisms in their environments. For human beings, it would follow, knowledge as prediction is fatuous and irresponsible; it is based on the assumption of our separation from the predicted. It also assumes that the predictions are to be used as instruments in our service, in the service of one species, or in the service of a disembodied, mastering consciousness. Responsible knowledge, by contrast, remains true to our communication with the natural world. Inquiring into the workings of the natural world, in this view, has to be seen as a moment in the larger process of earth-keeping, or acting *for* and *with* rather than simply *upon* nature.

These remarks must, for now, remain general and open to further elaboration. However, we are at a point now where we can move on to the two remaining items of business. First, I shall introduce a notion central in phenomenological philosophy, namely that of task. Then to conclude, I shall offer my own ideas about the practical and educational sides of the larger task to which phenomenology belongs.

Husserl, Merleau-Ponty, and some of the other phenomenologists speak so often of the "task of philosophy" that the unsympathetic reader might consider them obsessional. They tell us, for example, that philosophy is an "unending task," that "the task of philosophy is to re-awaken the power of expression," and that "philosophy is creation or re-creation" not of man or of prehuman nature, but of Being. Philosophy (and this means, for our time, phenomenology) is a task of "grounding" or resituating scientific constructions in the fundamental "speech" or *logos* of Being. No doubt this is all quite obscure. What matters to us is their understanding of philosophy as a task or call (vocation). They do not see themselves as technicians or specialists performing jobs definable in terms of either techniques or regions of phenomena (like the region of phenomena for chemistry, the region for neurophysiology, and so on).

To describe a task, we have to speak of the future, or of purpose, and we have to speak of debt or obligation. A task, as the history of the word clearly suggests, is work owed (the word *tax* has the same root). A task is performed for another, either definite (such as a feudal lord) or indefinite (such as living things). So if a task is worth doing, it is worth doing regardless of compensation. That is, its worth cannot be measured in terms of compensation. What counts is the meaning of a task, not the internal satisfactions that accompany its performance, or external rewards, or finished results.

Husserl and Merleau-Ponty both speak of philosophy in terms of being. They do not describe philosophy in terms of human faculties or problems, or in terms of reasoning and the making and clarifying of arguments, or in terms of linguistic uses and abuses. Their sense of the calling and end (*telos*) of philosophy links them with the beginnings of philosophy in Greece. Aristotle, for example, says that "there is a task or work for man as man, a task which is not exhausted by the different *technai,* the different skills and professions, a task which unifies human action and which gives life its human meaning."[7] This statement helps us see that the idea of philosophy as task links philosophy with all men by showing man's links with all being or by articulating what it means to be human.

Another, almost pre-philosophical, link exists between the work of the phenomenologists and the rest of humanity. Probably more human beings today than ever before in history have a sense of what tasks are, and the reason is not that a few philosophers have been restoring the idea of task for their own work. For example, the growing concern for the living world is for many people a discovery of tasks. For them, genuine concern for the ecosystem and for its animate members cannot be based simply on self-interest, economic considerations, or survival. If it could be so based, it would not be a task but just another job, another chore. The question answered by and in a task is, simplistically, "How shall I live as a real human being?" Is such a question merely personal or subjective in origin? Or is the question one we find posed to us by our world? I think phenomenology puts into words questions of the latter sort.

Phenomenology is limited, of course, in that it is restricted to words. Merleau-Ponty insists on this by saying that "philosophy is realized when it destroys itself as separated philosophy." The words become true by becoming flesh. The idea of a task brings together words and flesh; without reflection and interrogation, we can't know what we are doing, and without activity or praxis our words remain abstract. Similarly, the idea of task breaks down the separation between science, or cognitive process, and action. We discover our debt and our task by being open to the world, and not by deducing obligations or inferring prescriptions or having emotions. We begin to carry out our task by reflecting on our situation, by joining ourselves with others through speech, by getting down to work—and by continuing the reflection and the dialogues.

If, for example, we see that fellow humans and beasts are left out of political, economic, and ethical decisions on the tacit grounds that they are mere things with no intrinsic value, we can wake up to the task of relearning to see them. In order to begin the task we do not require "scientific" knowledge. For a skeptic there can be no such thing as a task; the knowledge at the base of a task is always inchoate. The leading phenomenologists are generally in accord that the final truth of man lies in his tasks, not in his absurd freedom or his superfluity. As Merleau-Ponty put it, echoing and criticizing his friend and fellow phenomenologist Jean-Paul Sartre, "man is condemned to meaning." The phrase is unfortunate, apart from its allusion to Sartre's "man is condemned to freedom"; for he means that human life, as contrasted with the existence of an object or the existence of a pure consciousness, is a meaningful life in relation to a multifarious world and in relation to generations unborn.

If there really are tasks, we cannot look "up" to the possessors of knowledge to prescribe to us what these tasks are and what we as individuals must do. Nor can we expect to find an unambiguous "book of nature" that tells us our duties. If there are tasks, we must discover them in our own experience and through our own questions. The work of Husserl and Merleau-Ponty calls us to this discovery. Americans, in particular, for whom exploration and discovery are still living parts of their historical inheritance, should easily respond to this call. Also, since wanton destruction—in fact a kind of metaphysical assault on life altogether—is also a main part of American history, we might well feel a special urgency to discover or recover our genuine tasks. The task, I suggest, is the only form of redemption in a world whose god is hidden. The idea of the task secularizes and deepens the religious idea of "good works."

To conclude this unavoidably sparse essay, I want to give some indications toward the "humane ethic" that proceeds from the writings of the phenomenologists. Since the phenomenologists rule out the possibility of a deduced ethic as well as an emotivist or feeling-based ethic, this is a challenging job. We must see, first, that any ethic or body of prescriptions has to be open and self-revising. Thus, we should not look to an authoritative ethicist, or to a mere argument, in order to find out the rules for conduct. The idea that a moral system is a device for controlling, suppressing, or limiting human action is one of those ideas that dissolves along with the idea of possessing nature through concepts. Whatever ethic comes out of phenomenology (and I doubt that a complete ethic can be brought out of phenomenology), it has to be as exploratory and open as phenomenological philosophy has tried to be so far. We might even say that, given the understanding of human existence presented in phenomenological writings, it is unethical, false to our being, to seek and to use recipe-like codes of conduct.

In the book cited earlier, John Hay gives a good statement of the attitude I find expressed in the chief works of phenomenology:

> We have not conquered nature, any more than I have conquered myself. Life unfinished is the rule for man or trees. What I go looking for is not nature under man's control but a wider, lasting range—that which we will have to live with in order to avoid a life in isolation, that which belongs to us only when we go out to meet it.[8]

86

"Life unfinished"—"go out to meet it." That, I think is imperative enough. What it means is not so simple to state. But there are, I think, numerous ways of "re-learning to see" and to live in accordance with our seeing. I shall suggest some "imperatives," but I think the word is anachronistic. Its meaningfulness depends in part on the assumption of a tightly deterministic natural universe, where every event must happen as it does. Our experience shows us a looser-jointed universe and prevents a sharp cleavage between moral and natural spheres. We might face ontological behests or tasks, but nothing so sharp as an imperative in the current sense of that term. I continue to use it here only because it is familiar.

First, and most important, we have to learn to see the ways in which the dynamics of the economy dictate the wholesale destruction and alteration of beasts as well as people. The major fault of the be-kind-to-animals movements has been blindness to the major assault on animal and human existence. If the economy forces me to become nothing but a consumer and a threatened job-holder, and forces cattle to be nothing but future steaks and hides, something is radically wrong. It is absurd to stay silent in the face of this destruction and content oneself with cleaning the ducks caught in oil spills and picking up stray dogs for the animal shelter. Rescue efforts and gestures of kindness have their place, but it is limited. What is at stake is not just the suffering or death of a number of living things, but the continued being of a complex earth that includes human beings too. If our ethic is confined to helping only certain individual beasts, we misperceive what they are and we remove them from their environments in order to make them our charity cases. In the end we serve ourselves more than we serve the animal victims. The first ethical imperative, I believe, is for the humane movement to become fully and militantly political.

Second, if we think beasts ultimately have the place in our lives that they do in our perception—that is, as our analogues and fellow animals—we should realize that we can make no arguments at all to people who have no experience in seeing animals. But how do people learn to see them? Let me start negatively. We cannot learn what an animal really is by looking at bright pictures in wildlife society magazines or by passing through a zoo once a year.

87

We make it very difficult for our children to see beasts as they *are* when we start them out on images of superhumanly benign and cute things like Smokey the Bear. Such images foster the human disorder called anthropomorphism and probably encourage in some people a foolish wish that humans would be as nice as animals. The animal images in "primitive" societies are universally closer to the truth, probably because one of their main functions is to present the being of the animals to humans. Now, speaking positively, we should consider it ethically imperative to provide opportunities for all people, but especially youth, to confront living things, to "go meet them." Day-tripping to woods and beaches will not do. What is needed is sustained encounter, which can be accomplished in many ways.

Perhaps the most important encounter is the experience of husbandry. By husbandry I mean the daily care and training of beasts, whether they be finches or pigeons or horses or elephants. Simply learning the names and appearances of beasts is of no value at all. But learning the feeding and mating patterns, the ways of interacting with other species, and the ways of responding to human actions is just what "learning to see" means. As a teacher in a college for affluent students, I have been appalled to discover how many of them graduate without ever having taken care of any living thing, human or nonhuman. Do such deprived persons even have ears to hear what we have to say about animals? Or about elders? Or about impoverished peoples? I doubt it. That is why I emphasize that we must strive to provide experiences rather than verbal imperatives—which, if they have any basis, ought to be elucidated from experience anyway.

A third imperative also has to do with learning. If Husserl and the others are right in saying that concepts are open, but that we might slip into treating them as closed and precise, we should allow ourselves to go out and meet concepts and ways of mediating the world that differ from ours. For example, instead of treating the American Indians' reverent use of beasts as a piece of history, we might ask what we can learn from their ways and how their ways might *not* be fully adaptable to modern conditions. Like the phenomenologist, we should not take conceptual frameworks for granted. A promising way to discover that we operate within a framework of presuppositions and to find out

88

what our framework amounts to is to entertain sympathetically and critically the variously expressed frameworks of other peoples.

A fourth imperative holds us to intervene in the processes of nature, taking risks and trying to gain knowledge at the same time. The reason for intervening, rather than turning nature back to itself, as some neoromantics beg us to do, is dual: (1) we cannot carry out such a withdrawal, and (2) there is no such thing as "nature left to itself," free from humanity. As part of this imperative, we might criticize the absurd anthropomorphism that consists in associating the concept of freedom with the concept of nature (and the related error of regarding all beasts in zoos as unfortunate captives). In short, our ethic must be positive and interventionist, or else it is no ethic at all but a form of abdication.

A fifth imperative brings many of us closer to home. We must speak out against certain forms of pet ownership as militantly as we do against the wanton slaughter of wild animals. The use of dogs as surrogate humans and ornaments diminishes the real value of the beasts. Taking care of a pet, in many cases, is a matter of prudent ownership to be classed with keeping crab grass out of the lawn and washing the car once a week. Therefore, pet ownership, even the healthiest kind, does not amount to carrying out a humane ethic, for an ethic is directed to all life, not just to the living things I own. A humane ethic requires us to think "zoöcentrically," to put our thoughts and practices in the service of the creatures who now so obviously need our resources.

A sixth and I hope temporary imperative is rather negative and unpleasant. It is to phase out (I'm not sure how) "nature lore" that is excessively child-oriented and usually unrelated to any practice. The image of nature presented in the typical "nature lore" class or club is utterly false: The cute little animals never copulate, fight, or tear each other to shreds. Too often, nature is presented as an alternative or corrective to human existence—which it isn't. Also, the tradition of "nature lore" avoids confronting the thing that matters, which is man in conjunction with other living things—hunting, training, slaughtering, farming, and so on.

A seventh imperative is related to the sixth as its generalization: All ways of thinking and practice that posit nature or natural things as entirely other than humanity, or as distant from us, need to be revealed for the fantasy they harbor. Nature nostalgia has very little to do with nature and has nothing to do for it; it is a way to mask hatred of civilization and to escape political responsibility. I imagine that if a kingdom of nonhuman animals were to appoint a spokesman, he would say, "When you get out of the woods, do politics!" Fortunately, the Sierra Club is showing the way.

For an eighth imperative, I suggest this: Do not allow the environment to become simpler than it is. Our world should include and maintain as many zoö-centered environments as possible. The great Aldo Leopold made this very case very well in *A Sand County Almanac*. The case can be made only by thinking "in the place of" the living inhabitants of the environment, a kind of thinking which, for phenomenology, is fundamental and not just affective or fantastic. Among the mad projects prohibited by this imperative would be the wholesale draining of swamps, the suburbanization of the Atlantic Coast, and the elimination of mosquitoes. Needless to say, there are many others.

Finally, we have to keep in mind that the imperative of all imperatives is to become human—or even, to restore an idea of Plato and Aristotle, to "become like divinity as much as that is within our power." However what I mean is that the creative tendance of all things is a human calling. We do have obligations toward the things we see, and we find those obligations already implicit in our seeing, as long as we do not try to explain seeing on some causal model.

If we are called to become human, and if we cannot become human in solitude, and if becoming human is an endless process, where do we see in our culture any kind of organized devotion to this idea of humanity? Speaking from my own experience, I can find only one place, and that is the American college system. But there I find it more in the requests of students than in the practices of teachers and administrators. Here is my final recommendation: Students and educators should vigorously condemn the image of man as job-holder, as species-centered animal (whence comes the "ethological fallacy" of using animal phenomena to explain man), as the object studied in objective "human" sciences, and instead make place for task-oriented

90

education as one of the main opportunities of late adolescence. Job training in schools is nothing more than the unsalaried phase of the later job. If it must happen, let it not happen at the expense of the priceless discovery that there is meaningful work.

The meaning in meaningful work lies in our coexistence with each other and with all living things. We are our bonds, and our "oughts" are embodied in what we are.

### NOTES

1. The purpose of this essay and the limitations of space do not permit one to give an inclusive sketch of phenomenological philosophy and its internal quarrels.
2. John Hay, *In Defense of Nature* (New York: Viking, 1969).
3. Immanuel Kant, *Lectures on Ethics* (New York: Harper Torchbook), p. 239.
4. Maurice Merleau-Ponty, "Eye and Mind," in *The Primacy of Perception*, ed. J. M. Edie (Evanston, Ill.: Northwestern University Press, 1964).
5. Quoted in *Touch the Earth*, compiled by T. C. McLuhan. (New York: Pocket Books, 1972), p. 90.
6. Henri Frankfort, *The Intellectual Adventure of Ancient Man* (Chicago: University of Chicago Press, 1946).
7. Quoted by Paul Ricoeur in "The Will and Philosophical Discourse," in *Patterns of the Life World: Essays in Honor of John Wild*, ed. J. M. Edie, *et al*, (Evanston, Ill.: Northwestern University Press, 1970).
8. John Hay, *In Defense of Nature*.

### SUGGESTED READING

Buytendijk, F. J. J. *L'Homme et L'Animal*. Paris: Gallimard, 1965.

Farber, Marvin. *Phenomenology and Existence: Toward a Philosophy within Nature*. New York: Harper & Row, 1967.

Hay, John. *In Defense of Nature*. New York: Viking, 1969.

Hediger, Heini. *Wild Animals in Captivity*. Trans. G. Sircom. New York: Dover, 1964.

_____ *Man and Animal in the Zoo*. Trans. Gwynne Vevers and Winwood Reade. New York: Delacorte Press, 1969.

Heidegger, Martin. *Being and Time*. Trans. John Macquarrie and Edward Robinson. New York: Harper & Row, 1962.

_____ *Poetry, Language, Thought*. Trans. Albert Hofstader. New York: Harper & Row, 1971.

Husserl, Edmund. *The Crisis of European Sciences and Transcendental Phenomenology*. Trans. David Carr. Evanston, Ill.: Northwestern University Press, 1970.

Leiss, William. *The Domination of Nature*. New York: George Braziller, 1972.

Merleau-Ponty, Maurice. *The Phenomenology of Perception.* Trans. Colin Smith. New York: Humanities Press, 1962.

———————————. *The Primacy of Perception.* Ed. James M. Edie. Evanston, Ill.: Northwestern University Press, 1964. "Eye and Mind" is included in this volume.

———————————. *The Structure of Behavior.* Trans. Alden Fisher. Boston: Beacon Press, 1963.

———————————. *Themes from the Lectures.* Trans. John O'Neill. Evanston, Ill.: Northwestern University Press, 1971.

———————————. *The Visible and the Invisible.* Ed. Claude Lefort, trans. Alphonso Lingis. Evanston, Ill.: Northwestern University Press, 1968.

Portmann, Adolf. *Animal Forms and Patterns.* Trans. Hella Czech. New York: Schocken, 1967.

Scheler, Max. *Man's Place in Nature.* Trans. Hans Meyerhoff. New York: Noonday Press, 1962.

Smith, F. J., ed. *Phenomenology in Perspective.* The Hague: Martinus Nijhoff, 1970.

Straus, Erwin. *The Primary World of Senses.* Trans. Jacob Needleman. New York: Free Press of Glencoe, 1963.

# Is Man Innately Aggressive? 5

*Ashley Montagu*

IN HIS FAMOUS REVIEW OF Hawthorne's tales, Herman Melville singled out as their most arresting quality "the great power of blackness" with which they were suffused, a power deriving from "its appeals to that Calvinistic sense of innate depravity and original sin, from whose visitations, in some shape or other, no deeply thinking mind is always and wholly free."

It is of some interest to observe that in no culture, anywhere in the world, does anything quite resembling the doctrine of original sin appear until its promulgation by St. Paul in his epistle to the Romans. The story of the Fall, as told in the book of Genesis, on which the Pauline view of original sin is based, was never interpreted by Judaism to mean that man was evil in the flesh. Rather, by virtue of its frailty the sinner's guilt was extenuated, and in any event his sinfulness entailed no hopeless compulsion to evil. As St. Paul saw it, however, sin is inherent in the body and the members thereof, in the very nature of man's flesh (Rom. 7:23; 8:3). It is, according to St. Paul, because sin and man are identical that the powers of darkness can prevail over him.

Through the unremitting, one might almost say relentless, exegetical exercise of the Church Fathers, their commentators and followers in medieval times, the Calvinists and the Puritans, not to mention all the other dismal sects down to our own day, the Pauline view of human nature has continued to exercise its baleful influence.

Exactly when the sins of men came to be projected on the whole of nature I do not know. The unraveling of that story would make a valuable contribution to the history of ideas. I have

**Ashley Montagu** is a noted anthropologist, social biologist, and author of some forty books. He resides in Princeton, N.J.

little doubt, for example, that Darwin, like most of his contemporaries living in what has been called the "Age of Conflict," was greatly influenced by the prevailing view of nature as in an unceasing state of strife, for which the most obvious support could be drawn from the doctrine of innate depravity. The phrase Darwin frequently uses throughout *The Origin of Species* is "the warfare of nature."

The publication in 1859 of Darwin's epoch-making book could not have occurred at a more favorable moment in the development of Western industrial civilization. The very title of Darwin's book has an oracular, even programmatic, ring about it: *On the Origin of Species by Means of Natural Selection, or the Preservation of Favoured Races in the Struggle for Life.* I have long suspected that when Darwin wrote the words "favoured races" he was not unmindful of the fact that he belonged to a people who might be so described. As for the term "struggle," Darwin used that loaded word in the sense of "competition." "Struggle" soon came to be understood in its extended meaning as "the struggle for existence," and the words "preservation of favoured races in the struggle for life," came to mean (in a phrase adopted by Darwin from Herbert Spencer) the "survival of the fittest." Indeed, Darwin preferred this expression to "natural selection."[1] But it was Alfred Russel Wallace, in a letter to Darwin dated 2 July 1866, who most clearly stated the view that came to prevail. "The term," he wrote, " 'survival of the fittest' is the plain expression of the fact; 'natural selection' is a metaphorical expression of it, and to a certain degree indirect and incorrect, since . . . Nature . . . does not so much select special varieties as exterminate the most unfavourable ones."[2]

The emphasis was on "extermination" of the "unfit" and "preservation" of the "fittest." Malthus had clearly formulated such ideas in his *Essay on the Principle of Population* in 1789. Indeed, in the original *Essay,* his judgments on those who had not been called were so harsh that he was prevailed upon by friends to soften them in subsequent editions. The message, however, was not lost on Darwin when he read Malthus in 1838. Darwin fully acknowledged his debt to the gentle clergyman and, whether he was aware of it or not, translated the prevailing severity of industrial competition (and the struggle for existence that economic theory made evident) into the language of biology and exalted it into a complete explanation of the organic process. This accomplishment was first clearly pointed out by Patrick Geddes in 1882, the year of Darwin's death, in an article on "Biology" in *Chamber's Encyclopedia* (vol. 4, p. 116). Charles Peirce made precisely the same observation in an article entitled "Evolutionary Love" published in 1893. *"The Origin of Species* of Darwin," Peirce wrote, "merely extends political-economical views of progress to the entire realm of animal and vegetable life."[3]

The struggle for existence among men was paralleled by the struggle for existence among plants and animals. It was not that the struggle among men was regarded as part of the competition inherent in nature, but rather that nature was regarded as mirroring the struggle for existence of men living or attempting to live in a ruthless industrial society in which the "fittest" alone "survived."[4]

The truth is that Darwinian theory from its very beginnings was greatly influenced by the social, economic, and political thought of the latter part of the eighteenth and the first half of the nineteenth century, and that its own influence worked principally to give scientific respectability in the form of natural law to what had hitherto been factitiously imposed social law.[5] In addition to providing the world with the first workable and verifiable theory of evolution, Darwin also presented the nineteenth century with a biological philosophy for industrial progress: the survival of the fittest through competition. It fell to Herbert Spencer to develop this doctrine as Social Darwinism. It was Spencer who, in 1852, almost seven years before the publication of Darwin's *Origin,* had coined the phrase "the struggle for existence."[6] In his book *Social Statics* (1864) Spencer wrote, "Progress . . . is not an accident, but a necessity. Instead of civilization being artificial, it is a part of nature; all of a piece with the development of the embryo or the unfolding of a flower."[7] In the "struggle for survival" among individuals and classes within the state, the unfit would be eliminated. "The whole effort of nature," he wrote, "is to get rid of such, to clear the world of them, and make room for better."[8]

The appeal of such ideas to the businessmen, politicians, and militarists of the Western world can hardly be exaggerated, for the doctrine of Social Darwinism gave them a biological justification, a scientific justification, for competition and aggression. Aggression was a fact of nature, "red in tooth and claw," as Tennyson had sung, and challenged the creed of man. The bestiaries of medieval times were updated to support the rationalizations of the new Social Darwinian creed, and the sins of man were fastened on the defenseless animals of the "wild," the "jungle," and, indeed, on all of nature.[9] The indescribable evils and conditions of life in the cities of the civilized world were projected on what was, in a highly gratifying and self-righteous rationalization, called "the state of nature," no less. In keeping with this view of "nature," as hominid fossil remains were gradually discovered, prehistoric man was pictured as a cannibalistic brute whose principal occupation was murderous violence and dragging women by their hair. I am not referring to the imaginative parodies of newspaper cartoonists, but to the reconstructions of serious "authorities."

The ridiculous models of prehistoric man's physical appearance were equaled by the assertions pertaining to his behavioral propensities. Human nature was seen as having been largely determined by a past history of "bestiality," from which many writers on the subject feared it would never be possible for man to free himself. During the same period, the most influential of all students of human nature, Sigmund Freud, who was born three years before the publication of *The Origin of Species* and died in 1939, was plumbing the depths and surveying the boundaries of the human psyche. In 1919, in his book *Beyond the Pleasure Principle,* Freud proposed the theory of the existence of a death instinct in man. This theory became the foundation stone of psychoanalysis. Very few psychoanalysts subscribe to it today, but it has had a very profound influence on all who have been exposed to it. In *Civilization and Its Discontents* (1930), Freud further elaborated on man's innate aggressiveness. In words not unreminiscent of Thomas Hobbes's *Leviathan* (1651), Freud wrote:

> Men are not gentle friendly creatures wishing for love . . . a powerful measure of desire for aggression has to be reckoned as part of their instinctual endowment . . . *Homo homini lupus:* who has the courage to dispute it in the face of all the evidence in his own life and in history? This aggressive cruelty usually lies in wait for some provocation, or else it steps into the service of some other purpose, the aim of which might

as well have been achieved by milder measures. In circumstances that favor it, when those forces in the mind which ordinarily inhibit it cease to operate, it also manifests itself spontaneously and reveals men as savage beasts to whom the thought of sparing their own kind is alien. Anyone who calls to mind the atrocities of the early migrations, of the invasions by the Huns or by the so-called Mongols under Jenghiz Khan and Tamerlane, of the sack of Jerusalem by the pious crusaders, even indeed the horrors of the last world war, will have to bow his head humbly before the truth of this view of man.[10]

Then in 1931, in the famous rectorial address delivered at the University of Aberdeen, "The Place of Prejudice in Civilization," England's leading physical anthropologist, Sir Arthur Keith, really shook things up. What did this gentlest and kindest of men have to say about human nature? What he said was that man is innately aggressive:

Without competition Mankind can never progress; the price of progress is competition. Nay, race prejudice, and, what is the same thing, national antagonism, have to be purchased, not with gold, but with life. Nature throughout the past has demanded that a people who seeks independence as well as peace can obtain these privileges only in one way—by being prepared to sacrifice their blood to secure them. Nature keeps her human orchard healthy by pruning; war is her pruning-hook. We cannot dispense with her services. This harsh and repugnant forecast of man's future is wrung from me. The future of my dreams is a warless world.[11]

In 1953 Raymond Dart, the discoverer of *Australopithecus*, wrote in an article entitled "The Predatory Transition from Ape to Man":

The blood-bespattered, slaughter-gutted archives of human history from the earliest Egyptian and Sumerian records to the most recent atrocities of the Second World War accord with early universal cannibalism, with animal and human sacrificial practices or their substitutes in formalized religions and with the world-wide scalping, head-hunting, body-multilating and necrophilic practices of mankind in proclaiming this common bloodlust differentiator, this predaceous habit, this mark of Cain that separates man dietetically from his anthropoidal relatives and allies him rather with the deadliest of Carnivora.[12]

In his book *Adventures with the Missing Link* (1959), Dart elaborates on the bloody-mindedness of our early ancestors. *"Australopithecus* led a grim life," he tells us. "He ruthlessly killed fellow australopithecines and fed upon them as he would any other beast, young or old. He was a flesh eater and as such had to seize his food where he could and protect it night and day from other carnivorous marauders."[13]

These ideas have been repeated by Konrad Lorenz and Robert Ardrey, and, indeed, it was Dart's ideas on the murderousness of the australopithecines, and Ardrey's friendship with Dart in South Africa, that converted Ardrey to the views he has so successfully disseminated in his books. The widespread appeal of these ideas is such that some of Ardrey's books have been made into films.

It seems that the new litany of original sin is going to be with us for a long time and is destined to receive substantial support from wholly unexpected quarters, as we shall soon see. As late as 1970, under the influence of Freud, we find Edward Glover, the dean of English psychoanalysts, republishing views of the nature of the normal infant as follows:

> Expressing these more technical discoveries in social terms, we can say that the perfectly normal infant is almost completely egocentric, greedy, dirty, violent in temper, destructive in habit, profoundly sexual in purpose, aggrandizing in attitude, devoid of all but the most primitive reality sense, without conscience of moral feeling, whose attitude to society (as represented by the family) is opportunist, inconsiderate, domineering and sadistic. And when we come to consider the criminal type labelled psychopathic it will be apparent that many of these characteristics can under certain circumstances persist into adult life. In fact, judged by adult social standards the normal baby is for all practical purposes a born criminal.[14]

We perceive, then, that the gospel of man's innate depravity, his in-the-flesh orneriness, competitiveness, and aggressiveness, have a long and unbroken history. In our day this gospel has been given a fresh boost by the writings of Lorenz, Ardrey, and others. These writers devote lengthy works to the thesis that man is innately aggressive, but they seldom trouble to define what they mean by aggression, usually employing the term in so many different senses that they succeed in adding nothing but confusion to an already turbid subject—"calling in ambiguity of language," as A. E. Housman put it in another connection, "to promote confusion of thought."[15] Nevertheless, from their descriptions of man's aggressive nature it is quite clear what they mean by aggression.

Lorenz maintains that aggression is an instinctive trait in man and, like all instincts, is characterized by "spontaneity," that is, the ease with which it is elicited. He gives as a special example "militant enthusiasm." It is because of its spontaneity, according to Lorenz, that man's innate aggressiveness is so dangerous.[16] Man, says Lorenz, "is phylogenetically programmed" to discharge aggression against his neighbors, for early man was faced with "the counter-pressures of hostile and neighboring hordes."[17] The australopithecines, the earliest men, Lorenz states, used weapons "to kill not only game, but fellow members of their species as well."[18]

Ardrey fully supports the views of Lorenz. "Man," he tell us, "is a predator whose natural instinct is to kill with a weapon."[19] All Ardrey's books are devoted to the attempt to prove this thesis.

What Lorenz and Ardrey mean by aggression is clear: It is an innately determined, phylogenetically programmed form of behavior designed to inflict injury and/or death on others. In brief, these writers assert that man is innately murderous. War, murder, juvenile delinquency, crime, international rivalries are all, according to them, largely the result of man's innate orneriness. Niko Tinbergen, the distinguished ethologist of Oxford University, rejoices in the success of such writings, because, he writes, "it is evident that the mental block against self-scrutiny is weakening—that there are masses of people who, so to speak, want to be shaken up."[20]

On the other hand, I think that the wide appeal of these books stems not from the desire to be shaken up but rather from the desire for reassurance. It is very gratifying to learn that we cannot be blamed for our orneriness since it is innately determined, that the fault lies not in ourselves, but in our genes. This at once relieves us of the burden of guilt we may have been enduring for, shall we say, those unamiabilities and animosities for which we need no longer feel personally responsible. After all, it *really* is only human nature. And so we can continue being ourselves, knowing that it is in the nature of things to be so and not within the control of ordinary human beings, as B. F. Skinner would have us believe, to change them.[21]

I believe one of the dangers of these popular writings is that they divert attention from the fact that no matter what or who was responsible for making us into what we have become, we are not for a moment relieved of the responsibility of endeavoring to make ourselves over into what we ought to be. Books like B. F. Skinner's *Beyond Freedom and Dignity* are symptomatic of the profound loss of understanding of what human beings are for. What, indeed, is the human enterprise all about if it is not the achievement of personal freedom and dignity?

In recent years the neural basis of aggression has been the subject of an increasing number of investigations. Many workers in experimental neurology and the neurosciences claim to have located areas in the brain that represent the neural bases or "substrates" of aggressive behavior. Such areas are the limbic system, the amygdala, the hypothalamus, and the reticular system.[22] The results of such studies will inevitably lead many to conclude the brain is "programmed" or "wired" for aggression and that those who claim that aggression is instinctive in man are essentially right. In short, if actual "centers" in the brain for aggression do not exist, something very like them do. Such investigations deserve careful consideration for several reasons. First, they will, I am convinced, help us understand better what is involved in aggressive behavior. Second, there is a danger that such studies, incorrectly interpreted, may lead to a kind of "Higher Phrenology" or faculty psychology. Indeed, the inferences that have already been drawn from such investigations concerning the neural bases of aggression have, in my opinion, gone far beyond

100

what the evidence warrants, and unfortunately they have already been misused. Combined with the claim that aggression in man is instinctive, the neurophysiological findings would appear to make the case for innate aggression bombproof.

The view seems to be gaining ground that the brain has areas that, when stimulated, give rise to violent or aggressive behavior regardless of situation, context, or previous experience. Therefore, the conclusion is too easily drawn that these areas of the brain constitute the neural bases or substrates of violence and aggression. The words *bases* and *substrates* seem readily transmogrifiable into *cause* or *causes,* a fundamental condition in the causation of such agonistic behavior. Since it is small interneurons that mainly occur in the areas of the brain that have been associated with aggressive reactions, however, it would appear most likely that plasticity is a characteristic of the areas involved, and that there exist no predeterminants of any kind in these cerebral areas.

I have dealt with the concept of instinct elsewhere at some length, and I can only repeat here that I find no evidence for the existence of instincts in man.[23]  If instincts exist in man, it should not be difficult to produce evidence for them. There seems, however, a singular reluctance to do so.

At a meeting of the American Association for the Advancement of Science in Philadelphia in December 1971, Allen Deets of the University of Pittsburgh and Harry Harlow of the University of Wisconsin reported that when infant rhesus monkeys are isolated for periods extending from six to eighteen months of age they become extremely violent when exposed to other monkeys, especially defenseless infants. The investigators concluded, contrary to the expectations of other theorists, that the capacity for violent behavior, at least in monkeys, is innate. It is the ability to control aggressive tendencies, they suggested, that must be learned.

"Cultural evolution has clearly outstripped biological evolution in shaping the nature of human social organizations," Deets said. "But this does not mean that man has escaped his biological heritage as a primate. As part of this heritage, we believe that innate factors *influence* the nature of human aggression and that the same maturational sequencing of affection, fear, and aggression occur in human [growth and development]."[24]

So there we have it. The evidence now appears to show that aggression is an unlearned, innately determined behavior. Notice that Deets says, "we believe that innate factors *influence* the nature of human aggression." He does not say *determine*. With his quoted statement there can be not the least argument. Innate factors probably influence every human behavior; aggression is no exception. But all this is very different from claiming that learning plays no role in the expression of that behavior. On the contrary, the evidence indicates that learning plays an important role in every form of human behavior, and this is probably true, to varying degrees, in many animals as well.

The spurious dissociation between "heredity" and "environment" is not dead yet. However, I believe that those who suffer from "geneticism" are much worse offenders than those who are described as "environmentalists," and are much more dangerous.

I do not think that the organism is "wired" or "programmed" to exhibit aggressive behavior as a response to the frustrations of its expected satisfactions. Rather, I think the evidence indicates that all organisms, when they lack the satisfaction of certain needs, especially a dependency need such as love, draw on similar organic resources for making their needs known. These resources will be not an area, center, or pathway for aggression, but a miscellany of organic functions—neural, muscular, hormonal—available to the organism. They can be mobilized, for example, for the purpose of directing attention to the organism's needs. As the infant grows older (whether or not his needs, especially the principal one of love, are satisfied), and is exposed to aggressive models, then aggressive behavior may become a permanent part of his personality.

The aggressionists do not seem to appreciate the full significance of man's evolutionary history, a history in which love, cooperation, and interdependency have been at a high selective premium. If man has any innate predispositions, they are directed toward cooperation rather than aggression.[25]

I suggest that the areas of the brain that have become associated with aggressive or violent behavior have been organized by the experience of the individual out of the environments in which he has been socialized. The evidence, as I read it, indicates that aggressive behavior is not a structurally innate function of the organism and that no innate basic aggressive neural circuitry exists. This is not to deny that there exist specific areas of the brain in which neural circuits can be organized by experience to produce aggressive behavior, just as various neural elements may be organized to function in the service of many different learned behaviors.

Certainly the evidence for man thoroughly supports the role played by environment in learning aggression or nonaggression. How else could one account for the extraordinary nonaggressiveness of the Tasaday of Mindanao, the Eskimo, the Ifaluk of the Pacific, the Semai of Malaya, and other peoples? Whatever predispositions the members of these societies may have had toward aggression, they have successfully learned not to develop them. Despite Lorenz's theories, their members exhibit no spontaneity toward aggression, but they do, like all human beings, exhibit a spontaneity toward cooperation. Despite, also, the wishes of still a sizable number of "true believers," the evidence unequivocally indicates that in the evolution of all animal forms, and most particularly in man, cooperative behavior has been a far more influential factor than aggressive behavior. Indeed, cooperative behavior has been selectively the most successful form of behavior in the evolution of all animal groups.

The outstanding species characteristic of man is his educability.[26] To suggest that man is born unchangeably aggressive, warlike, and violent is to do violence to the facts. To maintain that he is innately wired or programmed for aggression is to increase confusion and to exhibit a failure to understand the most consequential fact about the nature of man. That fact is not that man becomes what he is predetermined to become, but that, as a human being, he becomes whatever, within his genetic limitations, he *learns* to be. That, it seems to me, is the important statement about the nature of man.

*Now, what are the implications of these views for the humane movement and an ethic that includes man's consideration of his relations to other sentient beings?*

The important fact is that the whole of nature is a cooperative enterprise. There are no "superior" and "inferior" creatures; each is merely different. The whole of nature consists of one interconnected system of networks of relationships among living things, and no one, including man, stands above any of the others. All are part of one great harmonic scheme. Our relation to the whole of animate, as well as inanimate, nature is naturally one of involvement, for we are all part of the same world stuff organized at different levels of integration and complexity. A functional continuity in the behavior of all animals unites us and makes us, in a very profound sense, one. Man's relations to his relations, at the inanimate as well as animate, sentient level, should therefore be one of relatedness, of love. Love is to be understood as behavior designed to confer survival benefits on others in a creatively enlarging manner.

What is built into our genes is such a relatedness to the whole of nature, but since there is also built into our genes a supreme capacity for learning—the species trait of educability—we are capable of being blocked in the development of relatedness. In its stead we may be taught to become uninvolved, unrelated, disengaged, to regard ourselves not as a part of nature but as superior to it, and, indeed, to produce rationalizations to justify our destructive behavior to ourselves. Hence, we find militants of various sorts claiming, "Violence is as American as apple pie," and so-called sportsmen declaring, "Hunting is a great sport because it gives man the opportunity to express a basic instinct." In both instances the implication is that violence and hunting are natural. The truth is, of course, that violence in America is just about as natural as apple pie—it is entirely learned, just as hunting is. Man has no more instinct to violence than to apple pie or hunting—all three of these phenomena are, in fact, the product of socioeconomic factors.

What we have a right to expect in a humane society is that the child will be provided with opportunities supplied by his parents, teachers, and government to recognize the needs of man and his supreme educability in order that the child may understand that the most important of the humanizing needs is the need to grow and develop in the ability to love. Love, as previously defined, will enable him to become the continuing maker of himself as a humane being.

Man requires no further physical evolution to improve himself, observed biologist George Gaylord Simpson. What he requires is the wisdom to make himself over into what he ought to be, and as we well know he possesses the capacity to make himself into anything he is able to become. Toward this end our instructional systems need to be turned into genuinely educational systems, *not* for instruction in the "three R's" but for education in the art or science and relatedness or love.

Innumerable scientific observations show that the natural state among all animals is cooperation and that cooperation has been by far the most important factor in the evolution of living organisms.[27] It should surely be obvious, after a hundred or more years of field observations and research, that all animals are born for cooperation and not for conflict. Nevertheless, the weight of the outmoded ways of thinking about nature and man still bears down upon us and prevents most of us from seeing the truth, a truth to which intuition often breaks through where the errors of "reason" have failed. All nature is kin. As the Koran so beautifully puts it: "There is no beast on earth nor fowl that flieth, but the same are a people like unto you, and to God they shall return." We should, therefore, love and respect them, because they are worthy of our love and respect, because they are our kin, and because it is to suffer an irremediable impoverishment to forego the friendship of our fellow living creatures.

Since we, as sapient human beings, live at a level of abstraction vastly more complex than that of our fellow creatures, and since we are therefore capable of bringing about the most complex kinds of changes in the environment, we have a special obligation to all other living things, including plants and, as I have intimated, even the inanimate environment. As human beings we are the possessors of enormous powers for good and evil; hence, we must continually be on our guard that we not abuse those powers. The less capable other creatures are of exercising those powers, the more responsibly we must learn to use them. The rights of animals and plants are in a sense greater than the rights of our fellow human beings, because animals and plants are more vulnerable to extinction and more defenseless than we. Our duties and obligations are at the very least no less toward animals and plants than they are toward our fellow human beings, for without animals and plants we would not long survive. The care of others begins with caring for them, and the humane person uses his strength to strengthen the weaker and to defend the defenseless.

The myth of the beast is simply a projection upon animals of our own dehumanization. The myth has wrought untold destruction upon other creatures and justified our conduct to ourselves by saddling them with our own unacknowledged, acquired insensitivities to the needs of others. By this projection we have not only inflicted unspeakable cruelties upon other animals, but have deprived ourselves of the great riches of experience and friendship with them and the profound lessons we could learn from them for the conduct of our own lives and societies.

When we study animal societies we see that they are cooperative and peaceful, that man is the only violent creature of his kind, that there is no other animal that makes war on its own kind, and that innate aggression is the myth by which men attempt to "explain" and justify their murderous and violent behavior. Faulty attributions of this kind, based on pseudological rationalizations and unanalyzed theories and systems of value, make it obligatory for us to help the new generations to become acquainted with the world of nature through field trips, through reading, through observation, and above all through the compassion that is the highest form of intelligence; for while sound thinking is absolutely vital for man living in complex societies, compassion is at least as important—a compassion extended to the whole of nature.

Those who have lived among animals on farms or have kept pets know that animals are capable of expressing affection, loyalty, and love, that they are capable of suffering and sadness, that their friendship is unconditional and enduring, and that it is enriching to be able to communicate with them through the only language that surmounts all barriers and against which all frontiers fall, namely, through love. As it is written in the book of Job:

> Ask now the beasts and they shall teach thee; and the fowls of the air, and they shall teach thee:
> Or speak to the earth, and it shall teach thee, and the fishes of the earth shall declare unto thee.
> Who knoweth not that in all these that the hand of the Lord hath wrought this? In whose hand is the soul of every living thing, and the breadth of all mankind?

# NOTES

1. See Charles Darwin to Alfred Russel Wallace, 5 July 1866, in *Life and Letters of Charles Darwin*. In contrast to Darwin, Huxley, writing in 1890, spoke of "The unlucky substitution of 'survival of the fittest' for 'natural selection,' " and considered that it had "done much harm in consequence of the ambiguity of the 'fittest'—which many take to mean 'best' or 'highest'—whereas natural selection may work towards degradation *vide epizoa.*" *Life and Letters of Thomas Henry Huxley*, ed. Leonard Huxley (1901), p. 284. Huxley was, of course, perfectly right. It is, in any event, not the "fittest" but the "fit" who are most likely to survive. The "fittest" are generally too specialized to be able to make the appropriate adaptations in an immediately or mediately challenging situation. The specialized group will exhibit less and the unspecialized more of the variability on which selection may act.

2. Francis Darwin, ed., *The Life and Letters of Charles Darwin*, vol. 3 (1888), pp. 45-46.

3. Charles S. Peirce, "Evolutionary Love," *The Monist* 3 (1893): 176-200.

4. See Ashley Montagu's foreword to Joseph Townsend, *A Dissertation on the Poor Laws* (1970).

5. See Ashley Montagu, *Darwin, Competition and Cooperation* (1952).

6. Herbert Spencer, "A Theory of Population, Deduced from the General Law of Animal Fertility," *Westminster Review* 51 (1852): 499-500.

7. Herbert Spencer, *Social Statics* (1864), pp. 79-80.

8. *Ibid.*, pp. 414-415.

9. George Nasmyth, *Social Progress and the Darwinian Theory* (1916); Richard Hofstadter, *Social Darwinism in American Thought 1860-1915* (1944); John C. Greene, *The Death of Adam: Evolution and Its Impact on the Western Thought* (1961).

10. Sigmund Freud, *Civilization and Its Discontents* (1930), p. 86.

11. Sir Arthur Keith, *The Place of Prejudice in Civilization* (1931), p. 50. Keith describes something of the disturbance to which his address gave rise in *An Autobiography* (1950), pp. 565-566.

12. Raymond Dart, "The Predatory Transition from Ape to Man," *International Anthropological and Linguistic Review* 1 (1953):207-208.

13. Raymond Dart, *Adventures with the Missing Link* (1959), p. 191.

14. Edward Glover, *The Roots of Crime* (1970), p. 8. In a footnote to this passage Glover observes, "At the close of this lecture, the lady Chairman and magistrate, Mrs. St. Loe Strachey, remarked: 'But, doctor, the dear babies! How could you say such awful things about them?' " The learned doctor did not choose to comment on the lady Chairman's protest.

15. A. E. Housman, *The Name and Nature of Poetry* (Cambridge: Cambridge University Press, 1933), p. 29.

16. Konrad Lorenz, *Man and Aggression* (1966), pp. 49sq.

17. *Ibid.*, p. 253.

18. *Ibid.*, p. 239.

19. Robert Ardrey, *African Genesis* (1961), p. 316. See also the same author's *The Territorial Imperative* (1966) and *The Social Contract* (1970).

20. Niko Tinbergen, "On War and Peace in Animals and Man," *Science* 160 (1968): 1411.

21. B. F. Skinner, *Beyond Freedom and Dignity* (1971).

22. J. M. R. Delgado, *Physical Control of the Mind* (1969); B. E. Eleftheriou and J. P. Scott, ed., *The Physiology of Aggression and Defeat* (1971); S. Garattini and E. B. Sigg, ed., *Aggressive Behavior* (1969); V. H. Mark and F. R. Ervin, *Violence and the Brain* (1971); D. N. Daniels, M. F. Gilula, and F. M. Ochberg, *Violence and the Struggle for Existence* (1970); B. Kaada, "Brain Mechanisms Related to Aggressive Behavior," in C. D. Clements and D. B. Lindsley, ed., *Aggression and Defense: Neural Mechanisms and Social Patterns* (1967).

23. Ashley Montagu, "Introduction: *The Nature of Human Aggression*" (1976) and Ashley Montagu, ed., *Man and Aggression*, 2nd ed. (1973).

24. *New York Times*, December 29, 1971, p. 18. (Emphasis added.)

25. Ashley Montagu, *The Human Revolution* (1967); and Ashley Montagu, *The Direction of Human Development* (rev. ed., 1970).

26. T. Dobzhansky and F. Ashley Montagu, "Natural Selection and the Mental Capacities of Mankind," *Science*, 105, (1947): 587-590.

27. Warder C. Allee, *Animal Aggregations* (1931) and *Cooperation Among Animals* (1951); Petr Kropotkin, *Mutual Aid* (1955); J. L. Cloudsley-Thompson, *Animal Conflict and Adaptation* (1965).

## SUGGESTED READINGS

Allee, Warder C. *Animal Aggregations.* Chicago: University of Chicago Press, 1931.

_____ *Cooperation among Animals.* New York: Schuman, 1951.

Ardrey, Robert. *African Genesis.* New York: Atheneum, 1961.

_____ *The Territorial Imperative.* New York: Antheneum, 1966.

_____ *The Social Contract.* New York: Atheneum, 1970.

Blackemore, C. "The Limits of Learning." *New Scientist,* April 20, 1972, 145-148.

Cloudsley-Thompson, J. L. *Animal Conflict and Adaptation.* London: Foulis, 1965.

Daniels, D. N., *et al. Violence and the Struggle for Existence.* Boston: Little, Brown, 1970.

Dart, Raymond. *Adventures with the Missing Link.* New York: Harper & Brothers, 1959.

_____. "The Predatory Transition from Ape to Man." *International Anthropological and Linguistic Review* 1(1953): 207-208.

Darwin, Francis, ed. *The Life and Letters of Charles Darwin.* 3 vols. London: John Murray, 1888.

Delgado, J. M. R. *Physical Control of the Mind.* New York: Harper & Row, 1969.

Dennenberg, Victor H., and Zarrow, M. X. "Rat Pax." *Psychology Today* 3(1970): 47, 66, 67.

Dobzhansky, T., and Montagu, Ashley. "Natural Selection and the Mental Capacities of Mankind." *Science* 105(1947): 587-590.

Eleftheriou, B. E., and Scott, J. P., eds. *The Physiology of Aggression and Defeat.* New York: Plenum Press, 1971.

Freud, Sigmund. *Civilization and Its Discontents.* London: Hogarth Press, 1930.

Garattini, S., and Sigg, E. B., eds. *Aggressive Behavior.* New York: John Wiley, 1969.

Gardner, L. I., and Neu, R. L. "Evidence Linking Extra Y Chromosome to Sociopathic Behavior." *Archives of General Psychiatry,* 26(1972): 220-222.

Glass, D. C. ed. *Biology and Behavior: Genetics.* New York: Rockefeller University Press, 1968.

Glover, Edward. *The Roots of Crime.* New York: International Universities Press, 1970.

Greene, John C. *The Death of Adam: Evolution and Its Impact on Western Thought.* New York: New American Library, 1961.

Hirsch, J., ed. *Behavior-Genetic Analysis.* New York: McGraw-Hill, 1969.

Hofstadter, Richard. *Social Darwinism in American Thought, 1860-1915.* Philadelphia: University of Pennsylvania Press, 1944.

Huxley, Leonard, ed. *Life and Letters of Thomas Huxley.* New York: D. Appleton, 1901.

Jennings, Herbert S. *Behavior of the Lower Organisms.* New York: Columbia University Press, 1906. (Reprinted by University of Indiana Press, 1962.)

Kaada, B. "Brain Mechanisms Related to Aggressive Behavior," in C. D. Clements and D. B. Lindsley, eds., *Aggression and Defense: Neural Mechanisms and Social Patterns.* Los Angeles: University of California Press, 1967.

Kessler, S., and Moos, H. S. "The XYY Karyotype and Criminality: A Review." *Journal of Psychiatric Research* 7(1970): 153-170.

Keith, Sir Arthur. *The Place of Prejudice in Civilization.* New York: John Day, 1931.

Kropotkin, Petr. *Mutual Aid.* Boston: Porter-Sargent, 1955.

Levitan, Max, and Montagu, Ashley. *Textbook of Human Genetics.* second ed., New York: Oxford University Press, 1977.

Lorenz, Konrad. *Man and Aggression.* New York: Harcourt, Brace & World, 1966.

Mark, V. H., and Ervin, F. R. *Violence and the Brain.* New York: Harper & Row, 1971.

Meade, J. E., and Parkes, A. S., eds. *Genetic and Environmental Factors in Human Ability.* New York: Plenum Press, 1968.

Montagu, Ashley, *The Anatomy of Swearing.* New York: Macmillan, 1967.

_____ *Darwin, Competition and Cooperation.* New York: Schuman, 1952.

_____ *The Direction of Human Development.* Rev. ed. New York: Hawthorn, 1970.

_____ *The Human Revolution.* New York: Bantam, 1967.

_____ ed. *Learning to be Non-Aggressive.* New York: Oxford University Press, 1978.

_____ ed. *Man and Aggression.* New York: Oxford University Press, 1968. (2nd ed., 1973.)

_____ *The Nature of Human Aggression.* New York: Oxford University Press, 1976.

Rosenthal, David. *Genetic Theory and Abnormal Behavior.* New York: McGraw-Hill, 1970.

Skinner, B. F. *Beyond Freedom and Dignity.* New York: Knopf, 1971.

Spencer, Herbert. "A Theory of Population," *Westminster Review* 51(1852): 499-500.

_____ *Social Statics.* New York: Appleton, 1864.

Sperry, R. W. "How a Developing Brain Gets Itself Properly Wired for Adaptive Function," in Tobach, E., *et al.,* eds., *The Biopsychology of Development.* New York: Academic Press, 1971.

Townsend, Joseph. *A Dissertation on the Poor Laws.* Berkeley, Calif.: University of California Press, 1970. See especially the foreword by Ashley Montagu.

Tinbergen, Niko. "On War and Peace in Animals and Man," *Science* 160 (1968): 1411.

Whittlestone, W. C. "Physiology of Lactation," in Carey, H. M., ed., *Modern Trends in Human Reproduction.* Washington, D.C.: Butterworths, 1963.

Yerkes, R. W., and Yerkes, A. W. *The Great Apes.* New Haven: Yale University Press, 1929.

Zublin, W. *Chromosomale Aberrationen and Psyche.* Basel: S. Karger, 1969.

# Man and Nature: Biological Perspectives 6

*Michael W. Fox*

THE OTHER ESSAYS IN THIS BOOK deal primarily with a philosophical analysis of our relationship with and responsibilities toward other animals. A biological orientation, focusing on aspects of ecology, evolution, animal behavior, and consciousness, is a necessary inclusion. This biological orientation is important because we too are animals and are no less a part of evolution and ecology than is the rest of creation, and also because without a biological perspective, our world view and philosophy will continue to be partially or wholly human-centered.

This selection provides an overview and synthesis of biological phenomena relevant to our philosophical orientation. It explores the similarities and kinship among humans and other species and presents the ecological perspective that all life forms are interrelated.

These scientific findings will be used to form the biological basis for the subsequent elaboration of a unifying biospiritual ethic, the objective biological perspective supporting and complementing the more subjective and intuitive religious and philosophical one.

## ECOLOGY: THE BALANCE AND THE WEB OF LIFE

Ecology is one branch of the natural sciences that serves as a bridge between science and philosophy. For example, the ecological fact of the "oneness" of an animal, preadapted and adapting to maintain a state of harmony with its environment, is like the Zen Buddhist concept of oneness. Zen philosophy (the all in one and the one in all) emphasizes the interpenetration and

Michael W. Fox is Director of the Institute for the Study of Animal Problems, a division of The Humane Society of the United States.

111

interdependence of all things (another fact of ecology). Such thinking contrasts with the Western Aristotelian way of splitting and dichotomizing, of separating observer and observed, animal and environment. Actually both world views are correct and complementary, although historically the Western view (and the associated Judeo-Christian tradition of man's dominion over all of creation) has been more destructive in terms of mankind's relationship with nature.

The science of ecology seems to have come to our rescue, its Zen-like pronouncements offering a more balanced and harmonizing world view than our distorted and destructive Western mode of thought and action.

Ecology (and molecular biology) teaches that on the other side of the reality of individualism (of a separate you and me) is the reality of oneness—of a harmonizing, complementing, interdependent balance. For example, you, as an individual, are defined in terms of all your relationships—that is, you are defined in a social context. You are as much of others and the world as you are of yourself. The fact that you seem to be the center of your universe is just a coincidence because of the nature of your nervous system.

Another intriguing fact that destroys the idea of a wholly separate individualism is that we are all living communities—with amoebas in our blood stream, alien mitochondria in our cells, and symbiotic bacteria on our skin and in our intestines. Destroy these parts of us and we would die also (unless we were maintained in total infection-free isolation on a special diet!). Applying the ecological principle of "holism" to Western medicine may also help restore some confidence and improve effectiveness in medical diagnosis and treatment.

One of the most delicately balanced relationships in nature is that of prey and predator populations. All natural systems are self-regulating, and all interspecies relationships (as between moose and wolf, caribou and wolf) and social groups (wolf packs) have naturally evolved self-regulating systems. For example, quail and pheasant produce enormous numbers of eggs, and field mice and other rodents have many offspring. The reason some areas are not overrun with such birds and rodents is that natural diseases and predators, such as foxes and bobcats, control their numbers. The production of many eggs and young by these animals is an evolved adaptation to predation; without natural checks and balances, they would soon become extinct by eating up all the available food in their habitats. The same is true for the wolf's prey—deer, moose, and caribou. On the other side of the scale, foxes, bobcats, and wolf packs are very territorial and keep others of their kind away, thus regulating competition and preventing others of their kind from exhausting the supply of prey in their hunting ranges. Destroy the quail, rodents, or deer, and there would be no foxes, bobcats, or wolves. Destroy foxes, bobcats, or wolves, and there would be an overabundance of their prey and serious destruction of habitat through overgrazing and then a "crash" in the prey population. Prey and predator species are essentially interlocked, and thousands of generations of evolution bind them in total dependence and harmony. Any form of human intervention (by hunting or poisoning) may have disastrous consequences.

If modern man is to learn anything from ecology, it is this: he must act with humility and with the utmost caution, since the balance of nature is extremely delicate and to interfere with the "seamless web" of life is to court disaster. Even with the best scientific minds and equipment and years of field data, a national body of scientists was wrong in its prediction of a population explosion of lemmings in one area of Alaska. This lesson from nature teaches us above all that life is infinitely complex and more unpredictable than predictable. Therefore, we should exercise dominion and control over ourselves before we attempt to work in creative harmony with nature, and we should learn more of ecology before we interfere further with the order of nature.

## AGGRESSION (WAR) AND HUNTING

It is widely accepted that primitive man was a hunter, a killer of animals. Many people today believe that this is why the human species is so highly aggressive, engaging in war and killing of other humans without a second thought. There is little evidence to support this view, however.

Studies of other animals that hunt, especially social carnivores such as the wolf, show beyond question that hunting and killing prey are behaviors and motivations quite separate and distinct from aggression and fighting among their own kind. We

113

should not, therefore, regard our hunting ancestry as a natural (instinctive and therefore unavoidable) basis for human aggressiveness. We cannot blame human nature for the aggressive and homicidal qualities that characterize our species. The wolf teaches us that the best hunters, equipped with intelligence and powerful weapons, have a highly organized social structure in which aggressive conflicts are usually checked by certain rules of social order (the dominance hierarchy). The leader will often "police" others and intervene to prevent conflicts in the ranks.

Fighting in many animals has evolved to the degree that contestants rarely get injured, and this is in the best interests of both winner and loser. Hence numerous rituals have evolved, and weapons (teeth, claws) and defense structures (antlers, horns, quills, and venomous fangs) that are used to kill prey or fend off predators are used differently between members of the same species so as to reduce the chances of injury (and possibly more injurious retaliation). Ungulates use the tips of horns or antlers to ward off predators, but they use the body of these structures when they fight among themselves, pushing and wrestling but not stabbing or thrusting. Similarly, a wolf displays its teeth as a threat or challenge; if it does bite a companion, the bite is usually inhibited and directed toward a relatively invulnerable area of the other's body such as the thick cheek or shoulder region. These same teeth and powerful jaws can quickly eviscerate a caribou and slash and sever its limbs.

Such ritual controls in fighting are evident in many human sports such as fencing and wrestling, which evolved in generations past when men at war engaged in arm-to-arm combat. (One could surrender and display all the natural primate signals of submission and appeasement to cut off the aggressor who, in turn, might respond chivalrously.) Unlike in hunting, where the aim is to kill the prey, the aim in fighting for most animals, including man, is usually to dominate the adversary—to force him into submission. Killing is unusual. Sometimes it is accidental, as when the loser gives the appeasement signal inappropriately or too late; rarely is it deliberate.

It is easier for an aggressor to kill when he does not see the appeasement displays and signals for surrender. Animals fighting close together can hardly avoid seeing the signals, but once man

114

was able to use projectile weapons, these natural mechanisms to cut off the aggressor were weakened. The greater the range of combat, the easier killing became, and the push-button war of the twentieth century was the final step in distancing and depersonalizing adversaries.

Animals, including man, will kill their own kind for survival or to protect their territory and offspring. The survival motive underlies both the killing of other species for food and the killing of one's own species in the context of aggression. In human beings, however, the survival of ideals and political-religious beliefs has become synonymous with physical survival, thus broadening mankind's capacity and potential for aggression and war. A threat to such beliefs is often mistaken for a threat to one's actual biological survival; any perceived threat to the *status quo,* often paranoically motivated, may trigger the biological reaction of aggression with catastrophic results. Such a reaction is biologically ancient, yet it is anachronistic and inappropriate for the context. The evolution of the "cold war" has positive promise; it may represent a new and more appropriate ritual way of coping with international conflicts and fears over survival (ideological and economic) and of repressing the biological reaction of aggression and killing.

Finally, on a less global and political scale, the difference between aggression and hunting in relation to the modern sport and trophy hunter should be emphasized. The modern hunter is often branded as an unfeeling aggressive "biopath" who enjoys hunting and killing as an outlet for pent-up aggressive drives. Hunting in its pure form is, I believe, a natural outlet for a very ancient and principally male human drive. Second, it may be an outlet for emotional tensions and frustrations. Killing the animal is not primarily an aggressive act but a consummation of the challenge of the hunt, which provides ego-gratification as well as food for the family. Certain critics of hunters have inferred a sexual element of male "macho" domination over the prey, but hunting in its pure form is not an outlet for aggression or sex—and this is true for all animals that hunt and kill other animals for food.

Hunting in man does not often occur in a "pure" form comparable to hunting of prey by other species. For one reason, the weapon is used in exactly the same way to bring down the prey as it would be to kill another human being in an aggressive context. In animals, as pointed out earlier, the natural weapons are used differently in the contexts of hunting and fighting. Also, because animals are born and raised with such weapons, they have deeply ingrained rituals to insure their safe use; this is not true for man, as the high annual incidence of real and questionable "hunting accidents" attests. Early childhood training for gun safety would be insignificant compared to the hundreds of thousands of years of evolutionary selection and social training in animals equipped with weapons. Although a child, like any other animal, will learn to control the aggressive use of his or her natural weapons, a gun or other nonbiological weapon is something else. For man, it can be a separate symbol—of power, virility, and security.

Such symbolic attitudes, combined with the limited natural biological controls over the use of firearms, raise many serious questions. Also, there is a distance factor between prey and hunter—the child hunter may have a safe emotional distance from the animal victim and not fully see or hear the intensity of its fear and pain. And we must add another fact: since the brain regions associated with aggressive and sexual responses are partially overlapping, "cross-contamination" can occur. In other words, the "pure" motive to hunt and kill may be contaminated by aggressive sexual motives. The very close relationship between sex and aggressive behavior in man and other animals is well recognized— sexual sado-masochism being one abnormal development of the naturally close affinities of those brain centers. Often when young animals are playing together, actions normally associated with aggression, sex, and prey-hunting occur together, again emphasizing the close relationships between these different motivational states.

As Thoreau said, the embryo man has to go through the hunting stage in his development before he lays down his gun. We would be well advised to do this and return, with the advantage of mature enlightment, to the purity of our animal motivations, where sex, aggression, and hunting are indeed separate and uncontaminated. Surely our species can now survive with less preoccupation with the latter two motivational states and enjoy

116

life even more without causing further violence and suffering to our own species and to our animal kin alike. Such decontamination of our often confused motives is a purifying step in gaining control over our minds and actions and in understanding human nature.

### THE UNITY OF ORGANISM AND ENVIRONMENT

As a result of millions of years of evolution, each living creature, through the time-wrought chemistry of selection and inheritance, comes into the world essentially preadapted to live in a particular niche or habitat. Each creature has specific inborn preferences for food, for a particular terrain, type of vegetation, temperature range, and so on. No prior experience is needed, for example, for a woodland deer mouse that has been raised in a laboratory cage to choose the right living environment when given a choice between simulated woodland and prairie. Some species of snake that live in swampland will naturally prefer swamp food—frogs—when they first hatch rather than lizards, while newborn desert snakes prefer lizards over frogs.

These are dramatic examples of preadaptation for certain environments, and many subtle factors in the tuning and organization of their nervous systems fit them for a particular niche. The word "fitness" suggests not only survival (for the most adapted or "fit" individuals) but also the way in which the animal "fits" into a particular niche or set of environmental conditions. It is akin to a marriage, a unity in which the animal is as one with its environment. This unity is such that we cannot fully understand the animal without a full knowledge of the world microcosm into which it fits. The two are inseparable, and in a sense there is no such thing as an individual, since the individual is defined or shaped by the environment (which it in turn may change to some degree) and by social relationships that constitute its identity.

The fact that the organism-environment is a complex unitary whole, a gestalt, echoes again the philosophical concept of Zen: the one in all and the all in one, the inseparability of all—interrelated, interpenetrating, interadapted.

Fulfillment for any living creature would be its union with the environment for which it is best adapted and to which its whole being is receptively attuned. To deprive it of such natural

117

fulfillment would be as inhumane as if its instincts and potentials were never fully actualized but instead were frustrated, blocked, or denied. This is the core philosophy of humanistic psychology, which is concerned with the provision of an optimal environment for the ultimate fulfillment (self-actualization) of an individual's potentials.

Since there is no qualitative difference between the fulfilling unity of man and his world and that of any other animal and its world, certain humane and ethical questions must be raised. If a human has a natural right, by virtue of his very being, to be free (within the limits of moral and social constraints) to seek self-actualization in an optimal environment, then surely this right should be accorded to all other living creatures. They, too, in their kind, reflect (within the limits of social, interspecific, and other ecological restraints) a pattern of seeking self-fulfillment within the environment for which they are preadapted and best suited. To deny this fact would be both inhumane and an unethical violation of their rights, determined by their very existence. For reasons of health and ecological harmony, man, as steward, may assume the ultimate right and responsibility to intervene and regulate them (by destruction, containment, or other ecologically and humanely sound methods). However, his right to deny them fulfillment for other reasons must be questioned.

This argument opens to debate—on a sound evolutionary, developmental, and philosophical basis—man's previously assumed dominion over animals. If he must confine them and deny them an optimizing environment, this denial must be justified; and when and wherever possible, some reasonable approximation of natural environmental conditions should be provided—for animals in zoos, circuses, farms, and animal research facilities. If this is not possible, and if deprivation cannot be justified—as in circuses, some zoos, and many research studies—then such practices should be terminated. To deny the unity of an animal with the social and environmental milieu for which it has evolved is inhumane and unethical.

Few if any domestic animals have been so artificially selected or genetically engineered as to be preadapted to live in a barren cage or stall. Many, if given freedom even after

118

generations of domestication, have the capacity to revert to the wild.

A more sensitive stewardship and husbandry of wildlife and domestic and captive animals can be realized once the significance of the evolved unity of the animal and its environment is fully comprehended.

### EVOLUTION: KINSHIP IN DIVERSITY AND CONTINUITY

One of the most striking features of animal and plant evolution is diversity. Within each major evolutionary branch—insects, for example—are countless other smaller and smaller branches leading from the main stem of phylum to class, order, family, genus, species, subspecies, and even sexual and age variants or morphs.

Individual species may seem so different from others belonging to the same class, order, or family that the human mind, after classifying such a vast array of creation, can only wonder at the limitless creations of life. Even the subtle variations in structure and later in temperament and aptitudes within members of the same species disclose the evolutionary pattern of diversity. Consider not only the racial variants of our own species but the incredible range of variability within any single race.

We know that over a few generations exposure of organisms to different environmental conditions will lead to changes in structure and behavior. It is through this process that subspecies, and later separate species, evolve. Existing diversity and the potential for diversity are clearly adaptive, enhancing survival. When a species is protected or "buffered" from environmental and social selection pressure, so no strong forces shape structure and behavior in only one direction (like the more or less fixed and most adaptive body size of a wolf or a wild dog) even greater variation may develop. Our domesticated dogs, for example, protected by man in varying degrees from natural selection forces, manifest wide variations in size and temperament: contrast a chihuahua and a great dane, a beagle and a bulldog. Domestication, a special form of evolution, can increase diversity, and a comparable process in man—through his capacity for culture—can increase diversity in a comparable way by buffering us from the rigors of natural selection pressures. Very civilized cultures can support variants who would be physically and psychologically unable to survive as primitive hunter-gatherers. The evolutionary value of such diversity could be for the benefit of society in terms of optimal creativity and flexible potentiality.

Interestingly, surface similarities between species can give a misleading impression of relatedness. In order to adapt to similar conditions many diverse species evolve similar adaptive strategies in structure or behavior—such as the wings of flying birds and insects and the fins of fish and seals. Such convergencies or analagous structures must be distinguished from homologous or directly corresponding ones that can help us identify kinship similarities in recently evolved and more closely related species— such as the facial expressions of man and rhesus monkey and the similar behaviors of foxes and cats, who respectively share recent common ancestries.

In classifying things, the human mind makes distinctions between me and you, us and them, and surrounded by the vast diversity of creation may perceive only the surface differences that mask the deeper similarities. These superficial and often illusory differences have led to racist, sexist, "speciesist," and other separatist views of "in-groups," setting up a nexus of divisive and alienating forces and notions of superiority and inferiority. Even today people question whether blacks are less intelligent than whites, dogs superior to cats, and so on, not realizing that a cat is neither superior nor inferior to a dog: it simply *is* a cat. But unlike a leopard who cannot change its spots or alter many of its instinctual reactions, any person (irrespective of race or color) has a mind that *can* change his or her acquired values, attitudes, and beliefs. (This is the key through consciousness for a transcending unity for humanity, but to date, our values, attitudes, and beliefs have served more to divide humanity and to separate mankind from animals and nature.)

In sum, the diversity of life is only a surface phenomenon that can distract us from the underlying truth of our deep kinship with all life. When we go back in time, or explore the structure and components of our cells and those of slime molds, fish, and prairie grass, we find that we all converge. All species came from a common family root; different orders come from the same phyletic branch, and even those branches have a common origin. Tracing the thread of our past

120

lives back through evolutionary time, we discover that all of creation is of one essence and one origin.

There is indeed kinship in the present diversity and evolutionary continuity of all life. Perhaps humanity is going to reverse the pattern of increased diversification to return to a common core, a unity in heart, mind, and spirit of all nations and races, and with all creation. It would not be a backward step but a synthesis and integration to a higher plane. Our survival and fulfillment depend on it, and fostering the knowledge of kinship with all life and the ethical responsibilities that come with such knowledge is one of the most vital imperatives of the humane movement.

## EVOLUTION AND OUR ANIMAL KINSHIP

Don't let anyone tell you that evolution is just a theory.* Some people still believe that human beings are a special form of divine creation, something separate from and above all other life forms—the only one with a soul perhaps. How convenient this thinking is for those who adhere to the Judeo-Christian tradition of man's god-given dominion over all creation, entitling him to use nature as a resource for his own gratification and to think of all creatures as his to harvest and dispose of as his whims decree.

Even when Charles Darwin presented strong evidence supporting his theory of evolution, the continuity among species evolving toward greater mental abilities was accepted by few. Most chose to use Darwin's evidence to support their view of man's superiority and dominion over all creatures great and small.

It is more important today than ever before for human beings to be aware of their kinship with all of life. It is essential for our survival that we have a strong reverence for all forms of life as our kin and see all as part of creation (or of evolution as a godlike creative process if you wish). Our lack of dominion over ourselves and our dominionistic, egocentric world views are respectively suicidal and biocidal. Evidence from studies of the evolution of animals can give us the factual pieces to build a firmer foundation for an active and viable belief in man's kinship with all life.

*Creationists who choose to personify speak of *Mother* Nature and *Father* God; this differs fundamentally from the evolutionist view presented here, in which nature and god are not personified but are instead regarded respectively as manifestations of the processes of creation and evolution. A "personal" God belief system may be the immature antecedent of a nonperson process, which, when one becomes a part of the process, is experienced as a self-actualizing transpersonal (that is, ego-transcending) relatedness.

First, a look at human consciousness. It has been held for a long time by some philosophers (and other misguided people lost to the real world in the labyrinths of abstraction and scientific reductionism) that only man is a conscious being. Only human beings, they would say, have an awareness of themselves, a self-consciousness, because they have the power of speech. They can describe to others, verbally, how they feel and what they are thinking about. Language, it is argued, is the element that makes us qualitatively different from animals; man knows that he knows (because he can say so, in so many words) while an animal at most just "knows," and more likely has a very dim self-awareness that is subordinate to instinctual drives. What arrogance indeed! Until such men could understand that guttural utterings of primitive tribespeople like the Kalahari Bushmen, the latter, lacking any sophisticated technology or tools, were regarded as subhuman, as being only slightly evolved above the oblivious, instinctual unconscious of the animal world. Yet when we can understand their linguistic symbols, what eloquent philosophy and well-developed self-consciousness they have!

The many secret codes of nonverbal animal language are now being broken. Perhaps, when all this research is completed, we may know what many of us feel intuitively—that man differs very little from animals. They too use symbols—gestures, sounds, and smells— with which to communicate their inner states (feelings) and intentions. For one animal to understand another's signals, it must have some awareness of itself and of its own signal states in relation to the other and what the other feels or intends to do. Empathy and expectations are surely not exclusively human qualities. Man may be the only species that uses one specialized communication system (words) to communicate more than immediate, moment-to-moment reactions, feelings, and intentions. This existentially here-and-now state may be typical of most animals and young humans. The new ability, an outgrowth of the former, is the ability to bind time symbolically so that one can talk about the past and plan and share alternative ideas about the future.

Communicating (expressing socially) what one is feeling or intending to do is an animal and human ability. You might ask skeptically whether an animal really "knows" that it is happy, distressed, or afraid. Perhaps the answer is in its response to its own kind who are in similar states, but like indifferent people, some animals seem indifferent, too, or are so subtle in their reactions that they seem unresponsive to the human observer. I believe that all mammals are very much aware of their feelings or emotional states and that they have a sense of self, an inner awareness or mentality and show some insight, reasoning, human playfulness, creativity, and imagination. In my experience it is more a characteristic of the adult human animal than of other animals to be unaware of one's own or another's feeling and wants— a pathology of the suprarational, objective, or repressive side of our minds. We also confuse our own unthinking and unfeeling habits with the instinctual actions of animals who are probably more aware, most of the time, of their internal states and external worlds than most adult humans!

Some people who are more aware of themselves and others tend to ask themselves "why" a great deal. Why am I doing this, feeling this way, or responding or thinking that way? Not many people do this, and I wonder if we will ever know whether any animals ask themselves why. This is perhaps the major difference between man and other animals. Asking why is a reflective question; it is a consciousness turning it upon itself. Reflection goes one step beyond being aware of one's thoughts and feelings. Until more people evolve to this higher state of consciousness, most people who are governed by cultural instincts, blind habits, and unthinking traditions and beliefs will remain as something less than animal—a missing link between what is wholly animal and what could be a fully human being!

OUR ANIMAL ROOTS:
DISCOVERING THE ANIMAL CONSCIOUSNESS IN MAN

Another proof of our kinship with animals comes from studies of the human brain. Comparing its structure and function with those of other creatures' brains, we find that we differ in fewer ways than we may think: the similarities between the brain of man and the brains of other mammals are greater than the differences.

Take, for a start, the development of the human brain, which goes through very similar stages of development as does the developing nervous system of a lizard, chicken, or dog. In fact, the human brain is a composite accumulation of earlier brains from past lives or evolutionary epochs that we have brought along with us, the blueprints of which are encoded in our genes. The human brain has three distinct regions. One, the brain stem or core, is termed the "old brain." It differs little from that of a reptile or bird. An extended outgrowth of this is the middle brain or emotional center, the limbic system. This represents the final stage of development for primitive mammals like the kangaroo and opossum. We essentially have their brains in ours, but we also have more. The more recent brain, the forebrain or neocortex, is the latest evolutionary addition to the complex brains of placental mammals, herbivores, carnivores, and primates. In man, it is a relatively large mushrooming outgrowth. It subtly regulates activities in the middle and old brains and in addition is like a complex biocomputer, a storage center for information (encoded memories). In man, it also has a well-developed speech center.

What these comparative and developmental studies of the various brains reveal is a continuum of increasing complexity. This must be accompanied by a continuum of awareness or "mental" experience from the "lower" to the "higher" (more correctly, most recently evolved) animal species. All this supports irrefutably that man is kin with other animal species and that he is not so different from them qualitatively, but rather quantitatively, as reflected in the great mass of new brain he has acquired (and much of which he does not use). To reiterate, the similarities of the human brain to those of other species are greater than the differences. This means that the subjective, inner, emotional world (principally modulated by the middle brain) must be very similar for all those species that have a middle brain and even more similar for those that have a new brain or neocortex regulating this middle brain region. The inner worlds of a goat, a dog, a rhesus monkey, and a man must therefore have more similarities than differences. How then does this affect our responsibility toward those species with brains like ours?

Another striking similarity between human and nonhuman mammalian brains is seen in the electrical activity patterns or electroencephalograph (EEG) recordings. A dog, for example, has the same states of activity as a man, its EEG patterns being almost identical in wakefulness, quiet sleep, dreaming (REM, rapid eye movement—or "activated" sleep), and daydreaming.

As for the chemistry of the brain and endocrine systems, there is no difference in kind between humans and other animals. The biochemistry of physiological and emotional states (of stress and anxiety, for example) differ little between mice and men. Thus, having virtually the same body chemistry, it is not illogical to assume that associated emotional "mental" states are basically the same for people and their animal kin. The only major difference, perhaps, is that some may choose to interpret them differently!

These similarities in EEG readings and biochemistry, added to the structural similarities of human and nonhuman vertebrate brains, are further evidence that the brains of men and other animals function in virtually identical ways; it follows that their mental states are probably similar and often identical. Donald R. Griffin in his provocative book *The Question of Animal Awareness* observes that:

> . . . behavioral sciences have grown highly uncomfortable at the very thought of mental states or subjective qualities in animals. When they intrude on our scientific discourse, many of us feel sheepish, and when we find ourselves using such words as fear, pain, pleasure, or the like, we tend to shield our reductionist egos behind a respectability blanket of quotation marks.

I couldn't agree more, and one must seriously question why behavioral and biomedical scientists think in the way he describes. Perhaps they do to absolve themselves from the burden of responsibility and guilt they should feel toward the animals they use and "sacrifice" for knowledge's sake.

To doubt whether an animal can experience pain, fear, anxiety, satisfaction, and pleasure is to doubt the very existence of our own consciousness. And to reject the possibility that our most recently evolved animal kin—the carnivores and primates—cannot or do not experience comparable states of joy, depression, guilt, remorse, and love is as illogical as denying that you or I have such experiences.

Only the skeptic, divorced from his own animal self, like a robot tuned into its new brain biocomputer, would argue against the evidence of a continuity of animal awareness and inner

125

subjective mental states akin to our own. And for what reasons would he argue against such evidence? Perhaps, in the final analysis, to avoid the revolutionary consequences of such evidence; it is easier to think of other animals as different, inferior, and unfeeling, since to think and act otherwise brings with it the enormous responsibilities of humane stewardship, of benevolence to all life.

## SUGGESTED READING

Fox, M. W. *Between Animal and Man.* New York: Coward, McCann, 1976.

_____ *Concepts in Ethology: Animal and Human Behavior.* Minneapolis: University of Minnesota Press, 1974.

_____ *One Earth, One Mind.* New York: Coward, McCann, forthcoming.

Godlovitch, S. R., and Harris, J., eds. *Animals, Men and Morals: An Enquiry into the Mal-Treatment of Non-Humans.* New York: Taplinger, 1972.

Griffin, D. R. *The Question of Animal Awareness.* New York: Rockefeller University Press, 1977.

Harrison, R. *Animal Machines.* London: Stuart, 1964.

Krishnamurti, J. *Talks and Dialogues.* Berkeley, Calif: Shambala, 1969.

Maslow, A. H. *Towards a Psychology of Being.* New York: Van Nostrand Reinhold, 1968.

Reagan, T., and Singer, P., eds. *Animal Rights and Human Obligations.* Englewood, Cliffs, New Jersey: Prentice-Hall, 1976.

Regenstein, L. *The Politics of Extinction.* New York: MacMillan, 1976.

Rudhyar, D. *The Rhythm of Human Fulfillment.* Palo Alto, Calif.: See Center, 1966.

Ryder, R. *Victims of Science.* London: Davis-Poynter, 1975.

Schweitzer, A. *The Teaching of Reverence for Life.* New York: Holt, Rinehart & Winston, 1965.

Singer, P. *Animal Liberation.* New York: Random House, 1975.

Stone, C. D. *Should Trees Have Standing? Towards Legal Rights for Natural Objects.* Los Altos, Calif.: Kaufmann, 1974.

Teilhard de Chardin, P. *Man's Place in Nature.* New York: Harper & Row, 1966.

# Are We Right in Demanding an End to Animal Cruelty?

7

*Roger Caras*

OUR DISCUSSION HAS BEEN ENTITLED "Cruelty—So What?" What kind of a question is that? Do we, the Humane Society of the United States, need an explanation for what we do, what we believe in, what we fight for? Surprisingly enough, we do. We should pause, and we should determine whether we are right. Perhaps we take too much for granted, for who here has really questioned our cause in a very long time?

If we are right, we would see an end to the fur trade. What would an end to the fur trade mean? Many highly skilled and creative people would have to rechannel their efforts—marginal income people on the wilderness fringes would lose a source of income as retail and wholesale operations simply shrivel up and die. Do we have a *right* to work toward these ends? Are we right in even wanting them to come about?

That is the question, and here is my answer: Yes, we *are* right. Jobs will be lost—they would be lost if the drug trade shriveled up tomorrow, too. Narcotics officers would be fired; U.S. Customs could cut back on labor; the courts would be under less pressure and so would the public prosecutor; therefore, fewer would work in those quarters. Well, if it is right to ignore those imaginary pleas and work and pray for an end to drug addiction, it is right to say "enough" to the fur trade. Enough agony! Leghold traps, be gone! Furriers, close down your salons. Leave our wildlife alone and close your mink and fox torture farms, whatever the momentary cost (and it will only be momentary as these things go).

Roger Caras is a former Vice President and Director of The Humane Society of the United States. This is a reprint of an address delivered at the Annual Conference of The HSUS, Houston, Texas, 1975.

128

I say we are right. I say the fur industry must die, every last shred of it. And if we have ever tried to accommodate ourselves to that industry and said "Think mink" in the hopes that ranch-raising furs meant less suffering than wild-caught furs, we can forget that one. The only way to get people to stop wearing the wrong furs is to get them to wear no furs at all. Forget the lost jobs! We are right on that count.

But are we right in calling for humane slaughter? Do we come close to a dangerous edge with that one? Are we not on the verge of interfering with religious freedom? That would be a dangerous, not to say unfortunate, posture for the humane community. No again. We are right, for those things we hate—shackling and hoisting in uncontrolled slaughterhouses—have nothing whatsoever to do with religion. And we must never be deterred by false claims that there is a connection. There is none.

I have personally visited slaughterhouses in Israel and discussed the matter with the veterinarians in charge. They were horrified by what I had to tell them. And I was told that meat slaughtered the way it is done here in the name of the Jewish faith could not even be marketed in Israel, the Jewish state, because of the cruelties involved. As often as not, those uncontrolled slaughterhouses are not even run by people of the faith they claim to serve. Shackling and hoisting is an economic expediency with no basis in religion, and therefore it has no bearing on religious freedom. I would be glad to be questioned on that one. Again, we are right.

What about rodeo? Is it not Americana? Of course it is, much of it legitimate. But so was slavery, cannibalism in the Donner Pass, the Bad Day at Black Rock, Prohibition, the slaughter of the American Indians and the wasting of their priceless cultures, the slaughter of the bison, and the slaughter of the whale—all Americana. But which would you see persist? Lynching blacks and the Ku Klux Klan, Father Coughlin, Joe McCarthy, and the vigilantes—all Americana, like the rodeo, a part of our history. Is that excuse enough for a cultural artifact to persist? I should not think so. I think we are right.

I think rodeo can be modified so as not to torture animals. It need not go. It can accommodate itself. It can be a wild west show that will not cut into regional pride, will not deface self-image, and will preserve a fragment of history. But those accommodations must be made. They persist in our time not as history but as the huckstering of showfolk. They are quick-buck tricks, crowd-pleasers (they had real crowd-pleasers in the Roman arena, too—Caligula loved them). Let us not mistake huckstering for historical pride and national image. We are right in calling for a modification, a *profound* modification, of the present rodeo, and let the devil have our enemy, for that is good company for both.

Where else might we lay our heavy hand? In the laboratory, for one place. Are we right when we ask for modification in the research community? Again, yes. Unlike some of you, perhaps, I am not an antivivisectionist. My mother died of lung cancer, and I know what that means. I would see a lot of mice die of that disease before I would see another member of my family, or one of you, die of cancer. I do not know enough about medicine to know point-for-point what must be done with live animals and what can be done instead with cell cultures and computer models.

Perhaps none of us knows quite enough or quite as much as we should. But I do know this from long association with the scientific community (not as an adversary but as a friend): about 80 percent of what goes on in the laboratory has nothing whatsoever to do with the good of mankind. Only 20 percent can be exalted to that level. That remaining 80 percent is for the fun, profit, reputation, or other benefit of the experimenter. We may be a little less sure of ourselves beside the laboratory bench than we are by the rodeo chute or the slaughterhouse ramp or the leghold trap. But this I can tell you: we have enough right on our side to push on ahead, know it better, and clean that mess up.

What might we question ourselves on next? A very complicated one—hunting. That is a multibillion-dollar industry. The per capita incomes of some states are raised almost fifty dollars each year by out-of-state hunters. The transportation complexes in this country, the hotel and motel industry, the chemical industry, real estate values, the whole outdoor sport and equipment complex—all are tied up with hunting. Billions of dollars and some first-rate conservationists are involved.

And who are we to ask them all to stop? We are duck eaters who say do not shoot duck for your table, although you pay more for that duck in the shooting of it than we do while asking some unseen person to stick a knife in the throat of ours. We who say do not hunt and eat venison, eat beef and lamb and veal—mind you, *veal*! Do not hunt and eat pheasant, say we who eat chicken (a related bird, by the way, simply gallinaceous cousins under the feather). We who bring that twenty-five pound turkey to the table on Thanksgiving and Christmas say, "Hold! Stop! You are wrong!" to him who would gain a traditional bird by gobbling away in the woods and shooting his own. Our bird is antiseptic because we do not watch its death. He who will, we call wrong. It is not uncomplicated unless you are a vegetarian, and then it is very straightforward and simple. We who eat meat, though, had better search a little deeper before we sit in judgment.

Let us study a recent series of events that reflects on this matter. CBS television had a special. It was called "Guns of Autumn." Despite some spurious advertising claims, that show was not based on any one book, nor was it inspired by any one member of the humane community. It was an idea born in the mind of the show's producer, Irv Drasnin. My book *Death As a Way of Life,* as well as other books on hunting—thirty-eight in all—were consulted and used as source material. On top of that, my files were lent to CBS, and I was a paid consultant to the producers, as were other people with some knowledge of this field.

Word leaked early, and hunting groups, the National Shooting Sports Foundation and the National Rifle Association among others, began their campaign. They tried to coax and then later coerce CBS not to do the show—although they knew nothing of the content. When they failed there, they started on the sponsors and did in fact get all but one—Block Drugs—to back out. Even that failed, and on September 5 the show was aired. The scream went up—they howled and roared and moaned.

And from that carefully orchestrated outcry another show was born at CBS. It was called "Echoes of the Guns of Autumn," and on it our president, John Hoyt, deported himself handsomely—coming off as the reasonable, intelligent, and informed gentleman he is. Not everyone on the show did as well.

The claim made by the hunting community was that "The Guns of Autumn" lacked typicality—that was a word used by a lot of them: *typicality.* It did not show *all* of hunting, just what they call "slob hunters." When asked to react to the show by CBS, I was forced to agree with the hunters that the show did omit too much. I listed these points as missing from "The Guns of Autumn"—points that would have helped viewers have a more representational picture of hunting as it is in America. A picture painted by an Andrew Wyeth instead of a Paul Klee.

— There were no scenes in the morgue—not one picture of a hunter killed by another hunter. No dead teen-age kids shot by mistake.
— No interview with orphans or widows of men and women killed by hunters—no evidence of shooting accidents.
— No dead cows or horses—no livestock shot by mistake or in frustration or in retaliation for a farmer posting his land.
— No cut fences or gates—no trespassing by hunters.
— No farm houses or barns shot up and vandalized by hunters.
— No highway signs or "No Hunting" signs shot up by hunters—although hundreds of thousands of dollars a year are spent repairing that damage.
— No hunting from aircraft—we saw none of that.
— No misuse or abuse of off-road vehicles—no hunting from snowmobiles, dune buggies, four-wheel drive vehicles, or swamp buggies. All omitted.
— No drunk or careless hunters.
— No hunting out of season.
— No hunters exceeding the bag limit.
— No hunters shooting endangered species or nongame species like songbirds.
— No hunters jacking deer at night with a spotlight.
— No hunter turning a living animal into a pincushion with his bow and arrow—no animals being bled to death.
— No trophy hunters shooting six animals because they can't decide which one has the biggest set of horns or antlers—then picking one and leaving the rest to rot.
— No deer being run by hounds.
— No hunting dogs being given live racoons and other small animals to tear apart and practice on.
— No hunters threatening farmers or local law-enforcement officers who try to interfere with their plans.
— No carcasses left to rot because the hunter didn't want anything but kicks anyway.

No tally sheet from state or federal game officials showing what enormous percentage of the much-vaunted hunting license dollar must go to police the licensee and not help wildlife at all—and how much of the general tax revenue must be diverted into control of hunting and hunters.

Those are twenty points "The Guns of Autumn" never got to make, so I would have to agree with the hunters that the show did fall somewhat short of real typicality. Paul Klee won.

But there is something else about that show, and I think it reflects on what we are talking about. It was the reaction of the hunting community and the industrial complex that helps them bolster their fading self-image. Our libraries are chock-full of books that further the fiction that the hunter is the original and true great American. Hero-in-the-field type books are found in all public libraries by the hundreds.

Our newsstands are covered with *American Rifleman, Guns and Ammo, Guns Magazine, Sports Afield, Field and Stream, Outdoor Life,* and all of the other magazines that are filled with articles about how great the hunter is and how brave and how durable, how the hunter is the only real sportsman and the only real conservationist and the only real animal lover.

Most newspapers today have hunting and fishing columns—sometimes more than one. "The American Sportsman" was on ABC for years, featuring every imaginable kind of supercelebrity shooting everything that moved and always made to look the cool hero. Manufacturers from shoes to cigarettes, from camper trucks to tent pegs, feature hunters in their ads. Sporting goods manufacturers issue catalogs filled with the things for killing.

Now, has the humane community asked that those books come off the library shelves? Has the humane community asked that the hunting magazines stop publishing? Have we insisted that "The American Sportsman" be banned from public airways? Have those of us in the humane community tried to ban catalogs for killing gear from the U.S. mails? Then why are the hunters afraid? *We* are not afraid of free speech in America, but *they* are. We frighten them.

I have seen a lot of bumper stickers on cars, trucks, jeeps, and hunting rigs. The stickers read "Register Communists Not Guns"—charming and logical bits of contemporary American folk art. For shame. I think the hunters have acted a lot like communists. Isn't that what communists do, try to get the other side muzzled so that they can't be heard? Isn't that what the hunters did? Didn't they try to force "The Guns of Autumn" out of existence? I think the American hunter is too guilty of communist tactics ever to display such a bumper sticker with pride again, except perhaps in the middle of his forehead where it would look as silly as it really is.

Why do you and I frighten the hunter? He has his magazines, books, catalogs, national ads, television shows. He has a President that calls for National Hunting Day (1975). He has all of that; yet, unlike us, he is afraid to have us speak. While I, at least, welcome his voice, I have never heard a hunter talk for very long without making a fool of himself. It is not without reason that the National Shooting Sports Foundation and the National Rifle Association and other interested groups print brochures telling hunters how to reply if challenged by a nonhunter. Imagine you and me needing a guide to tell someone why it is wrong not to spay a cat or why it is bad to play coon-on-a-log!

I think it is very germane, very important for us to understand why we instill such fear in hunters when we do nothing more or less American than express our view or why they literally go wild when a network expresses a point of view that isn't dictated chapter and verse by their party line. The answer to all of that contains the answer to the question "How can meat eaters still object to hunting?" Think about this.

I, for one, believe a woman has a right to decide whether or not she is ready or able to become a mother. I firmly believe in birth control and abortion, but that doesn't mean I have to work in an abortion clinic in order to justify my belief. I believe autopsies should be done on the deceased for the proper determination of cause of death and for the further education of medical practitioners. Must I then want to work in a postmortem room? I believe that Charles Manson at least belongs in prison for the rest of his life—at least that. Must I then want to be a prison guard? In some cases I believe in capital punishment. Must I vie to become the hangman? I believe in a strong professional and honest police force to keep order in our cluttered urban lives. Must I rush after every siren and run to the scene of every mishap, crime, and disaster? I know our surplus dogs and cats must be euthanized in great numbers. Must I want to do the job? (At one time I did do it for a while, and I know what it is like well enough!)

Must I want to do every dirty job to be done in our society? Must I have leprosy to care about the leper? Must I be paralyzed to want to contribute to the handicapped? The argument that meat eaters are in trouble on this hunting thing only *seems* like a sensible argument. There is no sense to it at all.

Many of us still eat meat—most of us do, in fact. That does not mean that we cannot decry unnecessary killing and hurting. And it certainly does not mean that we cannot object violently when fellow men get their kicks out of inflicting pain and death, for when one of us does it we all do it. Let there be no mistake: we in the humane community are not isolated—we have no ivory tower and no corner in heaven. We are of man, of the union of man and woman, condemned like all men to a human life span, and we live in the company of our fellows. We share the glories and the disaster of being human. It is mankind we seek to elevate, not just our own egos.

Hunting is an absurd anachronism; it is a leftover. It is a shard of a buried culture, an unwelcome artifact of another kind of man. We are trying to excise it, or exorcise it, not reaffirm in some incestuous little cluster that we are right and someone else is wrong.

We all know you can photograph wildlife and not shoot it—or that you can just look at it. We all know these things, so what we are trying to do is get rid of something that is sick in society and something that retards the growth of all men and all mankind. It is a poison for our children. It is a shame on us who have failed for yet another generation to clean it up. Remember this: in your lifetime you will meet many nonhunters who were formerly hunters, men and women who have matured and stopped the nonsense. You will never meet a nonhunter who has matured into a hunter.

We could go on, of course. We have other fights—racing green-legged, two-year-old horses, racing greyhounds, dog fighting, cockfighting, the protection of our feral horses (mustangs and others), predator control, and a score more. But in each of them, you will find our side right. We err in occasional fact; we misjudge an enemy; we say things that don't sound as good as we thought they would before we started speaking. We lose our tempers, and we get intemperate. We fight among ourselves. We squabble like children. We disagree on procedure and technique, and we never seem to agree on priorities because as individuals we are each more horrified by one thing than another. And so we tangle on that again and again, as individual personalities.

But behind all of that, behind our efforts and mistakes and miscalculations, behind every misstep there is this one single overriding right. I have said it again and again, and I will say it on the day I die if I have time. *It is wrong to cause pain. It is wrong to cause fear, and to allow preventable pain and preventable fear to exist is no less an offense than causing it.* That is my credo. I will argue it in heaven or hell. I will face any man or woman alive and argue it forever. It is wrong to cause pain and fear—to allow it is as bad as causing it. And just as long as that credo and that belief can be introduced into any specific argument, we need never fear a test or a challenge. That is a clear and positive right. I am more sure of it than I am of my private view of God and religion. I am more sure of that than I am of anything else in my experience as a man. As long as I believe that that credo is a valid view of my responsibility on earth, I, for one, will fear no argument and no man—I can live by it and with it.

I hope others can find in their hearts a conviction as strong, for together we will strike fear in more than the heart of the hunter. We will one day eradicate all among us who are vestigial, all who are left over from the cave, all who have come forward into our time and threaten to contaminate the future of mankind (our children) with the stink and the rot of pain and terror glorified. They are wrong; we are right. I can state no other certainty with so much conviction.

# Beyond Anthropocentrism in Ethics and Religion

8

*John B. Cobb, Jr.*

THE ENVIRONMENTAL CRISIS IS MAKING us aware that
we should change our behavior toward other living things. The
need for change follows from our traditional concern for human
welfare, but it also raises the question of whether our traditional
anthropocentric ethics and religion are adequate or justified.
Should theory be revised to take account of the welfare of the
nonhuman world?

This general question gives rise to reflection on four more
specific questions that constitute the four sections of this paper:
(1) What is intrinsically valuable? Is humanity alone of importance
in itself, or do other living things matter also? (2) Whose good
should one seek? If nonhuman values are important too, how are
they to be related to human values? (3) Do other animals have
rights? If so, what are they, and how are they related to human
rights? (4) Is belief in God relevant? Are questions of value,
obligation, and rights independent of ultimate convictions about
reality, or are they related to them? If so, how?

## WHAT IS INTRINSICALLY VALUABLE?

The existence of some things makes little or no difference unless they contribute to harm or benefit beyond themselves. There are
other things whose existence is important in itself. The former have
instrumental value; the latter have intrinsic value. My typewriter is
very useful to me, but its existence in itself, apart from its use by
human beings, is of little importance. Its primary value is instrumental. On the other hand, a child's enjoyment of a new plaything is
valuable in itself, as well as contributing to further growth and

**John B. Cobb, Jr.**, is Ingraham Professor of Theology, the School of Theology at
Claremont (California).

137

development toward maturity. The child's enjoyment is both an intrinsic value and an instrumental one.

Whereas everything has instrumental value—that is, has some capacity to contribute to the good or ill of others—only *experience* has intrinsic value. The existence of something that is wholly nonexperiential is a matter of indifference except as it contributes to some experience. The occurrence of an experience matters in itself—that is, it has intrinsic value. It also has instrumental value for other experiences.

Experience has a subject-object or self-world structure. All experience is experience *of* something or, more accurately, of many things. It is the way in which what is given objectively becomes subjectively appropriated, integrated, and transcended. Within experience, therefore, we can distinguish *what* is felt from *how* it is felt. The "what" is the objective pole of the experience; the "how" is the subjective pole. This subjective side of experience is emotion. There is a general correlation between the richness and strength of this subjective form of experience, emotion, and the richness and complexity of what is felt, but the locus of intrinsic value is in the subjective form. (This is a technical term in the philosophy of Alfred North Whitehead, and it is used here in this sense.)[1]

Experience is much more inclusive than consciousness. Consciousness lights up some portion of the total experience largely on the basis of attention. The intrinsic value of experience is greatly affected by the role of consciousness, but the relation is complex. Generally in the most valuable experiences one is attending to what is given and is not conscious of one's emotions. One is more likely to be conscious of misery than of happiness. On the other hand, one can attend consciously to the subjective form of one's feelings in ways that heighten and enrich them. This self-consciousness of ourselves in our intrinsic value is a capacity that may be peculiar to human beings. But the value of an experience does not depend on such consciousness.

The doctrine that intrinsic value is to be found in the subjective form of feeling is not far removed from common sense or from traditional theories of value. Utilitarianism proposed to regard only pleasure (and pain) as valuable (and disvaluable). Pleasure is, of course, a form of feeling. Critics have rightly complained that either the notion of pleasure must be taken very broadly or else it must be recognized that human beings find other feelings besides pleasure valuable. But many agree that the locus of intrinsic value is in the sphere of feeling.

However, it is noteworthy that, despite a passing reference by Mill to the value of feeling in other sentient beings,[2] utilitarians generally limited consideration to human feeling. To be concerned about the feelings of animals has appeared sentimental, and philosophers are eager not to appear sentimental.

The most famous opposition to the teaching that intrinsic value is found only in feeling (pleasure or pain) comes from G. E. Moore. Moore argues that "good" is a nonnatural property and an objective ingredient in the various states of affairs. When we contemplate alternative states of affairs, he argues, we recognize one as better than the other. Our judgment, he insists, is not based on the amount of pleasure present in these alternative states of affairs.

Moore proposes that we consider two worlds in the following way:

> Let us imagine one world exceedingly beautiful. Imagine it as beautiful as you can; put into it whatever on this earth you most admire—mountains, rivers, the sea; trees, and sunsets, stars and moon. Imagine these all combined in the most exquisite proportions, so that no one thing jars against another, but each contributes to increase the beauty of the whole. And then imagine the ugliest world you can possibly conceive. Imagine it simply one heap of filth, containing everything that is most disgusting to us, for whatever reason, and the whole, as far as may be, without one redeeming feature.[3]

In order to separate the question of the value of these worlds in themselves from the question of their value for a human observer, Moore asks that we suppose that no human being can ever see either world. He then asks, Do we not still believe that it is better for the beautiful world than for the ugly one to exist?

Moore's position, however, has not proved convincing. The beauty and ugliness of which he speaks are relational qualities—that is, they exist in the relation of certain formal patterns to the human observer. When we imagine them as existing apart from observation, or the possibility of observation, we are still visualizing them. But we are asked to suppose them as having no effect, actual or potential, on any visualizing activity at all. In that case, it simply has no meaning to say that one is beautiful and the other ugly.

The view of value developed in this paper can be sharply juxtaposed to Moore's by introducing into the ugly world a number of worms and insects that human beings find repulsive. Let us suppose that no such life exists in the beautiful world. Let us assume further that the ugly world constitutes a suitable environment for our insects and worms and that they are able to secure adequate food and are free from excessive pain. In that case, the ugly world has more value than the beautiful one. For in the ugly world there exist experiences of a level absent from the beautiful world—namely, the positive feelings of the worms and insects. Since human beings are excluded in principle from both, the fact that they would prefer to see and live in the beautiful world is irrelevant. If, on the other hand, we filled the beautiful world with birds and animals, restricting the ugly one to insects and worms, there would be much greater value in the beautiful world, not because it would appear beautiful to human beings, but because the experiences of birds and animals are richer than those of insects and worms.

Thus, whereas Moore fails in his effort to locate value outside human experience in general, he is right in rejecting the anthropocentric tendencies of most value theory. Values do exist apart from human knowledge of them. Whether human beings know about it or not, there is more value in the experience of a dog enjoying itself than in that of a dog suffering from an injury.

To suppose that only humans have experience or feeling is arbitrary. The issue is where, if at all, a line is to be drawn. Surely monkeys, cats, and mice feel. But what about unicellular organisms, or individual cells in multicellular organisms?

In the West the major basis for drawing sharp lines separating what is valuable in itself from what is not has been the doctrine of the psyche or soul. For Aristotle, psyche was the principle of life and hence was attributed to plants and animals as well as to human beings. Even so, he made a distinction between vegetable, animal, and rational souls, limiting the last to humans. Christian theology stressed the uniqueness of the rational soul, associating it with the image of God that in Genesis is attributed only to humanity, and viewing it as the object of divine redemption. This religious and ethical point of view supported an absolute gulf between human souls and sentient beings at other levels. Indeed, the term *soul* came to refer self-evidently to the human soul alone. The hierarchy of levels of soul gave way to a dualism of ensouled human beings and soulless animals.

Evolutionary views of living things should have reintroduced a more hierarchical conception. The human psyche, as we now know it, must have developed from simpler forms of life similar to those now represented by other animals. Because of the differences between human beings and other animals, and because of the now restricted usage of the world *soul,* we may continue to limit the term *soul* to the human soul. But we must avoid the too apparent implication of a radical and abrupt difference. Functions and subjective experiences analogous to those of the human psyche are attributable to other complex animals as well. In very simple animals and in plants, on the other hand, a society of cells seems to exist without any centralized organ of perception and control analogous to the psyche.

Consciousness is probably found only in the psyche or protopsyche. In general, experiences that are partially conscious are the locus of the higher values. Hence, our concern is primarily with the higher orders of life found in the animal kingdom. However, since consciousness does not exhaust experience, intrinsic value cannot be entirely denied to the unconscious experience of simpler animals, plant cells, or even electrons and protons.

Utilitarianism affirmed that each human being should count for as much as any other. It expresses a deep Christian concern and embodies a fundamental democratic principle. Even so, there are difficulties in its application when we deal with extreme cases, such as the human fetus and the human defective. And the equality of individuals cannot be asserted when we consider nonhuman individuals as well. It would be quite arbitrary to count a dog's pleasure or pain as equally important as that of a human being. Yet criteria are needed to judge the relative intrinsic value of experiences across species.

Utilitarianism sought its criteria on the pleasure-pain continuum and assumed that each human experience could be judged by its locus on that continuum. It ignored the fact that among persons there may be significant differences in the amount of feeling that is occurring. For example, in a very intense experience the factors of pleasure and pain may be so nearly balanced that the utilitarian calculus would yield a negligible value either way. In still another experience, at a very low level of feeling, the feeling present may be purely pleasurable. This would be assigned a high plus score on the utilitarian calculus. The distortion thus introduced would be immeasurably magnified when the subjects compared were a human being and a unicellular organism.

For a satisfactory theory of intrinsic value we require a quantitative measure of the subjective experience as such, rather than of its pleasurableness. A human being enjoys more experience than does a mouse. How can this "more" be interpreted? The easiest answer is that humans experience more of their world in greater richness of detail. They also have much more awareness of what is possible in contrast to what is actual. Thus the content of their experience is far greater. All this rightly suggests that the happiness of a human being is far more important than the happiness of a mouse and that the misery of a human being is a far more serious matter than the misery of a mouse.

The comparison of experiences in terms of their objective content of actuality felt and possibilities entertained is not sufficient, however. Intrinsic value, as we maintain, is located in the subjective form of the experience. The measure of objective content is relevant, since it correlates highly with the value of the subjective form. But it is also necessary to indicate the disinterested preferences that provide rough guides for the direct evaluation of subjective states.

Other things being equal, rich experience is better than poor. Intense experience is better than dull. A harmony of feelings is better than unresolved confusion. Pleasure is better than pain. Richness, intensity, harmony, and pleasure are ideally mutually supportive, but at times they provide conflicting evaluations. Harmony, for example, may be achieved at the price of vast simplification. But intensity may be attained at the price of pain. In such instances, comparative valuation is difficult, if not impossible. Nevertheless, these criteria provide a generally adequate basis for the conjectural ordering of the relative intrinsic values of the experiences of living things.

## WHOSE GOOD SHOULD ONE SEEK?

With this brief indication of the locus of value and the criteria of evaluation, we come to the question of ethics proper. Should we so act as to maximize value? If so, whose value? Which, if any, of the following principles should direct our action?

1. So act as to maximize value for yourself in the present.
2. So act as to maximize value for yourself for the rest of your life.
3. So act as to maximize value for all human beings for the indefinite future.
4. So act as to maximize value in general.

Of these, the first is hardly an ethical principle. There may be those who suppose that this describes actual behavior and that the ethical call for widening the sphere of consideration is useless. But most recognize that we act with some regard for the future consequences of our actions, and not only for immediate satisfaction.

The second principle is the maxim of prudence and is recognizably ethical in character. Against the tendency to consider only shortrun consequences, it calls for full consideration of long-term consequences. Yet it, too, is highly questionable. First, it cannot be defended as describing actual human behavior. It is not evident that we do consider consequences for our own future selves while excluding consideration of more immediate consequences to our friends and children. If we do not act in this rationally selfish way, on what grounds can one say we ought to do so?

The third principle is the familiar utilitarian one. The ethical action is the one that seeks the greatest good of the greatest number of human beings. This is profoundly plausible and attractive to all who have been shaped by the Judeo-Christian and democratic traditions. Indeed, it is a restatement of the fundamental teaching that we should love our neighbors as ourselves.

The basic assumption is that it is right to increase value. That principle is sound. It does not mean that people in fact act as such a principle requires. But it means that the sense of rightness points toward this kind of action. I may disregard my neighbor's good and seek only my own, but insofar as I realize that my neighbor's good is in fact, objectively, just as important as my own, I recognize a disproportion between my action and what would be objectively appropriate. I see my action as inappropriate and hence morally wrong.

Despite its attractiveness, this view of morality is unstable. If the reason I should seek the greatest good of the greatest number of persons is that it is right to increase value, then the limitation to human beings is arbitrary. It could be justified only if nonhuman entities had no intrinsic value. But since intrinsic value is not limited to humans, only the fourth principle is sufficiently encompassing to be stable and acceptable.

The calculation of pleasure and pain and the multiplication by the number of persons affected, called for by the utilitarians, has never been practicable in detail. Although it has given a rough and useful guide for the making of decisions in a human, social context, the extension of such calculations to the nonhuman world would be impossibly complex. To be at all functional, we require an image of that state of affairs in which some optimum of value obtains.

We are helped toward such an image by the idea of the biotic pyramid, which represents the movement from the soil and the microorganisms therein through vegetation and the herbivores to the carnivores and the primates. The total amount of value in a pyramid is roughly correlative with the richness of the base, the number of levels, the diversity of forms and total numbers at each level, and the complexity of living forms at the top. These measures correlate highly with each other.

The more valuable pyramids include human beings at the top. Hence this is not an antihuman view of value. The ideal biotic pyramid would seem to be the one in which human beings were sustained by an optimum richness of life derived from all the levels beneath them.

However, human control over the environment is such that an important complication is introduced. To a considerable, not yet determined, extent, human beings, unlike any other species, can increase their numbers at the top of the pyramid by reducing the numbers and levels in the pyramid, thus reducing the overall diversity of life. For the rich biotic community of the American prairie that supported a small Indian population, Europeans substituted the wheat field and thereby could feed a much larger human population.

We are warned today that the highly specialized biotic communities produced by human beings are more precarious than we have often supposed and that for human survival it may be important to modify them. However, that is not now the issue before us. Without such specialization, the total human population would have to be much smaller than it is now. There is a tension between what is optimal for humanity alone and what is optimal when viewed in terms of the biotic pyramid. The problem we face is how to balance these. If we count only human values, the concerns raised in discussion of the model of the biotic pyramid will be relevant only as they support the economic and aesthetic values in human experience. They will be treated as only instrumental values. Unless we altogether deny the hierarchical ranking of values, a ranking implicit in the pyramid itself, we cannot discount the great increase of value given with a larger human population so long as population size does not impair the quality of human life. *But if we take seriously the fact that all forms of life have value, we cannot ignore the loss of value entailed by human simplification or attempted control of the pyramid.*

This discussion points to the need of moderating, without renouncing, the structuring of the world around human needs. We must, of course, develop a more realistic view of our actual long-term needs and seek to practice the utilitarian ethic more wisely. When we do so, the value of the biotic pyramid will be more adequately conserved than is now the case. But the force of the present argument is that ethical action will require still further moderation of our practice in favor of giving greater scope to the biotic pyramid. We must learn to balance our human values against the intrinsic values of others, rather than to judge the others as only instrumental to ours.

Thus far the ethical principles considered have been oriented entirely to the anticipated consequences of an action. Another tradition in philosophical ethics is sharply critical of this approach. This second tradition has been just as anthropocentric as utilitarianism, but its interest is in the intrinsic rightness of actions. The most famous spokesman of this tradition is Kant.

Kant's position is extreme. He seems to say, wrongly, that the advantages accruing from actions are irrelevant to their ethical evaluation. However, analysis of his thought indicates that important considerations are introduced by his approach that are neglected in the utilitarian position.

Kant points out that the principle exemplified by an ethical action must be amenable to generalization. It is not enough to calculate that the probable consequences of my acting in a certain way will increase value. I must also ask what the consequences would be if people *in general* acted in that way. For example, I might calculate that there would be more increase in value by picking and taking home some wildflowers than by leaving them in the woods. But that would not make this action ethically right unless I could also decide that value would be increased *in general* by people picking wildflowers and taking them home under similar circumstances. What Garrett Hardin pointed out in "The Tragedy of the Commons" graphically illustrates this principle in relation to the ecological crisis. If each considers only the consequences of his or her own individual acts for the general good, the general good will be undermined.

### DO OTHER ANIMALS HAVE RIGHTS?

An ethical theory couched in terms of the general good, including the good of animals, can be helpful in guiding the conduct of sensitive individuals. However, its wider application requires that it be translated into political and legal terms. To do that is to raise the question of rights. Can we attribute rights to other animals?

Rights in the past have been attributed only to human beings. We say persons have the right to do whatever the rest of us, including the state, ought to allow them to do, not for our sake, but for theirs. We ought to let each other live, be free, and pursue

146

happiness, and so we speak of the right of all people to life, liberty, and the pursuit of happiness.

Ought we to extend those rights to all other animals? No. It would not make sense to turn our dogs and cats free. It is not necessarily wrong to slaughter animals for human food, or to use a mule to plow a field, even if the animal might pursue happiness better in some other way.

Do our fellow creatures, then, have no rights after all? Yes, they do. They have the right to have the value of their existence and happiness weighed seriously in the balance. They have the right not to be exploited casually for trivial human purposes.

When dealing with human rights the emphasis is on individuals. We should acknowledge the rights of individual animals too. An animal has the right to a chance to live out its life according to its nature. If it must be experimented on or killed, it has the right to a treatment or a death that is as free from pain as possible. If it requires human management for its survival, it has the right to considerate and regular care.

These rights, like human rights, are relative. The human right to liberty may be overridden by a nation's collective need for military defense. Even so, the affirmation of that right to liberty is not empty. It is protected in many ways by legislation and court action, and only very fundamental needs can give legal justification to its abrogation.

Similarly, the rights of individual animals cannot be absolute. Individual and collective human needs, and those of other animals, can supersede them, but the legal definition of their rights would not be an idle gesture. It would reinforce and extend existing curbs on inhumane treatment of other creatures.

Nevertheless, the primary focus when dealing with the rights of animals is larger. Animals suffer at our hands through individual acts of intentional cruelty and exploitation, but they suffer far more from having their needs ignored.

We should learn quickly to respect two kinds of rights of nature. First is the right of species to survive in their natural habitat. The wanton and casual killing of individual animals is a minor evil in comparison with the extinction of a species. Whereas in the animal world the individual can be largely duplicated and replaced, the species, once gone, is irreplaceable. Its extinction

147

permanently impoverishes the biosphere. In a general sense, whereas at the human level the species exists for the sake of individuals, in the nonhuman world the individual exists more for the sake of the species. For humans to annihilate the species unnecessarily—by destroying its habitat, for example—is incompatible with the ethical principles just developed.

Second is the right of the nonhuman world to develop its own balance and harmony free from human interference—that is, the right of wilderness. Nature, when untrammeled by human beings, produces a balanced richness and variety humans cannot match. The biotic pyramid that develops in the absence of human interference has both complexity and stability. It tends to an optimum of living forms in mutually supportive interconnections. It is an achievement we should neither ignore nor destroy but from which we should learn and with which we need to find ways to relate harmoniously.

Our worldwide encroachment on the rights of other animals continues today at an accelerating pace. The recognition of these rights would not automatically stop the extinction of species and the exploitation of the dwindling wilderness, but it would provide a framework within which some of us could rally to the defense of other creatures.

### IS BELIEF IN GOD RELEVANT?

Ethical questions can be discussed apart from questions relating to beliefs about God. In a time when all talk of God is problematic, this is fortunate. Broadening the scope of ethics to include serious consideration of the welfare and rights of other animals can and should be urged on its own merits. Yet study of the history of ethical systems will quickly show how closely such systems are bound up with fundamental religious belief—in the West with belief and disbelief in God. Even today serious ethical convictions are closely associated with such beliefs. We will consider three ways in which belief in God supports, clarifies, or modifies ethical reflection in our time.

The first has to do with the value of maintaining the variety of species that now exist. Protection of species has already been urged without reference to God. When sensitive people contemplate the finality of loss involved in the destruction of a species, do they sense the wrongness of this destruction? If the answer is yes, their recognition of the evil of the loss goes beyond practical considerations. They sense an intrinsic impoverishment of the planet. Even if the members of some other species increase to fill the emptied niche, their doing so does not compensate for the loss.

The point of view from which the destruction of a species is regarded as a significant loss is primarily aesthetic. A rich variety, harmoniously related, is an aesthetic value. A planet on which the variety of species is reduced is aesthetically impoverished regardless of the number of individual animals that remain.

But from what perspective is this variety *of value?* From the perspective of the experience of individual animals its value is negligible. From the perspective of human experience there is some loss, since some humans do enjoy either actually seeing a multiplicity of animals or knowing that they could be seen. But this still does not account for the concern generated in sensitive persons by the contemplation of the wholesale destruction of a species. The impoverishment they sense is of the biosphere as a whole. They believe the world in its entirety is objectively impoverished whether any individual experience is harmed or not. Such a conviction makes sense only if there is a perspective for which the world exists as a whole and for which the variety of species is experientially real. The loss of conscious and explicit belief in God weakens our ability to assert holistic judgments of value, but the sense that there is a perspective more inclusive than one's own is not entirely eradicated. It is an implicit belief in God that would be strengthened and made more effective if that belief could be made explicit.

This belief that there is a perspective more inclusive than one's own is closely bound up with other aspects of the ethical position just presented. For example, the judgment that we should act so as to maximize value in general, rather than only our own value and the value of those we like, bears witness to an inclusive perspective for which value in general exists and cumulates.

A second way in which belief in God is important for ethics can be explained through an expansion of Kant's critique of a simple ethic of consequences. Kant shows that the judgment of the rightness of an action must include consideration of its relationship to the past as well as to the future. If I have made a serious promise, I should not simply ignore that fact when I decide what to do. Similarly, the context for reflection on what I should do is influenced by what others have done for me in the past. If I have been helped when in need, I am indebted to my helpers, and I ought to act in a way that takes account of my debt.

But there is no strictly objective way of determining what commitments I have made or what debts I have incurred. For this determination one's basic perspective on life and one's fundamental self-understanding are crucial.

Some people see themselves as self-made, owing little or nothing to society and family. Others see society as chiefly a corrupt and corrupting force and locate any power that works for good in their own virtue. A third group see all that is most valuable in their lives as given to them through society and deplore their own tendencies to be ungrateful and to violate the rules of society.

The question that is particularly pertinent here is whether people have any obligations or debts beyond the limits of human society. Here the diversity of basic convictions becomes still clearer. Certainly Kant had no perception of such a relation to the natural environment. And in this respect his position is typical of Western ethics. But there are exceptions.

It is possible to see one's life neither as self-made nor as the product of human society alone but as a gift of the total evolutionary process. If I understand myself in this way, it is appropriate to respond in gratitude. Then the fitting ethical action is service to that to which I find myself so comprehensively indebted. To serve the evolutionary process can be understood as furthering its inclusive work.

This religious vision as stated is very vague. Its clarification is a theological task. What is the "total evolutionary process," for example?

It would be possible to understand evolution in such a way that commitment to it would have quite unethical effects. For example, if one's vision of evolution is dominated by the notion of "survival of the fittest," then one might rejoice in the continuing success of the human species in stamping out all competitive forms of life. One might also encourage ruthless competition among human societies and individuals so as to accelerate the evolutionary process.

However, far more basic to the evolutionary process than survival of the fittest is the urge for survival itself. Living things have an urge for life, for continued life, for more and better life. Theories of evolution describe the results of this pervasive urge, which certainly produces competition as well as cooperation. But they presuppose the urge itself. It is to this urge, rather than to the formulas that describe aspects of its consequences, that one may reasonably feel indebted for one's existence.

If this urge is toward more and better life, one must have criteria for understanding what that means. Here we can return to the theory of value with which we began. More and better life is that in which experience or feeling is enhanced. Feeling is enhanced when it can be richer, more intense, more harmonious, and more pleasant. Consciousness marks and enriches higher levels of experience. We may reasonably understand the very rich potentiality of feeling that is ours as the product of millions of years of evolutionary development in which the urge for more and better life has been effective. This everlasting urge toward the realization of higher values is God. To acknowledge our indebtedness to God as understood in this way grounds and sustains the ethical concern to promote the maximization of values.

Theology has a third important relation to an ecological ethics, not fundamentally different from its relation to a purely humanistic ethic, but worth considering in this context.

Ethical theory focuses on clearly conscious decision-making. It tells us how we should balance the factors on which we reflect in connection with such decisions. It depends on calculations of probable consequences of alternative actions and on the relations of action to the situation as shaped by past commitments and obligations.

Ethical behavior is not to be disparaged. In comparison with the widespread tendency to thoughtless selfishness, mere conventionalism, and compulsiveness, ethical behavior is highly desirable. Yet ethical living also has its problems and limitations.

First, life is a constant series of subtle decisions, many of them unconscious, so it is easy to exaggerate the importance of those rather rare instances in which reflective decision-making takes place. To become reflective about every detailed and trivial decision would make wholesome living impossible.

Second, for a decision to be ethical it must be guided by rational reflection. In rational reflection, judgment must be in terms of available knowledge. Also, the knowledge that one can articulate takes precedence over subtle sensitivities and implicit understandings. The subtle lure of as-yet-unimagined values has little opportunity to play its role. Ethical action is generally conservative.

The problem can be illustrated in the characteristic tensions between art and morality. Moral principles tend to formulate and enforce practices supportive of fully apprehended goods—that is, the values recognized and established in the community. The artist is often exploring the fringes of sensibility in ways that cannot but be destructive of the established order of values.

If we place these considerations in the wider context of the whole evolutionary process, they become still more important. The urge toward continued, increased, and enhanced life has pushed and pulled living things through hundreds of millions of years toward new and unforeseeable forms. Unforeseeable ends cannot enter into the calculation of the utilitarian ethicist. Hence, to serve the evolutionary process cannot simply be identical with making ethical decisions calculated to further it.

What is the alternative? The alternative is sensitivity to the urge toward life as it operates both within oneself and in the entire world. It is attunement of the self to that creative process. This attunement allows one to be reshaped by the creative process in ways one cannot anticipate and control. It enables one to work with that process toward unforeseen and unforeseeable ends. It leads to a spontaneity that is informed by rational ethics but transcends it. Christians have called such attunement "trust."

### NOTES

1. See Alfred N. Whitehead, *Process and Reality* (New York: Macmillan, 1929).
2. J. S. Mill, *Utilitarianism*, chapter 2.
3. G. E. Moore, *Principia Ethica* (New York: Cambridge University Press, 1956), pp. 83-84.

# SUGGESTED READING

Cobb, John B., Jr. *Is It Too Late? A Theology of Ecology.* Beverly Hills, Calif.: Bruce (div. of Benziger, Bruce and Glencoe), 1972.

Leopold, Aldo. *A Sand County Almanac.* New York: Oxford University Press, 1949.

Schweitzer, Albert. *Out of My Life and Thought.* New York: Henry Holt, 1933 (Mentor Book, 1953).

Slusser, Dorothy M., and Slusser, Gerald H. *Technology—The God That Failed.* Philadelphia: Westminster Press, 1971.

Whitehead, Alfred N. *Modes of Thought.* New York: Free Press, 1968.

——————————. *Process and Reality.* New York: Macmillan, 1929.

# Foundations for a Humane Ethics   9
What Human Beings Have in Common with Other Higher Animals

*Charles Hartshorne*

**"H**IGHER ANIMALS" MEANS BIRDS and mammals or, at the widest, vertebrates. Of course, our relations to invertebrates are also subject to ethical evaluation, but no additional principles will be involved, only diminished application of the same principles.

What the higher animals most obviously have in common is multicellular bodies, including well-integrated, complex nervous systems. I wish to stress the "multicellular." The discovery of cells is three centuries old, and the "cell theory" more than 140 years old; but the idea is largely unassimilated in our general culture. We talk about bodies as though the word meant mere masses of fleshy and bony stuff, articulated into visible organs—limbs, lungs, heart, arteries, and skin. This is or should be an obsolete way of construing the subject matter in any serious inquiry. The body is a very complex society of societies of cells, each cell an individual in a far stronger sense than is an organ, such as heart or brain. Since ethics is concerned with social relations, the fact that our very bodies are cases of social organization and cooperation is not to be brushed aside as a mere detail; rather, it is an illustration of a basic principle on which all ethics must rest. If our cells were not unconsciously, instinctively ethical (in a minimal sense of that word), we could not be consciously so, and indeed could not exist. But in this sense all higher animals illustrate the same principle, that of life serving life, individual serving individual. Nature is in some sense (in just what sense is the question) a single enterprise. On this point virtually all science and all religion agree. The notion

**Charles Hartshorne** is Ashbel Smith Professor of Philosophy, *Emeritus,* University of Texas, Austin.

that nature represents a war of each against all is at least as far from the truth as the opposite oversimplification that nature is the absolute working out of a single omnipotent and beneficent purpose. Such crudities have little relation to the wonderful subtlety of the cosmic order.

A metazoan animal—that is, a multicellular being in which groups of cells are differentiated into tissues and organs—is an organized society of individuals. But it is more than that; as a whole it is also an individual. This is where the nervous system comes in. Trees, too, are multicellular organisms, hence societies of individuals, but so far as botany has yet shown, and in spite of Fechner and a few botanists of India, this is all that trees are. A tree, like a forest, is many things taken as one, but it is not really in a deep sense one. As a great writer put it: "A tree is a democracy." Lacking a nervous system, its many cells are essentially on their own. (True, they form essential environments for each other, but then all individuals have environmental requirements.) To cut down a tree is not analogous to killing a deer or even a fish, but rather to destroying a colony of paramecia or bacteria. Of course I am abstracting from questions of utility, the value of the tree for animals, including man, who benefit from its qualities. But in itself, the tree is not on the supercellular level of individuality found in the higher animals.

A nervous system is a subsociety of cells by which a society of cellular individuals is made into a single supercellular individual. As each cell is an individual, so is the supercellular animal, if endowed with a nervous system. To see what this finally means we must, I believe, consider the phenomenon of sleep, above all of dreamless sleep. Some deny that there is such a thing, but on weak grounds. Suppose they are mistaken; then in dreamless sleep the metazoan becomes what it would always be if it lacked a well-integrated nervous system—a colony of cells. Aristotle, wiser here than he knew, beautifully said, "A tree is like a sleeping man who never wakes up." (One must understand that the sleep is dreamless.) Thus I take sleep to put us on both sides of a great divide, between two profoundly different levels of reality.

The acute reader may have guessed that by individuality in the "strong" sense I mean something psychological, not merely physiological. The physiological is our objective evidence, apart

155

from our own personal case, for individuality; but the thing, or individuality, is itself psychical. Awake or dreaming, we are actualized as individuals, but when our experience lapses altogether, then only our bodies exist.

Biologists who are merely biologists, and strictly behavioristic psychologists, are unable, I believe, to see the ultimate meaning of the mind-body relationship. Experience is the final reality; all else is but shadow or appearance. If the higher animals are individuals consisting of individuals, and I insist that this is what they are, then there are two levels of experience in such animals, not just one. First are the experiences, lapsing in dreamless sleep, that make the animal as a whole during most of its life a single individual, and second are the experiences that make each cell such an individual.

In terms of purpose or value, what is the relation between the two levels of animal life or experience? In our human case we tend to think our bodily parts are there for us, not we for them. We object to physical pain because *we* suffer, not simply because our cells suffer. It is because *we*, not simply our cells, enjoy that we try to be in healthy and pleasant physical states. The parts, we seem to feel, are for the whole, not the whole for the parts. This is the opposite of the usual political view of whole and parts, according to which the values of the group are just its means of securing the welfare of the members. We shall have to return to this question of whole and parts. It is one of the ultimate dimensions of the ethical.

Setting aside, for the moment, consideration of cells, let us turn to the larger society of which the multicellular animal is a member, its group or species. Does the animal seek only its own preservation and enhancement, or does it seek the preservation and enhancement of its species as well? How are individual and group ends related? If a single member is to its group as cells are to metazoan animals, then the end is the group, not the single animal. Yet a vicious half-truth holds, "Self-preservation is the first law of nature." If "first" is taken, as it often is, to mean "absolute" or "self-sufficient," then we are being asked to give egoism the sanction of nature itself. This is bad biology. The absolute law of nature, if there is one in this connection, is preservation and enhancement of the species, or even of something infinitely more comprehensive—nature as a whole (or God). Individuals are driven by inherited structures (genes) to act, in the normal case, so as to produce and provide for the health and normal safety of offspring and sometimes of conspecific adults, mates, or fellow tribe members. A male spider risks his life in mating; he is dispensable once he has done his necessary work. All individuals are dispensable; in the long run so are species. If nature has ends, the ends transcend "self-interest" and even species interest. It is selfishness, conceit, and lack either of observation or of imagination that accounts for our failure to see this, for the facts are there. We shall have to examine the concept of individuality more deeply to get to the bottom of the problem.

What makes an animal, once born, always the same individual? Here our Western religious and philosophical traditions are one-sided compared to Oriental traditions. Once the words *soul* and *substance* (as used by Aristotle) were coined, these two steps in combination initiated more than two millennia of indulgence in an exaggerated metaphysical individualism that kept ethics in chains. In the Western view, an animal is always the same entity or substance, and at least in the human it always has or is the same soul. In amazingly uncritical fashion—compared to the Buddhists of the same period—the notion of an individual entity that is always just itself, an identical something, was combined with the scarcely compatible notion of perpetual change. "The more it changes the more it is the same thing." This French saying could be taken as the motto of the Western doctrine. It is obviously at best a paradox, not a literal and clear statement of truth. And it is solid common sense that "being oneself" is at most a matter of degree, and not absolute. "He was not himself yesterday"—myriads of such remarks are considered intelligible.

Yet philosophers and theologians have either ignored these significant hints that something is wrong with their doctrines or indulged in equivocation or shameful vagueness in dealing with them. And there are deeper difficulties. In what sense is one really "oneself" in dreamless sleep? One's body is there, but what else? We have not a scintilla of hard evidence that one's mind is there, if by mind we mean more than the brain and the potentiality of experiencing and thinking when one comes out of the dreamless, sleeping state. The knowable actuality of the moment is body, not soul apart from dreams or waking experiences. Thus the soul is far from a simple identity through time, if "soul" means a more than bodily actuality. The Buddha himself is reported to have recognized this; for he told a disciple that his body came closer to being something numerically identical through time than did his individual soul.

What then about the identity of the body? We know scientifically that it is nothing absolute. The most minute parts are constantly transformed or replaced. On the cellular level only the nerve cells endure throughout life, and even this endurance is a matter of abstract outline, not of concrete specificity. True, the gene structure found in every cell is largely fixed, but this is an identity of form, not of matter; in our present state of knowledge it is abstract, a pattern, not a concrete stuff, physical or mental. The entire history of Western individualism is the story of confusing abstract and concrete. The concrete units of reality cannot be either physical substances or spiritual souls. What then are they?

The Buddhists gave the answer long ago, and Whitehead, apparently independently, has recently come to a view similar to theirs, though in my opinion more adequately worked out. The concrete units of reality are unit-processes, unit-events, singular cases of becoming or creation. Reality consists of actions, not things. What then acts? To ask this question is to attempt to force, in too crude a manner, the structure of language on that which language is about. The action is itself the actor. There is here ultimately only a semantic distinction, unless what is meant by the active "agent" is the system of actions prior to the present one. What is there, ready to issue in the animal's next action, is the animal's career up to now, the sum of its past actions. Oddly enough the poet Longfellow expressed this, surely only partly consciously, in his lines:

> For the structure that we raise
> Time is with materials filled,
> Our todays and yesterdays
> Are the bricks with which we build.

What one uses in acting now are his previous acts, together with the previous acts of others, including among the others his own bodily cells. The actual things in the world are careers, or what relativity physicists, who tend toward the Buddhist view (though the Buddhists knew nothing of precise physical laws), call "world-lines." They are kinds of sequences into which unit-events, which Whitehead calls "actual occasions" or "actual entities," group themselves. Thus the primary concrete entities are happenings, unit cases of becoming or activity, which, as Bergson says, is reality itself.

Whitehead properly terms this ultimate principle "creativity," also "self-creation"; for in this doctrine, though all events are causally conditioned, none is precisely determined by its conditions. According to Peirce, who partly anticipated Whitehead, but with a more conscious recognition of Buddhist antecedents, the primary realities are feelings, and a feeling, though it reacts to prior feelings, is also "spontaneous," an addition, however slight, to the definiteness of the world, not a uniquely predetermined unwinding of causal necessities. I know that strict determinism is still somewhat fashionable among philosophers and at least some physicists, psychologists, and social scientists; but I hold with Wiener that this is a "rearguard action." The edge of intellectual discovery has moved beyond the classical idea of causality as an absolute determining of the outcomes of situations.

Some "neat and tidy minds" (Whitehead) who cannot resist the attraction of the grandiose simplification offered by strict determinism have met Heisenberg's "indeterminacy principle" either by holding that the indeterminacy is our lack of knowledge or by suggesting that the present state of physics is not likely to persist forever. To the first point it should be said that long before quantum mechanics Peirce and several other competent scientists and philosophers had argued against classical determinism on grounds that have still not been discredited. To the second it should be said that leading physicists have suggested that when quantum mechanics in its present form is superseded it will be by moving still further away from classical conceptions, including that of causality.

Causality is the limitation within which, subject to statistical or probabilistic laws, creative decision takes place. Not only man, not only animals, but the very atoms defy any absolute or more than statistical regularity in their actions. There is very good reason to take this, not as an expression of our ignorance, but as the very nature of causality and of process as such.

We shall consider later the ethical implications of the view of identity and freedom just sketched, a view sometimes called Process Philosophy. I also call it Creationism, since it means that each moment there are new units of reality that not only did not exist before but were not even precisely defined in advance by natural laws and initial conditions.

It is pleasing that Longfellow begins the poem from which I quoted above with the line "All are architects of fate." Longfellow knew as well as anyone that an architect is no mere executor of a design or pattern already laid down, but the chooser of the pattern itself. I am quite aware that determinists have their way of describing choice, but I have yet to encounter a strict determinist (whether philosopher, psychologist, or physicist) who really meets the criticisms posed by James, Peirce, and a multitude of other scientists and philosophers, all of whom have known very well what the deterministic theory has to say on these matters.

## HOW MAN DIFFERS FROM THE OTHER HIGHER ANIMALS

The many important aspects of the difference between men and the other higher animals center in one: the symbolic capacity, shown obviously in language (but not exclusively in it, unless the word *language* is taken broadly). Only man draws representative pictures, maps, and diagrams, uses musical and mathematical notations, points or draws an arrow to show direction, uses a color for an understood meaning as in traffic lights, and so on. Symbolic capacity is our human advantage and superiority. Is it a difference in kind from other animals or only one in degree? I answer: it is a difference in degree so vast that for many purposes one can safely forget that it is one of degree. However, recent experiences in teaching what seem to be primitive visual languages to chimpanzees show that for some purposes the difference may be relative. My guess is that the chimpanzee will turn out to be capable only of what a quite small child can accomplish semantically. And of course most animals are far below the manlike apes in their learning capacities.

A clue to the nature of our symbolic power is in its reflexiveness. If other animals can talk, it is about things other than talk. But we can talk about talk, we have the word *word*, also *language, foreign language, symbol, analogy, metaphor,* and innumerable others. Until nonhuman animals exhibit something comparable, we need not concern ourselves with the hypothetical possibility that they might attain our level of consciousness, participate with us in conscious ethical and political discussion, and the like.

An effect of symbolic power is the enhancement of freedom in the partially indeterministic sense. Freedom is not, in spite of Hegel and Marx, the consciousness of necessity; it is rather the consciousness of limited possibilities. The element of necessity is covered by the qualification "limited," but to reduce freedom to this aspect is like reducing a river to its banks. Between the banks the particles of water have options as to where they flow; bring the banks close enough together to deprive the particles of all options and there is no longer a flow or a river. This is what determinism does, unwittingly, with the idea of freedom. It tries to justify itself by pointing out what no one doubts, that without banks or limitations there is no river and no freedom. I could show that this account applies to scores of deterministic essays, old and new, through the centuries.

The foregoing being granted, the question remains how far apart are the banks, or how wide are the limits within which exist genuine options, alternative actions that are genuinely open to the individual, meaning by the individual the sum of antecedent sequences of action. (To say that the options are really open is not to say that they are equally probable continuations of indivdual careers; here we can refine our river analogy. Granted certain laws or forces, the banks will establish a probability distribution of particles. But there is no evidence for the view that it is only our ignorance that makes the probability schema necessary. Any nonprobabilistic conception of causality is sheer dogmatism, not a record of known or knowable facts.)

That symbolic power increases freedom is apparent on reflection. We know that a universal is neutral as to what instances of it there may be. To entertain the concept "house" as a desirable product does not determine of what materials the house will be built—brick, stone, concrete, glass, iron, aluminum, pounded earth, wood, and so on. Thus the greater our power to generalize, the greater the range of options we can entertain for carrying out

161

our purposes. To hold the concept "protein" as a necessary element in our diet is to be free to consider meat, fish, soy beans, and many other possibilities. It is clear that the use of symbols enormously expands the power to envisage universals as such. Indeed, it is easy to suppose that creatures without something like language can have no freedom at all because they cannot generalize. However, this is a mistake. Every animal has something like the generalization "edible substance." A fox may have the options of chasing a rabbit and searching for field mice. But without a system of symbols this power is narrowly limited. A man can go on a hunger strike, or become a vegetarian, or cease being a vegetarian.. He can choose among philosophies, religions, vocations, avocations, nationalities.

One of the wonders of the history of ideas is that so many could suppose that with all this power to envisage possibilities a human being could still, taking circumstances into account, be predetermined to a single wholly particular career from birth to death. To me this way of thinking is one of the most remarkable of all mental leaps in the dark. Show me an argument for making this leap and I will show you a mind that fails to distinguish between the river having banks at all and the question: "How far apart are the banks set?" By some criteria, perhaps even human freedom is slight. The rivers may be narrow; still, their banks are at finite, not zero, distances from each other.

ETHICAL IMPLICATIONS

The ethical importance of the idea of freedom in the partly indeterministic sense just explained is that it brings out the real nature of life as deterministic views have never succeeded in doing. If each moment of life is genuinely creative, at least in some slight degree, *then each creature is also a creator,* sharing, in a humble way with any deity that one may be able to conceive, the dignity of a maker of the world's definiteness. Partly through each creature the formless acquires form, the indeterminate, determinacy. Robinson Jeffers states the issue well, even if he decides it wrongly. The mountain ahead of the world, he says, is not forming but formed; the questions are answered before we take them up. But not so. We here and now effect some part of the transition from the nebulousness of possibility to the definiteness of

162

actuality. Human beings do this to a far higher degree than the other animals, not to mention the plant cells or the atoms. This, in one aspect, is precisely our superiority. But note: the difference is relative, not absolute. Every creature has to resolve indeterminacies, however trivial these may be in some cases.

Indulgence in the superstition of unqualified determinism—it is supreme among superstitions of a highly intellectual sort—has poisoned the wells from which theologians and philosophers have been drinking for thousands of years. The classic "problem of evil" is one of the results. Once the supposition is allowed that action could be wholly determined in advance, people want to know why so many things have been determined so badly. It seems that some cosmic decision or cosmic chance back at the beginning, if there was a beginning, must be responsible for all our troubles. To wish that one had made a different choice is thus to wish that the entire sequence of events as far back as you like had been otherwise. Our choices, on the determinist's view, settle nothing not already settled long before we were born. In this way all our concepts collapse. The idea of God very obviously tends to collapse, but so do others. For the entire universe is being viewed by the determinist as an interconnected system with no genuine alternatives anywhere, and yet the system as a whole is obviously arbitrary, merely one among an infinite number of conceivable systems.

Those who object to indeterministic freedom as having an aspect of arbitrariness forget that determinism only pushes the arbitrariness back and back but does nothing to get rid of it. Spinoza and Leibniz applied their great intellects to finding a way of banishing arbitrariness altogether. If anyone thinks one or the other of them succeeded, let him say so. If he is not willing to do this, and few today are, then let him show a third way to eliminate contingency or arbitrariness. If he cannot, he should stop defending determinism on the ground that it avoids the scandal of setting limits to the "principle of sufficient reason." The history of thought shows that this principle, taken without qualification, is itself unreasonable. Determinism is one form of this unreasonableness. Determinism is in a sense an absolute rationalism, but it turns, when pressed, into an absolute irrationalism.

If we grant that the question "Why did this happen?" is valid only within limits, then for every concrete situation there will be an approximate, though not an absolute, reason in the previous situation; whereas determinism makes the entire situation backward and forward absolutely without reason. It simply has been and will continue to be just the system it is. No decision was ever made between it and alternatives. The qualified determinist sees the decision between possible and actual as always and everywhere in the making, rather than as always and everywhere already made. He can regard evils not as divinely imposed, or the product of some mere blind chance or necessity, but as the intelligible, though not in detail predictable, mixture of chance and necessity involved in creative freedom as universal to reality.

If every act is partly indeterminate in advance, then no power, not even divine, can have designed the world in its details, good or bad, and there is no "problem of evil" in the classic sense. That problem is created by the denial of creaturely freedom, of nondivine creativity. If the creatures had no such freedom, how could they form the idea of an eminent or divine form of such freedom? The problem of evil thus implies the contradiction that there are two levels, divine and nondivine, of creativity, yet all is determined by the divine level, and hence the other level is not really there at all. Or the problem rests on the arbitrary limitation of nondivine creativity to the human form, which is no more reasonable than the Cartesian idea that only man has feelings or anything like thought or volition.

The greater freedom of man is enormously increased, for good as well as for ill, by science and technology. At one time building a house or fighting a battle offered few options as to the means and materials employed. Today new options continually emerge. As we all have come to realize, the additions to our powers are not in all respects beneficial: we have pollution; we face a baffling complexity of choices that must be made; we have created destructiveness, threatening to escape all rational control, in our methods of warfare and even our methods of satisfying our desires for luxuries.

The reality of genuinely open notions implies a fundamental aspect of tragedy in life. No laws of nature, no divine providence, no laws of man, no control by hypnotists or master propagandists, can guarantee perfect harmony among individuals, human or nonhuman. Set the banks of the rivers as close as you like, but there must still be some free play among the particles and hence chances of conflict as well as harmony. Condition all individuals to be mild and kind—and also sensible—supposing the conditioners can themselves be conditioned to do this (Plato's old problem). Nevertheless, life itself requires that there be some room for the self-determination of each moment of life in each individual career. And if this self-determination is limited to trivialities, then life itself becomes trivial and no great good has been accomplished after all. Only determinism gives extreme utopianisms any plausibility. No doubt this helps explain B. F. Skinner's fondness for the doctrine. (I am not denying the value of Skinner's scientific discoveries or of some of his practical suggestions.)

The source of all vital harmony among individuals is the same as the source of all disharmony, and that is freedom. Risk is inherent in life and cannot be eliminated. All any ruler, or any providence, can do is set wise limits to the options; but so long as there are options at all, and life at all, there will be possibilities of discord as well as of concord.

Man's dangerous freedom threatens not just himself and his kind but all life on earth. The American Indians seemed to be aware of their responsibility to existing life forms other than themselves. However, their methods could support only a small human population and set limitations to the development of human potentialities. The white settlers took these two restrictions, the quantitative and the qualitative, as excuses for appropriating most of the land of the Amerindians. They had perhaps a stronger case on the quantitative than on the qualitative side, but in my opinion they had a genuine case in both, however shameful and brutal the particular actions taken. The Indian problem is still with us, along with many other somewhat analogous problems, including the problem of man's crowding nonhuman forms of life out of existence. The entire question of quantity and quality, and of the competition among forms of life for the earth's resources, must be reconsidered.

What ethical principles follow from our analysis? To say "Man is the rational or thinking animal" is to say that he can entertain definite principles and reckon more or less remote consequences. The ability to distinguish universals from particulars symbolically implies the ability to see oneself or another as a mere particular case. If a child could not think of itself as object for other subjects, it also could not form symbols for classes of phenomena. The ethical view of values is that things are good and to be approved not because they are good for me, or good for you, but because they are good for someone or some class of individuals, and good not merely momentarily but in view of probable consequences. Thus reason generalizes the natural impulses of approval and disapproval, making them valid from an objective, interpersonal, and long-run point of view.

It is to me a curious defect of most Western ethics that it inclines to absolutize self-interest (along with causality and still other relative concepts) and tries to deduce altruism from intelligent self-concern. Thus if one enjoys sympathetic feelings one can rationally promote the good of others, since in this way one secures one's own happiness. The assumption is that reason is needed, not to enlarge our ends but to show us how to achieve the sole absolute end—one's own welfare in the long run. At the age of twenty I thought about this way of doing ethics and decided it was absurd. I still think so. The self, identity, or individuality that is thus taken as the absolute end is nothing absolute at all, but in many ways is highly relative. Each moment I am a new reality, identical only abstractly, or partially and in outline, with what existed before. In deep sleep I am not, as a conscious being, actual at all. And in death what will I be?

To make this drastically qualified and ephemeral entity, or pseudoentity, one's absolute principle seems a monstrous perversion of reason. The lower animals have a more balanced attitude. They absolutize neither their own individuality nor that of their fellows, but relate their momentary needs to some of the needs, not altogether momentary, of others. Along comes reason (as some conceive it), generalizing the legitimate self-regarding aspect to its limit, taking the long run into account and the subtle spiritual needs to enjoy sympathy and similar attitudes, and calling this procedure enlightened self-interest. What is not seen is that the absolutizing of self-interest as an end in itself is unenlightened superstition. Not self-concern, but the whole complex of self-regarding and other-regarding impulses is what reason, if true to itself, generalizes and raises above the merely personal or individual. Of course one values others partly for what they can do for oneself; but equally, and even more fundamentally, one values oneself for what one can do for others. In both cases, one considers long-run consequences. But in the long run it is posterity and the everlasting whole of things that will be there, not you or I. The final long-run accomplishment must radically transcend self on any scientific or, in my view, any rationally philosophical assumption.

What a dismal view of life it is that takes one's own mortal individuality as that for the sake of which one's every act must take place. When I saw, years ago, that no one could force me to adopt this dismal position, I felt a great release. I still feel it. Later I learned that the Buddhists, and two thousand years later, Peirce and Whitehead had reached the same decision.

We must return to our question, the treatment of the nonhuman animals. One difference between ethical principles relating us to our human fellows and those relating us to the rest of the animal kingdom is that both sides to an interhuman dispute can appeal to principles *qua* principles, while the nonhuman side to an infrahuman dispute cannot do this. How close to such a thing chimpanzees can come remains an interesting question.

It is important to realize, however, that a human infant, even more an embryo in early stages, is only potentially human by the foregoing test. The same holds of outright idiots in human form—or rather they are not even potentially human, at least given present medical means. During the first weeks an embryo is but a colony of cellular individuals, itself as a whole not an individual at all. And when, at eight weeks, brain waves begin and we may perhaps suppose unitary "human" experiences or feelings corresponding to the activities of the nervous system, these feelings are still at a vast distance from anything comparable even to those of a child barely beginning to talk. If such an embryo has actual rights, then I say that horses and apes have them in a stronger sense. Their nervous systems, and hence their experiences, are functioning on a much higher level. Those who blur these important distinctions are hardly to be trusted to instruct us in the ethics of abortion.

Man is an ethical being because he is a symbol-using being. He lives in an elaborately symbolized world, the elaboration including particularly reflexivity, symbols about symbols. Hence he has options not merely between single possible actions but between whole classes of actions and with respect to definite principles of classification. He has choices among ends as well as among means. He can see himself and his very existence as contingent, a mere illustration, and a temporary one, of reality. His very species is such an illustration. What follows for ethics? What follows is that man can do in a conscious, generalized fashion what other creatures do in unconscious and particular ways: he can make his contribution to the cosmic drama. Man understands the secret of nature just enough to know that it has values beyond those that he can enjoy. He knows that there is weal and woe for all sorts of beings, none of which is necessary to the existence of a world or of values. He can more or less clearly and vividly empathize with other creatures and definitely put the question: whose values ought to give way in the case of conflict? And he has some insight into what is good or not good for other creatures, even those very different from himself. What this all means is that man can see himself as trustee for a cosmic end, an all-inclusive value vaguely understood, but valid for the distant as well as the near future. With just this has religion at its best been concerned. At heart, scientists are concerned with it too, but the specialization to which most of them have been driven, together with the partial failure of philosophy to rise to the occasion, has generated the present difficulties.

When the "whole" is an animal organism and the "parts" its cells, we all cheerfully agree that the value of the cells is, at least primarily, if not entirely, their contributions to the experience of the animal as a whole. But when the inclusive or cosmic whole is considered, we hesitate. Part of the reason is the misleading political analogy. Political theorists largely agree that the state as a whole does not sum up our human values. A good state is one that fosters and protects good individual lives. There is no further good actualized in the state as an individual entity. Is the cosmos like this? Precisely here, I think, is the crux of the religious-philosophical question. I argue that the organic analogy, not the political one, applies to the inclusive or cosmic whole.

Much can be said for this assumption, but it cannot all be said here.

I shall, however, point out that the religious precept widely acknowledged in more than one major religion—namely, that God is to be loved with one's entire being, not simply with much or most of it—makes no apparent sense unless it means that what we contribute to the divine life is all that matters in what we do. If then we feel kindly toward the lower animals, the religious meaning of this must be that they, too, are valuable to God, so that in loving them we are loving something in God himself. To the extent that we fail to love life in its myriad forms, to that extent is our being outside our love for God. Have Christians, Jews, or Moslems done justice to this simple reflection?

Recently, in a controversy about animal experimentation, a scientist declared that he was skeptical of the relevance of ethical considerations to our treatment of nonhuman animals. I wish to register a protest against this short and easy way of disposing of the animal experimentation issue. And I doubt whether most scientists would be content with it.

It may help here if we put the following question: *Though human beings have (let us grant) a net superiority to the other animals, may it not be the case that there is a price for this superiority, so that in some significant respects we are actually inferior?* Rather obviously, this is the situation. For while the other animals cannot be conscious trustees for cosmic ends, they very well can and, I hold, *do* serve these ends unconsciously, and it is even reasonable to say that, compared to human beings, the lesser creatures are infallible servants of the cosmic cause. By inherited arrangements they are guided in the right paths; they do what we (though not they) can view as their duty—that is, as mentioned earlier, care for themselves and their young and try to help their mates and in some species their fellows. We may even document their cooperation across species: weaning the young of others, feeding and caring for life not of their making. It would not be hard to show that this is the most they could effectively do with their types and degrees of intelligence. Animals, with their equipment, are as altruistic as a competent naturalist would want them to be, no more and no less. By eating rabbits, foxes do rabbits as a whole good and not harm. Only with a high level of

169

competence, requiring symbolic powers such as man's, is an extended scope for altruism, other-regarding behavior, in order. But the price of these powers is the capacity to reject the duty as well as to perform it. We can refuse our implied trusteeship. The other animals cannot. They do their best. Man may or may not do his best. So man is the grandest and the sorriest animal there is. This is no new thought, but it fits the realities. And it may help us to think with some approach to objectivity about our duties toward the unspeaking or "dumb" brutes.

The question is: In what sense does the nonhuman have rights? According to Kant, only rational beings have rights. The sole reason he sees for being kind to animals is that being unkind to them tends to carry over into unkindness to persons. I agree with Schweitzer and almost the entire Eastern world that this will not do. A better reason for treating animals kindly is that their lives, too, have intrinsic value. As I see it, the rationality that Kant takes to be a precondition of value and to be unique to man among animals, is not the absolute thing Kant's argument takes it to be. How rational are even the best human beings? If there is an absolute quality of rationality that an ape simply lacks, then I hold that man lacks it also. It is indeed a metaphysical or theological concept and is appropriate only to a theory of deity, not to a theory of man by himself. From this point of view no animal, not even man, is finally an end in itself. All are dispensable, and therefore all are mortal. If there is an absolute end to which all else is contributory, it is not man but Nature or God, the Everlasting Reality, however one conceives this.

I conclude from the foregoing that in the sense in which any animal has intrinsic value, all animals have some of it, and the differences are matters of degree. Since man has the typical animal capacities—sensory, emotional, practical—plus an enormous addition of reflective consciousness and technical power, it seems reasonable to assign him a far higher value than the other terrestrial creatures (other planets may contain superhuman races, and I hope they do); at the same time it is also reasonable to proclaim the ideal that man should, where possible, regard himself and his value as additional or complementary to the others, rather than as competitive with them. This is not easy for modern man to do. He has only begun to think seriously about it, whereas many

170

primitive peoples gave the matter considerable thought. All honor to them. Most of us, when we think about it, tend to feel that there is a significant analogy between a dog in pain and a man in pain and that the analogy means, other things being equal, that we would like to prevent or mitigate animal pain wherever it occurs or threatens. I hold that Kant's attempt to deny the intrinsic value of all animal life was a grave error. Terrestrial, nonhuman life is not the final end of all existence. Is human life? I think not.

I wish, before I end, to make one confession. I have discussed difficult issues with what some will no doubt regard as surprising confidence, not to say dogmatism. But on a very crucial point I am far from confident or clear. It is easy to say that while all animals have intrinsic value, man has more value than the others. Irresistibly, the question arises: How much more? "Ye are of more value than many sparrows." Is it forbidden to ask how many? Is the answer any number, no matter how great? I cannot think so.

No matter what we say, our actions constitute answers to such questions. Our cities are seated on the ruins of natural ecosystems, and our germicides obliterate multitudes of micro-organisms. These are but two examples. Man does take his kind as more valuable than other species, infinitely more valuable, it almost seems. Of course, if one knew that a human individual was an "immortal soul" (including the complete idiots?) while no nonhuman animal possessed this infinite attribute, there might be a case for taking the difference to be infinite. But we have no such knowledge. Further, I hold that we have sufficient grounds for regarding ourselves as mortal in the same sense as the other creatures, with the sole but important difference that we alone can *consciously* contribute to the beauty of the whole of things, a beauty which, according at least to my faith, infinitely survives us. The other animals make their contributions, but not consciously.

Fortunately, it may not be necessary to quantify in any very definite manner the differential values of human and nonhuman. For even in our own human interest we need to set limits to population growth and to our luxurious habits. Perhaps in this way we can to some extent sidestep the qualitative question.

If we avoid absolutizing man's difference from the rest of nature, we can more easily open our minds and hearts to the really infinite difference, that between any mere animal or mere transitory creature and the Primordial and Everlasting, however we conceive this, the Cosmic Life, the Ocean to which all streams somehow make their contributions. Who can suppose that the many beautiful, obviously self-enjoying nonhuman creatures contribute nothing to this Ocean?

Life in the present is self-enjoyed but this very self-enjoyment is momentary, and beyond the present its value can only be in what it contributes to the Really Permanent and Really Inclusive Good.

Finally, we are all but contributions to the mysterious cosmic future. With proper humility we may be able to cease flattering ourselves with the fancy that we or our species is the Everlasting. And then we should be able to see that it is not we human beings alone who contribute to what really matters, but we and all other creatures, each in its way and measure. We should then have the wisdom—but in a more sophisticated form and with more scientific clarity—that Asiatics, including those wanderers from Asia, the Amerindians, have for ages possessed.

## SUGGESTED READINGS

Cobb, John B., Jr. *Is It Too Late? A Theology of Ecology.* Beverly Hills, Calif.: Bruce (div. of Benziger, Bruce, Glencoe), 1972.
Hartshorne, Charles. *Beyond Humanism: Essays in the Philosophy of Nature.* Lincoln: University of Nebraska Press, 1968.
——————————— *Creative Synthesis and Philosophic Method.* LaSalle: Open Court (London, SCM), 1970.
——————————— *Born to Sing: An Interpretation and World Survey of Bird Song.* Bloomington: Indiana University Press, 1973.
Sherburne, Donald W. *A Key to Whitehead's Process and Reality.* New York: Macmillan, 1966.
Whitehead, Alfred North. *Modes of Thought.* New York: Free Press, 1968.
Wright, Sewall. "Biology and the Philosophy of Science," in *Process and Divinity: Essays presented to Charles Hartshorne,* eds. William L. Reese and Eugene Freeman. LaSalle: Open Court, 1964.

# Naturalistic Realism and Animate Compassion

# 10

*F. S. C. Northrop*

Today IN NORTHERN WISCONSIN, on a chain of lakes amid extensive undisturbed forests, there lives an exceptional person. His name is Carl Marty; the place, Northernaire. There he has helped nature's creatures bring into being a remarkable, compassionate community.

Of it he says:

> As I walk in the forest in the darkness of the night and the bear, deer, fox, and raccoons walk up to me in friendship and lick my hand, when the porcupine climbs up my arm and gently nuzzles my ear, when the beaver swims in from the lake, stands up and grasps my leg, crying like a human child to be held in my arms, and when the fox jumps through my open window to lie on my bed, I feel that they are asking me to help their misunderstood brothers in the woods to a better understanding between their kind and man.

Clearly, were such understandings prevalent, there would be no need of societies for the prevention of cruelty to animals or for a book such as this one.

Carl Marty adds: "Without exception, the animals of the forest are reaching out for human friendship. It is we humans who are not conditioned to accept this friendship." His own habitual behavior, as experienced above, demonstrates that we might be conditioned otherwise.

It also recalls another occasion. The time is the sixth century B.C.; the place, the luxuriant grounds of a high caste Hindu maharaja's palace at Kapilavastu in Northern India near the Nepal

F. S. C. **Northrop** is Sterling Professor of Philosophy and Law, *Emeritus,* Yale University.

173

border; and the person, Siddbattha Gautama. He is the maharaja's eldest son, assured by high-caste primogeniture of patriarchal birth to take over, on his father's retirement, the theocratic kingship of the state, the public leadership of the Hindu Aryan religious ceremonies, the command of the army, and the juridicial declaration of the laws of caste and tribal custom, as well as the enjoyment of the sumptuous perquisites of palace and military fortress that accompany these responsibilities.

The circumstances, however, that confronted this young man were somewhat unique; for as he stood there in the palace garden, a flock of white swans flew over, and suddenly the leader, with wing bloodstained and pierced by a hunter's arrow, fell frantic and helpless at his feet. After stroking and calming the trembling creature with his left hand and carefully extracting the arrow with the right, he tested its barb in his own flesh to wince with fellow-feeling pain and forthwith vowed:

> For now I know, by what within me stirs
> That I shall teach compassion unto men
> And be a speechless world's interpreter . . .
> [Thus] . . . Our Lord Buddh
> Began his works of mercy.[1]

Immediately, his movements outside the palace grounds took a new course and were seen with different eyes. Instead of riding in his chariot with military pomp and splendor along the Royal Highway, deferred to by those of the higher castes, while those of lower caste, the aged, the hungry, the crippled, the diseased, the beggars and the untouchables, were pushed to the rear or out of sight beyond concern—instead, he put on the humble person's simple garb—a single cotton sheet draped around his body—to seek out, face objectively, and share with fellow-feeling the bodily ills and pains of his fellow men. He thereby cultivated, first in himself and then in others, the natural compassion for all living creatures that such understanding and shared pain and suffering elicit. Thus was born of an initial fellow-feeling for an injured swan a spontaneous newly conditioned habitual compassion for the speaking as well as the speechless world's animals.

It is little wonder that for anyone who has taken the time to study his deeds, observations, teachings, and achievements; to know personally some of his countless followers in Southeast Asia;

and to experience from within their compassionately egalitarian democratic and quietly joyful familial, religious, and village communities, as well as their national political, religious, and educational leaders with their personal habits of mediation and meditation, the young Gautama has earned not merely the right to be called the Compassionate Buddha, but also the affectionate loyalty of the largest number of followers, both secular and religious, any single leader has ever enjoyed.[2]

To understand the dynamism behind this remarkable reconditioning of himself and others, we must pursue the Buddha's observations and behavior in greater detail and depth. Notable first is that his experiences are objectively initiated and biologically grounded rather than being merely introspective and accessible only to one's own wholly subjective interior. For it was not his own subjective private pain or his self-centered existential agonizing that initiated the Buddha's concern with the cause and cure, so far as there be one, of the fact of suffering. Instead, it was the outer-focused, biologically objective impact on his attention and complacency of the pained and agonizing swan that fell at his feet. This fact prevented him from falling into the error of the ancient Indian Mimamsa Dualists, or the Charvakian Materialists of his day, of supposing that feeling awareness is privy to human persons.

The Buddha's story should also enable us today to escape (i) the Cartesian or early Lockean dualism of Broad, Lovejoy and Sir John Eccles, between feelingless material substances and disembodied mental ones, thereby never allowing its insolvable pseudo body-mind problem to arise and then generate the following succession of attempts to "solve" it, each one more futile, in its diverse phantasms, than its predecessor. These pseudo-answers, all persisting and conflicting dangerously, in our world today, are:

(ii) The Hobbesian, Marxist and Skinnerian behavioristic phantasy that only feelingless material substances exist, both thought and feeling awareness being phantasmic projections.

(iii) The similar (body, now phantasmic) notion of the "Idealistic" personalistic pluralists Berkeley, Leibniz, Lotze, the early McTaggart and countless others today, that only disembodied windowlessly monadic psychies, i.e. Ghosts, exist; each one trapped claustrophobically in his private psychied interior, being

175

unable to contact, know, or feel his own sweetheart, or spouse, to say nothing about our pained bodily swan.

(iv) Kant, who knew his Newtonian linear mechanically causal mathematical physics, saw all these implications of (i) (ii) (iii), and to avoid them (a) denied the existence of both (ii) and (iii) assigning each phantasmically to the so-called "outer" and "inner" sensa called *a posteriori,* with all else categorically *a priori,* and then (b) launched a rescue mission, not joined by McTaggart, to release the pluralistic personalists of (iii) from their window-lessly monadic psychic jails, by (c) substituting for them a Monistic Idealistic disembodied Self, i.e. a Ghost named The Transcendental Ego which is identical not merely in all human persons but also for the Categorical *a priori* understanding of all the entities terrestrial and celestial in the cosmos including pained injured swans and even one's own human nature, calling all these diverse subject matters when thus "understood" in terms of this Monistic Idealistic disembodied Ghost, in somewhat Pickwickian fashion "Natural Sciences," i.e. *Naturwissensschaften;* only then (d) to find and prove (due largely to this Monistic Idealistic disembodied Ego's Category of linear 100% deterministic mechanical causality) that not merely purposeful, i.e. teleological animate or human behavior, but also *interpersonal* normative subjects such as ethics, legal persons, and the humanities generally and their history including even Kant's moral "freedom God and immortality" are left meaningless—clearly, a disembodied Monistic Idealistic Ghostly one's own Self, as Pickwickianly spurious in its "Idealism" as in its "*Natur*alism."

Moreover, in order to give what turns out to be a wholly phantasmic *a priori* "regulative" meaning to the interpersonally pluralistic normative humanistic persons of (d) above and an even more phantasmic "as if" meaning to goal-guided embodied animate or teleological human behavior, Kant and each one of his Monistic Idealistic followers added to this self's *categorical,* or the Neo-Kantian, Karl Popperian *hypothetical, a prioris* of their Pickwickian *Naturwissensschaften,* the additional set of phantasmic "regulative" *a prioris* and "as ifs," "necessary" for the understanding of the interpersonal humanistic subjects. They thereby require their disembodied Ego's normative self to generate another set of diverse autonomous disembodied sciences, this time called more frankly the sciences of ghosts, *Geisteswissensschaften.* Some species are not merely the (v) Neo-Kantians but also (vi) Husserl's (bracketed external object) phenomenology, (vii) von Hartman's philosophy of the Unconscious, (viii) his successor Freud with his three unconscious Ghosts, usually not on speaking terms with one another, in the unconscious basement of his own consciousness, (ix) all other psychoanalytical Continental European and Anglo-American psycheists who, derogating logic as "rationalization," suppose one can have a scientific psychology, i.e. logic of psyche without either any logic or any embodiments, the axiological and existentialists (x) Kierkegaard, (xi) Heidegger, (xii) Sartre, (xiii) Marcel and (xiv) Tillich's theological existentialism—all these being instances, one after another of the "jumping from the frying pan into the fire" modern and contemporary world's Ghostly Sciences.

There are many more, among them (xv) Kant and today's Harvardian Professor Friedrich's legal and international political science with its "Perpetual Peace." Also directly from Kant, (xvi) Fichte's Voluntaristic Monistic Idealistic Moral Ego *wills* the Ghostly Sciences and their human history as primary, thereby making the *Natur* Sciences subservient to them as an explanation of why all their Idealisms and Perpetual Peace have not occurred. Then (xvii) Hegel, taking his dialectical logical humanistic "causality" directly from Kant's *Natur* Category of linear 100% deterministic causality (as does today's Professor Blanshard) has his absolute Monistic Idealistic Ghost come dialectically to self-fulfillment with linear 100% deterministic mechanical causality, in, of all places, all-too-human, occasionally sublime, often detestable and frequently indifferent and unpredictable history spelled of course with a capital H, called *Historismus.*

As if all this were not a sufficient *reductio ad absurdum,* (xviii) the feelingless material substances only "lack of refined sensitivity," and hence *bourgeosie* Marx of (ii) swallows without choking, not merely the disembodied Monistic Idealistic Voluntaristic taking-over-everyone Ghost of Fichte (xvi) but also that of his successor Hegel's (xvii) Monistic Idealistic Absolute time serial linear dialectically 100% deterministic mechanical causal disembodied Ghostly *Historismus,* purportedly to necessitate that every sensitive bodily human being in today's ordinary history the world over is destined to march to the Marxist made-in-mid-19th Century Germany's materialistic goosestep of a muddled monistic metaphysically ghostly and frequently ghastly disembodied history.

The reader may pardon one for being reminded of a sober remark made by the Harvardian scientist Professor L. J. Henderson in 1921, who then directed the scientific portion of the present writer's Ph.D. thesis (1924) on The Problem of Organization in Biology.[4] This remark given in his lectures on the history of science referred to the unfortunate impact of all this 19th Century *Geistes-Natur* philosophy on his own Gibbsian-minded experimentally verified science of animate including human physiological chemistry, and was: "A German metaphysician can go down the deepest, stay down the longest, and come up the muddiest of any human being on earth." In this, Karl Marx is clearly the all-time World Series Champion.

It is equally clear that two other things today are the case. The first has to do with another present consequence of Kant.

They arise largely from the fact that his humanistic sciences are autonomous. Consequently what begins with him as a rescue mission to save the personalistic pluralists from their disembodied windowless monadic interiors and also purportedly to give the definitive "solution" of the insolvable pseudo body-mind problem, entailed by the feelingless material substances disembodied mental-physics dualism, ends by substituting for the latter dualism an even more unbridgable and dangerously demoralizing one between the natural sciences and the humanities. A dualism, moreover, which Sir C. P. Snow, well nigh alone in our times, has seen and correctly described.

It is equally clear that, in the midst of all the foregoing (i) through (xviii) Marxist metaphysical mud described above, the bodily sensitive biologically minded Buddha and his injured swan have been lost. What a relief it is to return to them.

The outer focused biologically objective initiation of the young Buddha's sudden overt discovery that pain is not privy to human persons prompted him immediately to reconfirm this conclusion experimentally and behavioristically, in a manner anyone can repeat. This occurred when, taking the barbed arrow which clearly had been the cause of the swan's fearful trembling and suffering, he pierced his own bodily person to wince with similar fellow-feelingfully shared muscular constriction and pain. Thereby he demonstrated the second biological fact that fellow-feelingly shared animate pain and suffering naturalistically

178

and behavioristically generate compassion. The generalization to the case where both animals are bodily sensitive persons followed spontaneously, motivating him to seek out the bodily ills and pains of his fellow men whoever and wherever they may be.

Thus, the Buddha and his spontaneously *assenting* followers arrived at their biologically based and behavioristically self-conditioned conclusion that moral, religious and legally just man is universal man, some several centuries before the Greek and Roman Stoic mathematical physicist and logician Chrysippus,[5] the moral scientist Epictetus, and the Roman lawyer Quintus Mucius Scaevola (and also, much later, the English Bracton) arrived at the similar conclusion, by their different interpersonal relational analytically stated contractually-legal scientific linguistic methods[6] in their creation of Western egalitarian democratic[7] contractual-legal science in what the 18th century legal scientist Jefferson called "the pure form of Epictetus."[8]

The young Buddha's sequence from the objectively focused discovery of feeling awareness of pain and suffering in an injured swan to compassion for his fellow men points up the importance of rearing children with some of the speechless world's animals as companions and with habitual daily responsibility for their bodily needs and care. This may well be as important for their later compassionate concern for the bodily sensitive feelings and needs of their fellow men, and for their own co-relative responsibility as citizens to accept spontaneously, thereby learning what moral, legal and political freedom means, their obligations to as well as their rights from society, as it is for the prevention of cruelty to their fellow animals.

The Lord Buddha's compassionate seeking out of the ills and suffering of all his fellow men reminds one of the late Earl (Bertrand) Russell's observation in our own century that there will not be a proper or effective personal or social morality until human beings are as emotively moved by the dry and dull statistics of human pain and suffering as they are by the particular local instances known by immediate acquaintance.

Whether Earl Russell's deprecation of objective naturalism in ethics and his introspective differentiatedly radical empirical merely psychical and subjective identification of the *content* of the positively good with the privately pleasant and its youthful insistence on "the right to be happy," and similar identification of

179

the *content* of the negatively evil with the painful—identifications which as his own British empirical Hume correctly observes, makes the content of what is judged to be good and the *content* of what is judged to be evil "relative to each human breast"[9] —whether this notion warrants, or will generate, the outer focused biologically objective *com*passion for all animate creatures, is another matter. The differentiatedly radical empirical, merely introspective psychic theory may well be a necessary, but not a sufficient condition and warrant, for an adequate and effective interpersonal or social ethic.

The second thing to note about the Buddha's objectively focused and biologically all-embracive experience and spontaneous subsequent behavior suggests one reason why. Originating and being continuously grounded in his two biological demonstrations that (1) even an injured swan has feeling awareness of pain and suffering, and that (2) *fellow-feelingfully-shared* bodily pain and suffering naturalistically generate and behavioristically condition compassion, his is not a merely egocentric and introspectively private rooted sensation of pain or pleasure, merely added up statistically as a non-internally related aggregate, instead, being a *fellow-feelingfully-shared* inter-man and animal and inter-man and man morality and law, is, from the outset and always, an *irreducible many animate-entity termed relational compassion.* This is the stuff of which emotively moving community can be built[10] —the irreducible fellow-feeling relatedness making emotively felt rights and emotively felt obligations two faces of the same communal coin, the latter the precondition for the former. These spontaneous obligations showed immediately not merely in the young Gautama's introspectively psychic interior, but also in his bodily movements with the injured swan and among his fellow men.

They showed also in the radical changes in the communal relations and institutions—social, legal, political, religious, and familial—which the young Buddha initiated and which became behavioristically and interpersonally conditioned throughout Asia everywhere his spontaneously loyal followers became the majority biological and social influence. This became evident first when, having decided to make it his life work "not for men alone, But for all things which speechless share our pain."[11] He faced, with

180

characteristic biological realism and self-reconditioning behavior, three social facts:

(a) To attempt this effectively from within his Princely Palace and restricted regal rounds would be to blind one's eyes to, rather than objectively and fellow-feelingfully share, the bodily needs, ills, and pains of all his fellow men.

(b) This is even more impossible within his Princely and his Father's theocratic Kingly Aryan Hindu religious, legal, political and social caste system in which marriages, or even contacts, of those of the higher castes with those of lower castes are severely restricted if not legally forbidden and in which, in the case of the outcasts who suffer most, any high caste Hindu's body is polluted, should the shadow of such an untouchable fall upon it.

(c) Nor could he embody his vow to the speechless world's fellow creatures, if as Prince, or later as his Father's successor, he presided, as required regularly, at the Aryan Hindu religious ceremonies (even in 1950 A.D.) in which regularly there occurs,

> . . . a sacrifice of goats five score.
> And five score sheep. . . . Round about the pile
> A slow, thick, scarlet streamlet smoked and ran . . .
> The blood of bleating victims. One such lay
> A spotted goat, long-haired, its neck bound back
> With munja grass; at its stretched throat the knife
> Pressed by a priest.[12] . . .

Witnessing what is here described, the young Buddh arose, turned to the presiding Aryan Hindu Maharaja and softly said . . .

> "Let him not strike, great King!" and therewith loosed
> The Victim's bonds, none staying him, so great
> His presence was. Then, craving love, he spoke
> Of life, which all can take but none can give,
> Life, which all creatures love and strive to keep,
> Even to the meanest; yea, a boon to all
> Where pity is, for pity makes the world
> Soft to the weak and noble for the strong.[13]

Faced with the three foregoing social implications of his present Princely and his future Kingly religious, social and political obligations, the young Buddh's deeds were immediate: stripping his body of all Princely regalia and its use of the Prince's chariot: in humble garb, on his own fond horse's back, in the dark of the night, thereby avoiding all bitterness, any use of force, sit-down

181

prayer meetings or public pollution defecations, or any intemperately passionate crowd-rousing or martyrdom-seeking self-ostentation, he rode away from this Princely past and his Father's Royal Palace and Fortress, leaving behind his young wife and his patrilineally pure-bred Sakiya tribal and Aryan Hindu racist first-born son, who is by primogenitural "law of status"[14] birth, the next generation's maharaja. Thereby, the young Gautama behavioristically embodied, first in himself and his local followers, and then in millions upon millions of *freely assenting* and devoted followers throughout Asia, the first, the largest, and the longest still-persisting egalitarian democratic social, political, religious, and familial communities this earth's surface has ever contained, which are rooted in (1) compassionate fellow-feeling for the speechless world's animals as well as human beings and (2) the unequivocal rejection of tribal, racial, color or caste,[15] sexual (patriarchal or matriarchal) or economic class differences as the basis for ordering human relations and institutions, be they political, religious, social or familial.

Restricting ourselves to those overwhelmingly Buddhist peoples and leaders whom the present writer knows over several decades at first hand, the Buddha's social achievements and reforms, persisting today, speak for themselves. The national order of the professional teaching Buddhist monks, centered at Bangkok, has no hierarchy, and is, in both its written constitution and practices, unequivocally egalitarian and democratic. Socially this Buddhist people have no caste. Also, in the "rice roots" village of Lam Poon, some twenty-odd miles from Chieng Mai, some two hundred and fifty miles north of Bangkok, at the end and edge of a high mountain range's traveled trail that leads up, over into Burma and on into Kunming, China, these Lam Poon Buddhist villagers' politics and their secular as well as religious decision-making is completely democratic, taking place beside the simple Buddhist village temple. Even more important, the elementary and high school age education is under the direction of those previous Buddhist students, all wearing the common draped humble yellow robe of the Buddha, a few of whom remain on to spend their lives teaching their youthful similarly robed student successors. Equally remarkable is their aesthetic, religious and even recent economic behavior.[16]

To be sure, the Thai villagers have a King whose legal and political status, after the manner of democratic Britain's Queen Elizabeth and the Japanese today, is that of a constitutional monarch; even so he would not be the Buddhist villagers' King enjoying their devoted loyalty had he not (1) when a student, robed like them, sat amid his fellow students in the humble yellow robe of the Buddha, and (2) received his advanced modern Western education in democratic Switzerland. Later after becoming King, in 1956, during the present writer's presence in Bangkok, he returned from a three-week Buddhist retreat in which he sat among the younger fellow Buddha-robed students before their similarly robed Buddhist teacher. The Thai federal legal leadership is similar. In 1950, when the present writer was first in Bangkok, the Western egalitarian democratic contractually-legal minded Chief Justice of the Supreme Court of Thailand was not merely a sincere practicing Buddhist but also the President of the Buddhist Society of his country. The similarly educated Chief Justice of the Federal Court of Appeals was in his law as well as his religion a practicing Buddhist. Beside the door of every courtroom in their respective court buildings they pointed out to me a large bronze statue of the lotus-seated Buddha signifying for all litigants who enter, as do these justices themselves explicitly, that fellow-feelingfully self-resolved, or, if that fails, third party mediated[17] compassion, rather than all-black or all-white litigation[18] to the death, is the wise and proper method for settling interpersonal, as all other, disputes. One is reminded of the late Federal Judge Learned Hand's spirited remark, "Avoid a law suit as you would the Devil."

To the Thais above must be added the vital dynamic democratic Princess Poon, President of the World's Buddhist Association, who in 1957 had just returned to Bangkok from Northeast Thailand where for weeks in its villages she, with others, were showing the villagers how to preserve their traditional democratic ways against infiltrating disrupting "peace-makers" from Laos and points further east and north, while modernizing those non-sex prejudiced matriarchal and patriarchal ways with modern free world western scientifically agricultural, rice hulling and milling, and freely consensual federal legal instruments. In fact the entire overwhelmingly Buddhist Southeastern Asian peoples from Burma through Thailand, Cambodia, to South and North Vietnam are matriarchal-patriarchal in their living law customs.

This shows in both urban and rice-roots Burma today explicitly with the wife's family name as well as the husband's being that of their children and with the wife's specified decision-making duties and rights being shared with the different specified ones of the husband, as is instanced in the following young present day Buddhist Burmese freely consensual democratic legal political and educational leaders: (1) The legal Rangoon, Hague, London Inns of Court and Yale Law School Dr. of Juridical Science educated Mr. Chief Justice Maung Maung of the Supreme Court of Burma;[19] (2) the UN's U Thant; (3) Burma's Buddhist President Emeritus U Nu; and (4) the Burmese Buddhist Yale Ph.D. in Philosophy educated Dr. Khin Maung Win,[19a] recent Chairman of the Philosophy Department in the National University of Rangoon, who today (1977) is the National Minister of Education with its program being implemented after the manner indicated in the previous paragraph, not merely at the national and intermediate levels, but also throughout the villages, except their local schools and democratic leaders, which are not disrupted and liquidated by muddy-footed Marxist Metaphysical "peace-making tourists" coming down the borderland mountain trails from the north and east and the steeper ones of Everest-peaked Tibet to the west.

Similar dozens of Asian Graduate students, not merely from these Southeast Buddhist cultures but also China, Korea, Japan, the Philippines, Taiwan, Hong Kong, Indonesia and other lands, who came expert in the positive and living laws of their respective peoples into Professor Myres MacDougall's Seminars and the present writer's in the Yale Law School and Graduate Schools, have returned to their homelands with this method for combining in a viable realistic practical way their traditional respective homeland values while also modernizing them with 20th-Century Western naturalistic scientific thinking and its normative democratic correlative obligations-rights contractual legally scientific instruments and institutions.

Returning again to the Buddha and his swan, need one wonder, consequently, that when majority non-Right Wing Aryan Hindu New Delhi-centered Free India in 1948 chose a symbol for

184

her similar Anglo-American common law egalitarian democratic contractual-legal Government and Constitution which, in its *Fundamental Freedoms,* repudiates Aryan patriarchal and tribal racism with its castes, she selected the lion pillar, that of the Third Century B.C. Buddhist Emperor Asoka—the *sole native* Indian in the geographical Indian subcontinent's entire history to unify its people into a single nation. Nor is it remarkable that the English and American educated lawyer Ambedkar, the leader of India's millions of untouchables, who chaired the Committee that wrote Free India's Constitution and was Prime Minister Nehru's first Congress Party Minister of Law, came to believe near the end of his Ministry in 1950 that the *sole indigenously Indian* basis for the peaceful solution of the communal problems between the Muslim Indians and the Hindu Indians of overall Pakistani India and New Delhi-centered India must be that of the Buddha. Why? Ambedkar had two reasons: The first one was that against his strenuous objection the Hindu members of the Constitutional Committee who wrote with their right hands the *Fundamental Freedoms,* with their left hands added a *Preventive Detention Act* giving the Chief Executive the right to put anyone in jail without any legal protection. The second even more important reason was that because of the caste habits of the Hindus in practice, vis-a-vis his 85 million untouchables, the Hindu Atman-Brahman "without differences" doctrine which is identical with that of the *Buddhist Nirvana* to which Gandhi appealed was being defeated, as Prime Minister Nehru's behavior in Kashmar and his daughter's behavior now fresh in our memory unequivocally confirm.

With Ambedkar in 1950 the Liberal Socialist Party leaders Jaiprokash Nayoran and Asoka Mehta agreed. They added that were they *Free India's* party in office, an attempt by diplomatic peace-making negotiations with Pakistani India would occur to achieve an over-all geographical Indian single Asokian nation[21] based on the proposal made before his death in 1938 by the Anglo-American Lincoln's Inn common law educated, the McTaggart philosophy trained and the Ph. D. in Persian (non-racist or caste) Muslim philosophy expert Punjab lawyer, legislator and statesman[22] —Muslim India's representative (with Gandhi and Nehru for Aryan Hindu India) at the London Round Table Conference in 1923—the remarkable Iqbal of Lahore.[23] For proof of his non-racist Islamic convictions the following verse 82 from his *Tulip of Sinai* testifies:

> Leave childishness, and learn a better lore;
> Abandon race, if thee a Moslem bore;
> If of his colour, blood, and veins and skin
> The Arab boasts—an Arab be no more![24]

It would seem that the Buddha and the Buddhist Indian Asoka's persisting impact upon all the above-mentioned Asian and Western nations and its future is secure, especially in the light of the latest (1977) events in India. This is the case *but only providing* two other things are done: one of them by themselves, the other by the rest of us.

In order to be specific and concrete with respect to the former, let us restrict ourselves to the isolated democratic villagers of North Thailand's Lam Poon (near Chiang Mai) visited by the present writer in 1950. For themselves and countless villagers like them through Tibet and all the other Southeast and East Asian villagers referred to above, their afore-described local and national leaders today must find a way to prevent their democratically elected village leaders from being disrupted and then liquidated by "peace-making" tourists coming down Chieng Mai's mountain trail via Burma from Kunming China and points much further east and north, or over a different mountain trail, via Laos, from Hanoi to the northeast.

But if the native Burmese and Thai villagers and their federal leaders, except when invaded by armed attackers as in Tibet, have been able in considerable part to do this *by themselves,* what is there for the *rest of us* to do? This brings us to the young Buddha's equally remarkable influence on Nepal, Tibet, Outer Mongolia, China, Korea and Japan, and via the latter largely in Zen form upon the U.S.A., Great Britain and even Continental European art, psychology and architecture.

Simultaneously with his 5th Century B.C. achievements the young Buddha's ways spread northward from his Indian village to nearby Nepal, and then on up the highest Himalayas to Lhasa and overall Tibet where, in the Llama Buddha-robed form, they became the communal fellow-feelingfully peaceful pervasively aesthetic, wool-growing-and-weaving utilitarian economic, political and religious ways of their people, not up to the present moment, but up to *October 26, 1950* when Tibet was taken over. It is when they heard of this day's events over the radio that the Tibet-neighboring Burmese and all the natural scientific minded democratic contractual legal lawyers specified above became concerned about whether they can do it all by *themselves*. Here also, the rest of us begin to come in. Why?

Because on that grim October day, they knew that the same kind of peace-makers who came down Chieng Mai's mountain trail from Peking's north, had previously gone up Tibet's higher Everest-peaked mountain trails, and on this October 26th day were followed by, since they moved for South Dakotans and Ivy League Presidents from north to south, the "peace-making" armed forces and heavy hardware of a military invasion, which liquidated Tibetan Buddhist teaching and student monks and their Llasa leaders, precisely after the manner in which the peace-makers coming down Chieng Mai's mountain trail had tried, for the most part unsuccessfully, to liquidate Lam Poon or other Thai, Burmese, Cambodian, Laotian and South Vietnam village leaders and their teaching and student Buddha-robed monks. Clearly, if Peking's Mao and Hanoi's Ho Chi Minh can *peace-make* heavy-hardware-wise uphill like this from north to south, what chance do the democratic villagers and their national leaders have, when isolated South Dakota-wise *by themselves*, to defend their democratically elected village leaders and their teaching and student Buddha-robed monks from going the way of those on October 26, 1950 in Tibet?

What happened in New Delhi to the official good office's offer made by Prime Minister Nehru before, on and after this climactic peace-making event, as reported by India's major newspapers[25] will hardly interest today's youth, out-of-office politicians, or Ivy League University Presidents with their present concern for only what is relevant. Hence, we omit it here.

In any event, this would seem to be the point at which the *rest of us* come in. Or, more specifically, it is where the *responsible* rest of us come in who, like Harry Truman, are not gullible pseudo-intellectual suckers for muddy mid-19th century German metaphysical myths and their goose-stepping peace-makers backed by Moscow, Peking and via Laos, Hanoi.

This, however, is but the beginning of where the *responsible rest of us* are involved if Buddhists everywhere are not to be betrayed, and if the shortest and quickest possible road to World War III is not to be traversed by the irresponsible as well as the responsible rest of us. To see in specific realistic detail why another direction of the Buddha's influence is most relevant.

Simultaneously with his impact on Thailand, Burma and Indian, his ways spread north from Tibet, with spontaneous peaceful acceptance of them on their merits, to Outer Mongolia, between the present-day Soviet Union and Mao's China, where in Llama Tibetan Buddha-robed form there were, *just before World War II,* some 250,000 teaching and student Buddhist monks. It is hardly to be expected that a major portion of them have not gone the way of their Tibetan brethren in post-October 1950 Tibet. From Tibet the young Buddha's ways also became one of the three major naturalistically realistic, aesthetic, religious, and communal factors in China, Korea and Japan.

In China the other two factors are (i) the Confucian patriarchal large joint family, epitomized and culminating hierarchically in the Confucian Emperor's Heavenly City First Family, and (ii) Taoism; in Korea, the patriarchal familial Confucianism[26] and a more democratic and matriarchal Shamanism; and in Japan, Confucianism and up to 1850 when a patriarchal familial Japanese racist Shintoism was restored. It was this patriarchal and hierarchal racist Shintoism with World War II culminating in the First Familial Mikado which power-politically invaded Korea before World War II and culminated in the attack upon Pearl Harbor which brought even the McGoverns, Georgians and Ivy Leaguers into World War II. The latter fact should remind all contemporary Americans mid-western short-distance isolationists and MIT Hanoi long-distance travelers that an American foreign policy which is not *a Pacific-oriented and based Asian,* as well as an Atlantic European and Middle-Eastern foreign policy, is no foreign policy at all. It was Pearl Harbor which enabled the present writer to predict in 1943, the post World War II shift of the world's political focus from East Coast America's Atlantic Europe through the Middle East, toward the Far East-Pacific Ocean and its Hawaii, Alaska and West Coast U.S.A.[27]

It is easy, as most post-1912 westernized Chinese and Koreans and some Japanese do, to underestimate the prodigious influence of Buddhism and its compassionate naturalistic ways in these Asian countries. This influence shows aesthetically in the biological naturalism of typically Chinese bamboo and Japanese animal painting, and in its deeper Nirvana continuum character in certain land- and river-scape paintings;[28] also in the Chinese painter's dictum that to paint bamboo one must fellow-feelingfully become bamboo. Religiously and socially the Buddha's influence shows also in that as late as World War II, there were some two hundred and fifty thousand Buddha-robed teaching and youthful student monks in Outer Mongolia, after the manner of Llama-Tibetan Pre-October 26, 1950 Tibet, and of Burma and Thailand today. The recent Korean Younghill Kang's *The Grass Roof* (1931) bespeaks the same thing for village "grass-roots" Korea, as does also for Japan the notable impact since World War II which Buddhism, especially in its Chinese and Japanese Suzuki Zen form, has had not merely upon East-West American and European philosophers and today's American youth, but also upon professional painters, musicians, choreographers,[29] psychiatrists, psychologists and Western theistic religious person-to-person practitioners, and even at least two professors of Western Anglo-American common law contractual legal sciences[30] in the United States.

Conversely, the post-war World War II Japanese Emperor and his Crown Prince, married to a commoner, have shifted their status (after the manner of the Buddha, the Buddhist King of Thailand, and Queen Elizabeth II of Great Britain today) from a Shinto-racist and chauvinistic patriarchal oldest Son of the Shinto Sun Goddess to that of a village democratic, federal representative by a republican contractual legal Constitutional Monarch; thereby again submerging Shintoism with Buddhism and with modern mathematically physical and contractual legal scientific ways. No Asian or single European nation matches this Japan in its modernity. Its only possible equals with respect to both consumers' goods and efficient contractual legal business, and other economic institutions, as well as potential military weapons, are the U.S.A. and the British-European Union Common Market.

Equally influential and even more important today for all Americans is another geographical direction of the Buddha's socially transforming naturalistically realistic and fellow-feelingfully compassionate ways. Reference was made above to the Buddhist Emperor Asoka's importance for a unified ancient and possible present-day India. He is equally notable for extending the young Buddha's fellow-feelingfully responsible compassionate ways to international relations.

This the Right Wing Aryan Maharajas could not do, since each derived his political authority from both Aryan racial and local tribal patrilineal primogeniture of birth; thereby making the political national sovereignty of each maharaja absolute. To confirm for one's self their starkly power political foreign policies, one has but to read the legal rules for foreign policy in their three major Aryan Hindu Law Books of Manu, Gautama and Apastama. The consequence was that there were as many power-political independent national states in geographical India after the Right Wing Maharajas counter-revolution had pushed Buddhism underground to retain caste in each Princely Hindu State, as there were different absolutely sovereign Aryan Hindu Maharajas. It was these power-political Aryan Hindu nations which left India such a prey to a divide-and-conquer invasion by the remarkable Muslim emperors who again approximated a united overall geographical India centered in Old Delhi.

To be sure, Asoka, like the Buddha's father, was originally an Aryan Hindu Maharaja. Also he (Asoka) achieved the recovery of northern India after its conquest by Alexander the Great in 322 B.C. and the political unification of overall geographical India by copying Alexander the Great's method of political organization as implemented defensively by Asoka's own military arms. Moreover, records recently translated into English[31] tell us that he became so deeply disturbed by the horrors and suffering of war that in the ninth year of his reign he became Buddhist, repudiated any further military conquest such as that of the recent British, who after uniting British India over an area approximately that of Asoka's day, went on to include Burma and Ceylon; instead the Buddhist Asoka dedicated his life to sincerely studying and practicing the Buddhist's compassionate ways, recommending them to all his subjects and even sending Buddhist missionaries abroad to acquaint others, by peaceful example and teaching, with their compassionate worth. It was Asoka's son who carried the Buddha's domestic and foreign policy ways to Ceylon. There, untrammeled by any Hindu Maharajas' caste system, these compassionate ways became the practice of the Singalese people. From them, they spread to Burma and to Thailand, but as described above, and in the sequel, and then on to Vietnam to become the fellow-feelingfully religious and social practices of the people at the village level and also their national leaders, *wherever Buddhists,* over the whole of mainland southeast Asia including Ceylon to the present moment.

*In this very important sense,* following the departure of the French Riviera's non-Buddhist Bao Dai, could it be?—that even Saigon's continuously maligned Buddhist general Ky and especially his Western TV reporters' ignored and recently underestimated Buddhist self-defensive democratic village troops, not merely represent the "rice roots" villagers (i.e., the overwhelming majority of the people of North as well as South Vietnam), but also *perhaps* may determine whether the overwhelming majority of the Buddhist villagers' teaching and student monks and their liberal democratic contractually legal leaders, as far west as not merely Thailand's Lam Poon, but also on through Burma to geographical India and East Pakistan's frontier, go the way of the Buddhist teaching and student monks and their leaders in Tibet and also, in all likelihood, the two hundred and fifty-thousand in Outer Mongolia. It is at this point that what the rest of us do again becomes important.

The shortest way home to the answer is, since our concern is with Southeast Asia, by way of additional biological research made by (1) Asoka and the post-Asokian Hindu Maharajas; (2) the young Buddha's further biological observation; and (3) non-Buddhist Adit living law villagers of Indonesia.

(1) Unfortunately, in his homeland, the Buddha and Asoka's Buddhist compassionate ways and peace-making methods were defeated by the counter-revolution of the Right Wing Hindu Maharajas which preserved until 1948 both their countless power political absolute national Princely States and the Hindu caste system in each. This reminds us that especially in an irreducibly relational concept of the moral, religious and political person,

unilateral withdrawal in the case of war, is *ipso facto,* no peace-making at all. Especially is this the case when the non-Buddhist other-party-to-the-war is committed to a muddily metaphysical 19th-century German Historismus 100% Determined, and hence peace-making uncompromising, feelingless material substances dictatorial chauvinist heavy-hardwared and world-embracing international policy, as well as a Buddhist village leaders and monks liquidating next-door-neighbors policy.

In any event we can understand why, in his Foreword to the *Edicts of Asoka,* Professor Richard McKeon writes that this Indian Buddhist foreign policy classic seeks "truths within the scope of reason and goods within the scope of action." This restriction of their conception of what is good, just and in accord with the will of the Divine for his human creatures, is very important. It enabled the Buddha and his followers to escape the wide gulf between one's Sunday-morning and one's every-day-of-the-week behavior which many Asians of every religion and color believe to be a serious weakness in the West; not thereby implying, however, that they don't have other weaknesses.

(2) This biologically objective and behavioristically conditioned restriction "within the scope of action" led the young Buddha to a more general natural history biological theory in his research into the "far sources" of the cause and cure for suffering. This advanced research produced two conclusions; the one causal, and the other with regard to life's origins. Causally his bodily sensitive biologically objective method of investigation required him to face the full temporal range of any living creature's existence—not merely its more pleasure-laden and hedonistically plausible springtime and early summer of life, but also its falltime withering away and wintery ending in death. This made it evident that if scientifically objective and confirmable truthful love of wisdom consists in learning how to face realistically and handle gracefully the full temporal range of any animate living creature's existence, then, as all his classical fellow Asians affirm, it is only the elderly and those most brain-wise, healthy and fellow-feelingfully sensitive of them, who can possibly know, in facing helplessly the loss of dear ones, the withering away of memory and one's frailties ending in inevitable death and in the nearing of one's own death, not merely how to live but also how

to die. One is reminded of the wise Socrates who, when asked about the aim of all his inquiries, replied, "I am trying to learn how to die." This prevented the young Buddha from falling into the present-day youthful preachers, psychiatrists and teachers on the quick-make, easy scapegoat error of locating *the entire* cause and cure for the facts of pain and suffering in one's elders or The Environment. It prevented the Buddha from back sliding into his Princely and his Maharaja father's theocratic Aryan Hindu racist and Sakiya tribal power-political absolute nation state theocracy with its caste system. The latter he realized to be an inhumane *partial cause* which he immediately proceeded to remedy and succeeded in actually removing in ordinary everyday history, spelled without a capital letter, whenever his followers were allowed to become the overwhelming majority of the people.

His stark naturalistic biological realism did not end even here. He turned his attention from the fall and winter of any living creature's life to its birth and springtime beginnings. Here are his first-hand biological findings as reported by a later follower:

> . . . . . . . . looking deep he saw
> The thorns which grow upon this rose of life: . . .
> How lizard fed on ant and snake on him,
> And kite on both; And how the fish-hawk robbed
> The fish-tiger of that which it had seized . . .
> . . . till everywhere each slew a slayer and in turn was slain,
> Life living upon death: So the fair show
> Veiled one vast, savage, grim conspiracy
> Of mutual murder, from the worm to man,
> Who himself kills his fellow; . . .[32]

Thus, some 25 centuries before Darwin's *Voyage of the Beagle* and his "struggle for existence," the young Gautama faced the zoologically objective and inescapable fact that any animate creature lives only as other temporally antecedent and contemporary animate creatures die. To this we in the modern West can add that plants are the only non-parasitic living creatures, since all animals, directly or indirectly, live off plants, not being able to synthesize from the sun's radiant energy the inner organic materials necessary for any zoological living creature's existence. Clearly, in his humane treatment of animals, here was no futile vegetarian purring about rabbits while nibbling cold carrots.

Even so, and because of his grim conclusion, and also because he brought to it the two additional biological and behavioristically self-conditioned facts that (1) bodily feeling awareness is not privy to persons, and (2) irreducibly relational fellow-living-creature-shared pain and suffering naturalistically generate spontaneous *self*-behavioristically conditioned habitual compassion, he reached a conclusion in addition to the one noted some 25 centuries later by Darwin—the conclusion, namely, that (3) this establishes a respect in which all living creatures are one; we are one in a fellowship of suffering; one in living only at the expense of other living creatures' deaths and consequently (4) the first key to the wise handling of pain and suffering is to face it, in all its starkness, with all our fellow living vegetation as well as animate creatures with compassion. Thus the Buddha found his first cure or prescription with respect to the wise handling of non-man-caused or responsible naturalistic pain and suffering.

In other words, he not merely biologically observed, but also demonstrated behavioristically, initially with a bodily sensitive injured swan, that facing fellow-feelingfully shared pain and suffering, while also accepting pleasure when it is there *and fellow-feelingfully shared as good,* is not merely more biologically and psychologically realistic, but also a more naturally wise, aesthetically and religiously sensitive and *philo* of *sophic* way to face and live "within the scope of action" the full temporal range of any living creature's existence, leaving one with a less soured and cynical disillusionment later on and a greater richer equanimity during the fall and winter of anyone's life, than does either (a) the focusing on merely introspectively psychic pleasure, even when added up statistically, or (b) the trusting in one's own, or anyone else's kinship anthropological genealogy of birth and culturally conditioned "law of status" familial, tribal and racist breeding. This is what makes the naturalistic realism of the compassionate Buddha unique even among Asians.

His biological research did not end here. He also extended his naturalistically realistic observations from the zoological to the botanical "world's speechless creatures," thereby generalizing his natural history field theory beyond Darwin. This occurred when he walked, ever-fellow-living-creature-wise observantly and feeling-fully, into the forests and up his nearby North Indian Nepalese Himalayan foothills, not merely to observe their sprouting seedlings and their giant dying trees, but also seat himself Buddha-wise on a hillside under a living giant Eucalyptus, after the manner of a later Chinese Buddhist painted landscape in order to further observe and to meditate "this deep disease of plant and animal life, what its far sources and whence its remedy."

To experience, more nearly at first hand, what he observed and with what he fellow-feelingfully communed botanically, and also to expand our Southeast Asian national, religious, cultural and legal horizon, let us leave the Buddha seated amid and feeling his giant Himalayan foothill topped forest with its view which his locus there provides, and with his observations and his meditative reflections. Parenthetically, to these reflections he brings a previously reached moral and religious conclusion. It is that no answer to this question of stark non-human-being-responsible naturalistic pain and suffering is provided by *any one* of the theistic religions' monotheistic Gods. This has been realized in the West today in the recent God-is-dead theology. Why? Because, as McTaggart, well-nigh alone of all modern philosophers of religion, clearly stated and as the young Buddha even more succinctly wrote:

> . . . . . . . . I would not let one cry
> Whom I could save! How can it be that Brahm
> Would make a world and keep it miserable,
> Since if all-powerful, he leaves it so,
> He is not good, and if not powerful,
> He is not God.[33]

The Buddha's reflections with this in his mind should be interesting, when in a moment we return to him Buddha-robed and Buddha-seated on his forested mountainview hilltop.

Our non-Buddhist, non-Northern India occasion is a recent forest ceremony in a Javanese Indonesian village, as described in the present writer's graduate lawyers Yale Law School Seminar by a modern Dutch civil and Anglo-American common law egalitarian, democratic contractual legally trained Indonesian lawyer, as witnessed by him previously in his own Indonesia's forest village. Because of the villagers' necessity to cut down a portion of their forest in order to grow enough grain and vegetables for their fellow-helping animals and themselves, this ceremony is performed. In it they literally, so to speak, fellow-feelingfully beg the forest's pardon for having to destroy part of its botanical life, and moreover, they promise explicitly as well as implicitly to take that destruction as a moral and legal trust. If they should merely slash the trees down, leaving an aesthetically ugly mess, not using that land for their own and their fellow animals' *necessities* of food-getting and livelihood, they would be in their own judgment guilty of not merely an immoral but also an interpersonal legally unjust act.

What is their warrant for this? It centers in their cosmic as well as in their zoological and botanical natural science. Their reason is that "Otherwise, we would upset the cosmic equilibrium." This entails for them the co-man and vegetable compassionate moral and legal obligation that if anyone has the irreducible correlative right to take anywhere and anywhen, anything out of cosmic equilibriated nature as we all do, life living on the death of other lives, one has the correlative obligation to put something else back again. Clearly, we have here *an irreducibly two-entity termed relational fellow-feelingful compassion for the vegetative as well as the animate "speechless world's" creatures* and in addition we have something cosmically so, geologically mother earth-wise and even mountain-view-wise. This brings us back to the Buddha, Buddha-seated on his forested Nepalese Himalayan hilltop.

For what one Chinese Buddhist saw and reflected upon from his similar mountain hillside in China, re-examine the Illustration XIII referred to in the *Meeting of East and West*. Clearly, as in this Chinese Buddhist-Taoist painter's case, the similarly seated and robed young first Buddha, some six centuries B.C. previously, had walked, ever-fellow-living-creature feelingfully beyond injured swans, other persons, vegetables, flowers and up through the Eucalyptian forests, over Mother Earth from which all biological life springs and to which "dust-to-dust" it returns. There in that locus on his mountain-view hilltop sits our first Buddha observing its monsoon rain-drenched water-worn-away hillsides and raging river valleys, and precipitous rocky aging Everest-peaked white glacier frozen rocky mountains, the vapors and dissolving mists and clouds surrounding them, and even later in the undifferentiated blackness of night into which all the differentiated aesthetic qualities of afternoon had withered away through twilight into dissolution and death; of a sudden there falls from high above these Himalayan peaks a brilliant blazing fiery speck—a falling star to its dust-to-dust death in the valley below. At last he has pursued in his naturalistically realistic research the farthest non-man-made or man-responsible causes of bodily sensitive naturalistic pain and suffering to their utmost cosmically all-embracive and astronomically heavenly source.

This cosmic fact, as stated in 1939 at the first East-West Philosophers Conference, by The Pali, Sanskrit, Tibetan, Chinese, Korean, Japanese, German, French and English linguistically erudite Japanese Buddhist scholar, Takakusu, in the opening of the first of his fifty lectures on Buddhism, is "Buddhism rests on the evident fact that all directly observable *differentiated* things are transitory. From this it follows that *all* bodily sensitive creatures are doomed to suffer." The word *all* (italicized by the present writer) in this great scholar's first sentence bespeaks the fact that the Buddha seated on his local hilltop, has reached the geologically and astronomically farthest cosmic cause of non-man-made or responsible inter-entitied pain and suffering. By the similarly italicized word *differentiated* is meant anything which is distinguished from some other things by some inner or outer sensed quality or qualities.

"Nevertheless," Takakusu then continued, "the Buddha also demonstrated that there is a cure for suffering," i.e., for even this non-man-made heavenly caused pain and suffering. We already know, from the earlier portion of this essay that this cure is twofold, and also what the first-fold cure is—namely, that, because the Buddha also demonstrated two other biological and self-behavioristically conditioned facts: (1) that feeling-awareness is not privy to persons and (2) that fellow-feelingfully shared pain and suffering generates spontaneously, self-behavioristically conditioned compassion—in the Buddha's case between a swan and man—and between man and man, and in the non-Buddhist Indonesian case, between man and the botanical "speechless world's creatures;" hence, for all of these factually and

197

behavioristically demonstrable reasons, we are all one in a fellowship of suffering; and this specifies the first prescription for the wise way to handle pain and suffering—namely to freely self-condition ourselves both bodily sensitively and behavioristically, to fellow-feelingfully share it with all cosmic creatures—swans, the untouchables, flowers, mother earth, forests, vegetables and even cloudy mountains and falling stars, with compassion, trying as hard as we can never to upset the ecological "cosmic equilibrium."

What about the Buddha's second-fold cure? So far we have the farthest cause, but not its deepest cure. To answer this question, let us return to the Buddha immersed in his sensuously differentiated existentially imminent cosmically all-embracive natural history field continuum with its transitory geological mother earth, rocky mountains and astronomical dying stars, as well as its biological transitory entities, among which his is another bodily sensitive instance.

He also noticed that this complex differentiated naturalistically entitied field continuum is not irreducible, but analyzes by abstraction into two components, the one the cosmically all-embracive, *per se* undifferentiated, existentially imminent non-transitory entitied naturalistic cosmic continuum itself; the other abstractable factor, the inner and outer sensuously differentiated tertiary and secondary qualities which distinguish these borning and dying natural history entities from one another. The latter factor makes them the transitory astronomical, geological, botanical and zoological entities differing from one another which all of them are. The former undifferentiated imminent and all-embracive feeling awareness factor gives them their undifferentiated cosmically compassionate feeling awareness which their distinguishing transitory perpetually perishing sensuous qualities differentiate diversely in each particular cosmic natural history borning and perishing entity's immediacy experience.

The Buddha's nomalistic black-lettered mark for *denoting* the former of these two abstractable field continuum factors is, when translated into English from the *Pali, Nibana,* and from the Sanskrit, *Nirvana.* In the paper of the 1939 First Hawaiian East-West Philosophers' Conference published as Chapter VIII in its Symposium Volume[34] and later in *The Meeting of East and West*

(1946), the present writer, concentrating on this *Nibana* (1) cosmic radically empirical natural history field continuum factor *per se* apart from its (2) radically empirical aesthetic perpetually perishing tertiary and secondary qualified differentia, and using the adjective *aesthetic* in the radical empirical sense of recent impressionistic painting, called it "the undifferentiated aesthetic continuum," with its plus (1) and (2) being named appropriately "the differentiated aesthetic continuum." Earlier in 1931, in sections entitled The Nature of the Psychical and the reducible "complexity" of the differentiated tertiary and secondary aesthetic qualities of the present writer's Science and First Principles,[35] this *Nibana* undifferentiated aesthetic continuum factor was denoted as "bare indeterminate experienced quality," better called *quale* (as Whitehead noted in a personal conversation later), that is "bare *quale* with the *ity*-nesses of the qual-ities abstracted away."

Stated even more specifically, what this means is that any sensed tertiary or secondary quality is not the elementary factor of immediately apprehended and felt naturalistic fact, as Hume and most modern positivistic scientists and well-nigh all Aristotlian, Medieval and present-day Neo-Aristotlian logic of predictable notioners and also most ordinary language modern humanists have supposed; instead any *qual-ity* is a complex of two abstractable factors—(1) an irreducible *per se* temporally and spatially undifferentiated all-embracing and unlimited, and hence eternal now existential and imminent feeling awareness *quale,* or to use *The Meeting of East and West* usage, "undifferentiated aesthetic continuum," and (2) also its playfully generated bornings and perishing diverse transitory *ity*-nesses each of which is not merely relative to each perishing natural history cosmic field entity, but also to each "perishing particular" moment as the radical empirical Locke of the *Essay* clearly sensed and stated. The remarkable American many-entity-termed relational mathematical and pragmatically minded Charles Sanders Peirce, in his analysis of naturalistically realistic knowledge into its irreducible components, called this feelingful, this non-*ityness* differentiated *quale qua quale,* "Firstness," and denoted it as follows:

> The idea of the absolutely First, must be entirely separated from all conception of or reference to anything else. The First must therefore be present and immediate, so as not to be

Second to a representation. It must be fresh and new, for if old it is second to its former state. It must be initiative, original, spontaneous and free; otherwise it is Second to a determining cause. It is also something vivid and conscious [in the radical empirical sense of feeling awareness] so only it avoids being the object of some sensation. . . . It precedes all synthesis and all differentiation; it has no unity and no parts. It cannot be articulately thought; assert it and it has already lost its characteristic innocence; for assertion always involves a denial of something else. Stop to think of it, and it has already flown. What the world was to Adam on the day he opened his eyes to it, before he had drawn any distinctions or had become conscious of his own existence—that is First, present, immediate, fresh, new, initiative, original, spontaneous, free, vivid, conscious, and evanescent. Only remember that every description of it must be false to it.[36]

To this, the present writer attempted once unsuccessfully to add: "Remember also that it is not an it," ity-ness being radical empirically differentiated and perpetually perishing.

The important point to note is that any entity in nature (human beings as well as all other cosmic creatures) is this undifferentiated *Firstness* or *Quale* cosmically all-embracive natural history field factor of fact in the radical empirical (ii) feeling awareness component of its existential being. Each and every natural entity—old, young, male, female, whether swan, butterfly, hummingbird, snail, forest tree, earth, shore, mountain, valley, or star, brings this *Nirvana* cosmic continuum *factor,* to use Kantian language, as an imminent *a posteriori* unity-of-aperception factor to the radically empirical component of his differentiated cosmic natural history field continuum being.

Schrödinger,[37] the creator of the many entity-termed mathematically functional time equation of quantum wave mechanics, expresses the same irreducible radically empirically felt and feelingful timeless factor in the cosmic all-embracive continuum of any naturalistic entity's being as follows: after stating that the "pluralization of consciousness or minds" leads almost immediately to the invention of souls as many as there are bodies, thereby generating the afore-described insoluble problems of how one such person can contact or know another or how anyone can know or have the content of his consciousness affected by his own body, or conversely, he then adds that "the only possible alternative is simply to keep to the immediate experience that consciousness is a singular." In short, even in bodily sensitive psychology, a *singular* monistic field theory of embodied *per se* undifferentiated fellow-feeling awareness must replace the traditional modern introspectively psychic disembodied single entity-property egocentric personal pluralistic monadic Ghosts.

The above references to the mathematically minded Gibbs, Henderson, Schrödinger, Heisenberg and Peirce warn us of certain necessary cautions: the foregoing natural history feeling-awareness scientific field continuum conception while analogous to, and epistemologically corelatable with, the mathematically functional many-entity termed Gibbsian Henderson bodily sensitive biochemical person, and the Schrödinger-Heisenberg not-100% Determined Quantum Mechanical physiology, physiological animal, must be distinguished from the latter type of naturalistically realistic field science. This the present-day similarly minded H. J. Morowitz, the Professor of Molecular Biophysics and Biochemistry in Yale University, knows very well, as his recent "Biology as a Cosmological Science" clearly and concisely shows.[38] It by no means follows, from the Buddha's and McTaggart's anti-theistic conclusion above, that no meaning remains for a theistic component of the Divine in both cosmic heavenly astronomical nature and in bodily sensitive human nature. What does follow is that if so, it must (a) be a *limited* powerful theistic component, after the manner of the not-100% deterministic Definition of State in Quantum Mechanics, and (b) also an irreducible many-entity termed relationally defined embodied component rather than a naive realistic "logic of predicables" single entity-property defined substance, be the latter monistically or pluralistically notioned. What specific content this *limited relationally conceived component* of the Divine possesses has been published in part elsewhere[39] but its complete specification must await another occasion.

In any event two things are clear: first, as both the Buddha and the Greco-Roman Stoics affirmed, in their linguistically different ways: no *physic,* then no *psyche;* and conversely, no

201

*psyche*, then no *physics*. Hence, no Ghosts, and no ghastly feelingless material substances. Also no bodily-insensitive swans, no insensitive forest trees, no geological rocks, and no stellar nebulae that are "only for a disembodied Ghostly mind." In short, no muddy metaphysics of species (i-xviii) above.

Second, the Buddha's influence, persisting vitally for some 27 centuries to the present moment, as described above, demonstrated the practicality and lasting vitality of Carl Marty's behavior and suggestion which opened this essay: it was, that given a people traditionally conditioned otherwise, it is both biologically and behavioristically realistic and socially achievable for any people anywhere by freely consensual, spontaneously accepted and peaceful means to self-recondition their bodily sensitive selves to world-embracing fellow-feelingfully compassionate and habitual social relations with both their fellow men and the speechless world's living creatures.

## NOTES

1. Edwin Arnold, *The Light of Asia* or The Great Renunciation, Being the Life and Teachings of Gautama, Prince of India and Founder of Buddhism (as told in verse by an Indian Buddhist), *LoA* (Boston: Robert Brothers, 1891), pp. 17-18.

2. *Ibid.*, Preface, vii-xi.

3. See Moscow picture in *Life* Magazine, June 2, 1972.

4. Ph.D. Thesis, Harvard University (1924), later published as the Deems Lectures (1929) in F.S.C. Northrop, *Science and First Principles (SaFP)* (New York: Macmillan; and Cambridge University Press, England, 1931). The philosophical portion of this Thesis (1924) was directed by W. E. Hocking, 1920-1922 and J.M.E. McTaggart, 1922-23, Trinity College, University of Cambridge, while simultaneously its philosophy of mathematical physics portion was directed once weekly by A. N. Whitehead in The Imperial College of Science and Technology of the University of London. See Chap. IV for Henderson's Gibbsian mathematical biochemistry.

5. S. Sambursky, *The Physics of the Stoics (PoS)* (London: Routledge, 1959).

6. J. C. Smith, "The Unique Nature of the Concepts of Western Law." *The Canadian Bar Review (CBR)*, XLVI, 1968, 192ff; his "The Theoretical Constructs of Western Contractual Law." *Cross-Cultural Understanding (CCU)*, Chap. 15 (New York: Harper & Row and London, 1964). See also *Yale Law Journal (YLJ)*, Vol. 71 - 1962, p. 1042; and F. S. Lawson, *The Rational Strength of English Law* (London: Stevens, 1951).

7. For the proof that Western contractual legal science is compatible only with egalitarian democratic content at the village level and with freely assented to representatively republican content above that level, see the present writer's "The Relational Personalities of Western Legal Science" in *Contemporary American Philosophy, Second Series (CAP)*, edited by J. E. Smith (London: Allen and Unwin; New York: Humanities Press, 1970), pp. 135-150.

8. "Jefferson's Conception of the Role of Science in World History." *The UNESCO Journal of World History (JWH)*, Vol. IX, 1966.

9. David Hume, *A Treatise on Human Nature*, edited by T. H. Greene and T. H. Grose (London: Longmans Greene, 1886) Vol. I, p. 389 and Vol. II, pp. 245-46; also see *YLJ, op. cit.*, pp. 1017-1023.

10. This also avoids the necessity in any introspectively psychic ethical or legal theory of having to resort to non-cognitive hortitory, exclamatory and command sentences in order to find even a private, to say nothing about an official legal meaning for obligation. See also Alf Ross, *Towards A Realistic Jurisprudence* (Copenhagen, 1946) for the similar weakness in Continental European Sein-Sollen "is-ought" legal facts and theory. Ross's definitive criticism applies equally to Professor Lon Fuller's *The Law in Quest of Itself* and his "Human Purpose and Natural Law" in *Natural Law Forum, Vol. III*, 1958, pp. 68-76, as shown in YLJ *op. cit.* fn 6 pp. 1031-1037.

11. *LoA*, fn 1 *op. cit.*, p. 107.

12. *Ibid.*, pp. 1, 2, 3 and 129-131. In October 1950, during the annual Aryan Hindu Holy Week when the present writer was in Jaipur, the otherwise modern-minded Maharaja of Rasputania presided over the Aryan Hindu religious sacrifice which was exactly as described in this reference.

13. *Ibid.*, p. 130.

14. In the sense of Sir Henry Maine's *Ancient Law: Its Connection With the Early History of Society and Its Relation to Modern Ideas* (London: Murray, 1908), p. 151.

15. The root Sanskrit word for color and for caste is identical, indicating that initially caste differences were rooted in tribal or racial color of skin differences. According to post-Bhagavitan Aryan Hindu religious doctrine the castes derive from the anatomical "head-shoulders-stomach-feet" differences in the theistic Divine Aryan Hindu Brahm's Body. For the Buddha's conception of this theistic Brahm's body, *see LoA, op. cit.*, 80, to be quoted in a moment.

16. F.S.C. Northrop, *The Taming of the Nations* (ToN) (New York: Macmillan, 1952), pp. 79 and 131; Reprint (New York: Hafner Pub. Co., 1971), Chaps. 4-8.

17. *Ibid.*, Chaps. 5, 7, and 9; and "The Mediational Approval Theory of Law in American Legal Realism," *Virginia Law Quarterly*, Vol. 44 (1958), pp. 347-363.

18. See "Compromise and Decision Making in the Resolution of Controversies," *Northwestern Univeristy Law Review (NLR)*, Vol. 58, No. 6 (Jan-Feb. 1964).

19. Maung Maung, *Law and Custom in Burma and the Burmese Family* (The Hague: Martinus Neihoff, 1963) and re *de facto* society today its Chapter "Buddhism and the State."

19a. Khin Maung Win, *Some Philosophical Problems Contemporary Burma* Ph.D. Thesis (Yale University Library, 1958), with its Chapter on "The Epistemological Analysis of the Burmese Language" pub. as Ch. 13 in *CCU: Epistemology in Anthropology op. cit.* fn 6.

20. F.S.C. Northrop, *Logic of the Sciences and the Humanities* (New York: Macmillan, 1946 P. B. Times Mirror 1974): "Naturalistic and Cultural Foundations for More Effective International Law" *59 Yale Law Journal* Dec. 1950 pp. 1430-1450.

21. F.S.C. Northrop, *Philosophical Anthropology and Practical Politics* (PAPP) (New York: Macmillan, 1960), pp. 14, 84-85 and 156 for Nayoran and Mehta.

22. See biographical note, v-vii, *The Tulip of Sinai (ToS)*, translated from the Persian of the late Sir Muhammad Iqbal by A. J. Arberry, Professor of Persian in the University of London (London: The Royal India Society, 1947).

23. For Iqbal and his political and other publications, see Chap. 5, "The Resurgence of Islam," *ToN, op. cit.*, pp. 100, 149-172, 313, 341-343.

24. *ToN, op. cit.*, p. 82.

25. For some few antiquarian elders who prefer the irrelevant see *ToN, op. cit.*, Chap. 3 esp. 35-38 & 44-45.

26. See Korea chart, *ToN*, op. cit., p. 117.

27. F.S.C. Northrop, *The Meeting of East and West* (MEW)(New York: Macmillan, 1946) Colliers PB 5th Prtg. 1974.

28. *Ibid.*, Illustrations XII, XIV, and for 16th century Chinese Buddhists (Tibetan style), XV.

29. "Towards a General Theory of the Arts." *Journal of Value Inquiry*, Vol. I, (1967), 76ff, esp. 105-116.

30. Charles Reich, *The Greening of America* (New York: Random House, 1970).

31. *The Edicts of Asoka*, translated into English and edited by Professors P. T. Rahu and Richard McKeon (University of Chicago Press, 1959).

32. *LoA, op. cit.*, p. 21.

33. *Ibid.*, 80.

34. Philosophy: East and West, ed. Charles A. Moore (Princeton Press, 1944) ch. VIII; & (MEW) *op cit*, fn 4, pp. 253-262.

35. F.S.C. Northrop, Cambridge Univ. Press England (New York: Macmillan, 1931), ch. VI.

203

36. *Collected Works of Charles Sanders Peirce,* edited by Professors C. Hartshorne and P. Weiss (Cambridge, Mass.: Harvard University Press, 1931), Vol I Par 357.
37. Schrodinger, *What Is Life?* (N.Y. and London: Macmillan, 1946), pp. 89-90.
38. Harold J. Morowitz, "Biology As a Cosmological Science." *Main Currents in Modern Thought,* Vol. 28 (1972), pp. 151-157.
39. F.S.C. Northrop, *Man, Nature and God.* (New York: Simon & Schuster, 1962), Chaps. 13-18; and *Science and First Principles, op. cit.,* Chap. VI. Also the Introduction to Werner Hersenberg, *Physics and Philosophy.* (New York: Harper and Brothers, and London: Allen and Union, 1958) pp. 1-26.

204

# A Game for All Seasons  11

_Amy Freeman Lee_

Do YOU REMEMBER A GUESSING GAME called "Twenty Questions: Mineral, Vegetable, Animal, or Man?" that we used to play as children? Since this game of identification is symbolic, we should continue to play it throughout our life, not only as a means of identifying other people, places, and things but also as a way to discover and define the core of ourself. At the moment, it is imperative that we play it, because brutality, cruelty, and violence constitute major motivations in our society. Surely, it is past time for us to recognize the obvious connection between innumerable forms of brutality in many phases of our daily lives and the violence that climaxes in such acts as the assassination of our late President, John F. Kennedy, and our late religious leader, Dr. Martin Luther King, Jr. We cannot accept the pat and simplistic answer that such horrendous crimes were committed by one mentally ill person, but rather we must examine objectively the factors in our society that produce such an individual.

Lately, I have been encouraged by the fact that the existence and operation of our innate violence are being considered by our mass media. A *Time* magazine essay was devoted to this subject in a penetrating editorial entitled "Violence and History":

> And yet foreigners can and should expect the United States to rise far above its present status as the world's most violent advanced country . . . Houston is the U.S. murder capital: 244 last year, more than in England, which has 45 million more

---

Amy Freeman Lee, artist, author, critic, and lecturer, is Secretary and Director, Board of Directors, The Humane Society of the United States.

205

people . . . Even grimmer is the psychological impact of the King assassination: his killer, however twisted his mind, clearly felt that he had a mandate for murder. The appalling result suggests that all too many unstable Americans unconsciously identify with a kind of avenging western hero, and believe that one man with one bullet can and should change history . . . The U.S. must utterly reject this grammar of violence just as it must urgently enact effective laws against the dangerous, absurdly outdated sale of firearms to all comers . . .

Today every parent who cares about peace ought to be guiding his children to militant enthusiasm for some humane cause, the most beneficent outlet for aggressions.[1]

While brutality and violence exist in almost every aspect of our environment, some areas, such as commerce and entertainment, provide shocking and blatant manifestations. The world of business and its constant companion, advertising, are fraught with symbols of violence. Right now I have a "Tiger in my tank," a Mustang in my garage and a Barracuda in my carport! For every Dove on the market, we have a hundred Jaguars! Two newspaper articles provide a succinct insight into our psychology of using brutality for commercial appeal:

In the *San Antonio Light,* the approach to car styling is accurately described:

The tiger in the tank is climbing out and taking over the entire car . . . the feline look of the softer contours and the appearance of the big cat about to spring will dominate car styling.[2]

The *San Antonio Evening News* reported that Dr. Jeffrey O'Connell of the University of Illinois, a noted psychiatrist, had peppered an address by quoting some automobile ads:

For stab and steer men there is a new three-speed automatic you can lock in any gear. Make small noises in your throat. Attaboy tiger. This model is just a friendly little saber-toothed pussycat. One of these at fast idle sounds like feeding time at the zoo . . . Drive it like you hate it, it's cheaper than psychiatry![3]

Who wants to spend his hard-earned American dollar for gasoline that is merely "Humble," when for the same price he can buy Exxon, bursting with energy and zip? When Marlboro cigarettes were seen being smoked by chic couples in an elegantly appointed setting, no red-blooded American would be caught dead smoking them. Now that cowboys are shown inhaling Marlboros on the open range in "Marlboro country," sales have zoomed.

In summary, it is perfectly obvious that brutality and violence in any form—potential, titular, implied, or actual—have strong appeal to the U.S. consumer. Evidently, if you wish to make a really successful pitch to the mass of the buying public, one effective way is to give your commodity a name that implies brutality or violence.

The world of U.S. entertainment offers an even richer source of examples of cruelty, brutality, and violence in the life of Western man in the twentieth century, for when you examine our *status quo* through our modes of entertainment, you will find that our "civilization" can be described as having an arena ambience, a coliseum culture, and a safari society!

Have you ever observed a popular form of entertainment called demolition derby, in which the purpose is to wreck automobiles for fees and fun while at the same time risking human lives? Here is part of an ad from a Kennebunk, Maine newspaper, although it might have been from almost any newspaper in the country, since this neurosis is national in scope:

Wanted

Young Men Not Afraid to Die!* If you think you have plenty of guts, lots of nerve and can stand the pressure both mental and physical of Crashing and Wrecking automobiles, deliberately, then you are the man we want. The requirements are simple: You must have a valid driver's license and supply a junker car that will be demolished—with you in it. We have 23 entries now, leaving 27 openings left. You must be prepared to take extraordinary risks as you will be a part of a 50-car DEMOLITION DERBY at the Arundel Speedway near Kennebunk. . . .[4]

In the area of contemporary "entertainment," what about body-contact sports such as boxing, wrestling, and football, in which participants needlessly risk severe injury and even death in the name of sportsmanship? While I do not condone these activities, at least we can assume as in the case of demolition derbies that all the participants are acting voluntarily, which certainly is not the case with the animals we capture, terrorize,

---

*At first glance I thought this must be a military recruiting poster!

207

and kill. Lately, however, we seem to have abandoned the old line that winning is secondary to the way you play the game. Now we have taken up a stand at the new, hard, fast line demanding that you win in any way you can, but win you must. In the words of the basketball coach in that commanding play, "The Championship Season," "You have to hate to win."

Some mass media have devoted lengthy coverage to individual athletes who specialize in brutality. Recently, when I addressed a regional conference for athletic directors, some of the deans among the football coaches shared their concern with me about the obvious philosophy of win-at-any cost among trainers and participants as well as the sock-it-to-them activities of disgruntled audiences. If the trend continues, maybe we will return to the form of body-contact sport known in the Roman trade as throwing Christians to the lions. We may well be closer to this revival than you think, for we have not only the arena syndrome, but the ancient, brutal appetite for playing for keeps and watching the players suffer.

Of course everything is comparative. At least in the demolition derby we have reason to think that the participants are volunteers. Unfortunately, this is not true in many forms of entertainment, including the so-called bloodless bullfights. Recently Texas distinguished itself again in one of its inimitable ways by legalizing bloodless bullfights and took another giant step toward primitivism and sadism. There is plenty of evidence to substantiate the fact that we are still in the cave. All the rationalizations about bullfighting as a necessary test of man's bravery and virility, as a means of providing harmless outlets for his so-called innate aggressions, or as a form of pageantry, art, or religion, is intellectual dishonesty in its most glaring form, for the real name of the game is sadism made manifest through the terrorizing and torturing of bulls. It is hideous enough that such human activity exists in countries where it has been a custom for centuries, but to have it promulgated in the United States is a national disgrace. If the Vatican can take an official stand against bullfighting *per se* regardless of ethnic and/or cultural patterns, then certainly the U.S., which claims to base its moral structure on the Judeo-Christian ethic, has the obligation at least to do as much in an ambience where bullfighting has never been a part of the cultural activity.[5]

If I had to name one major origin of our general lack of humaneness I would say that, ironically, it stems from a religious source and that, specifically, it has to do with our misinterpretation of the Judeo-Christian ethic. Through centuries, many people have operated on the principle that God created the earth for man to subdue and to use as he sees fit. If you really follow the Judeo-Christian approach to life consistently, you will realize that you never receive anything for nothing, and that there is always a price to be paid in relationship to your potential and the quality of the gift. Since man has been endowed by the Creative Spirit with the richest potential, he owes the greatest debt of responsibility. When, in the role of *Homo sapiens,* he inherits the privilege of existing on the earth, he has the responsibility to cherish the earth, and if he realizes himself on the genuinely human level, he is concerned not with subduing his environment for his selfish interest but rather with subduing his own lesser self in the process of spiritual refinement in the temporal order. Has organized religion missed the boat called the Ark? Unfortunately, yes! Many priests, ministers, and rabbis answer this challenging question by pointing out that their primary job is to save human souls. Certainly, their own common sense must make evident the fact that any and all acts of brutality, cruelty, and violence degrade the human spirit. If, as they claim, they are so concerned about human beings, a great deal of their effort should be concentrated on combating brutality in nonviolent, legal ways.

Even if the bullfights in this country were bloodless, and they are not, they are a national disgrace if for no other reason than the influence they bring to bear, especially on children in the audience, who comprise what the professional promoters hope will prove the lucrative audience of the future. If you think I exaggerate this influence, let me remind you of the Associated Press report of a U.S. marine who said he shot a Vietnamese civilian and then cut off his ear because he thought "it was a common thing to do after a kill." How quickly the tactics of the bullring invade everyday life! Is there any wonder that the so-called deranged individual who commits a brutal act keeps popping up in our society? Certainly a human being should wake up every morning knowing that he is smarter than a bull or any other animal by virtue of the fact that since he has been created a

*Homo sapiens,* he automatically has been endowed with greater potentials. To desire to torture an animal, even by just frightening, much less stabbing it, is a result of a deathly sick soul.

Of course, we do not have to move outside our own indigenous culture to discover one of the most widely accepted yet crudest forms of cruelty extant—the rodeo. As a native Texan, I am particularly familiar with this type of big business masquerading as a sport. In this man-versus-animal game, thousands of animals are tortured, but since the net profits to participants amount to hundreds of thousands of dollars, and to sponsors, millions, most of us who do not participate even as spectators choose to remain silent, and so the brutality and violence continue unabated. The California Branch of The Humane Society of the United States summarizes the *status quo* accurately in a pamphlet entitled "Rodeo, Commercialized Cruelty":

> Each year thousands of animals are maimed, crippled and killed in rodeo arenas.
>
> Animals are shipped, clubbed, kicked, goaded by electric prods, cut by lariats, and slammed to the ground, flesh is torn, bones are broken, animals are killed.
>
> Most spectators think that the "wild bucking broncs" and "vicious bulls" are acting up because they are naturally ornery. This is far from the truth.
>
> It is the calculated infliction of pain and terror moments before the chute gate opens that triggers the crowd-pleasing exhibition of bucking—an exhibition actually of pain and panic.
>
> Few spectators are familiar with the cruel instruments responsible for the animal's behavior. The bucking strap is suddenly cinched tightly on a sensitive area* to make him buck. Spurs must be raked over the mount's shoulders if a cowboy is to win, and miscellaneous clubs and prods** are used brutally.
>
> An individual mistreating an animal for his own amusement would be censored as cruel, but if he does the same thing for a crowd's amusement, and to enrich rodeo promoters, there is hardly a protest.
>
> Rodeo is a multi-million dollar business. In its present form it requires an annual sacrifice of thousands of dead and crippled animals on the altar of the almighty dollar.

*Genital organs
**Electric prods

Personally, all I ask is that you read the rules and regulations set forth by the Rodeo Cowboys' Association establishing requirements for each event in order to qualify and win, and then tell me how it is possible to comply with these rules without being cruel. If that big, brave rodeo cowboy would relinquish his bucking strap, electric prod and spurs, he would not only be out of business, but we would have a chance to see him for what he really is—someone who, in my opinion, needs prolonged psychiatric treatment.

Now that women have demanded their share of the spoils and are promoting and participating in "All-Girl Rodeos," they have substantiated the self-evident truth that the female of the species can be and often is as brutal, cruel, and violent as the male. It is bad enough that adults permit this activity to continue, but it is a genuine abandonment of life on the human level to encourage children and youth to engage in this barbarism and thus perpetuate such sadism. Rodeos constitute one of the greatest disgraces in this country.

Perhaps the most popular form of subhuman activity in the United States is hunting. Some 20 million of our 218 million citizens hunt, and, no doubt, others would if it were possible financially and otherwise. I have spent a lifetime collecting the hunters' stock statements and answers:

First, they are apt to say they love to hunt not because they care if they kill anything, but because they love nature and like to get out in the country. If this is true, why don't they take walks or camp and not carry a gun at all?

Second, they often pose as true conservationists and if pressed on the point will reply that if they did not kill the animals, the beasts would starve anyway. Hunters fail to tell you that two prime reasons for the overabundance of some animals such as deer are that they have already killed most of the deer's natural predators and that they have been feeding the herds to increase their numbers and to make the animals less fearful of man. Suddenly, one day, the man with the grain becomes the man with the gun, bringing suffering and death. How many hunters really know or care anything about ecology? How many hunters are actually engaged in helping to solve any pressing conservation problems, from air and water pollution to soil erosion? How many hunters would contribute funds to preserve a species if they knew

211

they would not have an opportunity to kill some members of the species for fun? Definitively, hunters are not conservationists; they are reservationists, for they reserve the right to kill. When carried to its fullest enactment, the principle of killing the starving animal could, with a little more brutality mixed with a little more rationalization, be applied to people.

Third, some hunters justify their pleasure in killing by saying that since man is by nature an aggressive animal, he works off his natural hostilities in a harmless way by hunting. Such an eminent social anthropologist as Ashley Montagu has challenged the theory of man-as-aggressive-animal. Recently, when Dr. Montagu addressed a Los Angeles symposium entitled "Twentieth Century Violence and the Physician," he said,

> Aggression is simply love frustrated. The human being who is aggressive is saying in another way, "I want to be loved." It has nothing to do with instinct, everything to do with environment.[6]

Fourth, once in a great while, when a hunter's guard is down, he will confess, usually with great hesitancy and embarrassment, that the male of the species finds satisfaction in proving his virility through hunting. How can one possibly respond to this pitiably ephebic statement except to say that it is past time for this individual to be briefed about "birds and bees."

Fifth, it would not be fair to fail to mention one of the favorite rationalizations of hunters—namely, that he never kills anything that he does not eat. Since man's survival in our present society scarcely depends on his ability to track down, kill, and bring home his supply of meat, would it not be far better if the time, money, and energy spent in hunting were spent instead on securing humane slaughter legislation, because in our country, as in most countries of the world, many of our commercial enterprises devoted to the slaughter of animals do not practice humane methods?

When the tables are turned, and the hunters in self-defense respond with questions rather than with answers, they generally suffer under the delusion that they have trapped their humane opponents with the following two questions: "Since you are so opposed to hunting, are you a vegetarian?" Obviously, they fail to see the difference between killing for fun (whether for food or not) and the consumption of meat for nutritional purposes. Their second line of defensive interrogation rests in the question, "Since according to your way of thinking, all entities have life, where do you draw the line; will you also refuse to eat vegetables?" True, one has to draw the line somewhere, so I personally draw the eating line after minerals and vegetables; in other words, I am willing to eat minerals and vegetables but not animals.

Not all hunters by any means are men, so to point the finger exclusively at the male of the species as the brute is not only unfair but also inaccurate. Many women in our society have not only abandoned their role as the guardians, teachers, and practitioners of tenderness, refinement, and cultivation but also sponsor forms of brutality and engage in them. One of the most striking examples of this female retreat from the human level of existence occurs annually during the hunting season, when they go forth along with their children to kill for fun. Seasonally, the society and sports sections of the newspapers are filled with photographs, often in full color, of mothers and their children proudly holding the bleeding animals they have shot and killed. No doubt an appropriate slogan would be: "The family that shoots together may well live to slaughter together"!

Even in some superficial aspects of her life, the female leads the brutal way, as for example her desire to wrap herself in the skin and fur of animals to keep warm and to keep up with the Joneses. Nor does her desire to adorn herself and insure her status decrease even when she knows the animal whose fur she demands is becoming extinct. In some cases, the motivation on her part is not brutality but ignorance and/or thoughtlessness. Perhaps if she were made to witness the slaying of the animal, parts of which she wears, her attitude would be different. How many women, or men for that matter, would enjoy watching hunters club baby seals and skin them alive as they do in the Pribilof Islands? The fact remains, however, that women *per se* and as wives and mothers leave a lot to be desired when it comes to having a commitment to a humane approach to life or to making a witness of this commitment. One of the great mysteries of the world is why so very many parents have the time, money, and energy to teach children how to kill but not how to care for animals. I find this particularly puzzling in light of how much a child can learn about responsibility *per se* from the care and feeding of live animals. As

213

an artist, I have been a "hunter" all my life—a hunter of the minds, hearts, and souls of other human beings. This is a pursuit in which all participate voluntarily, in which no one is harmed and in which everyone gains! The well-known naturalist, Bill Gilbert, summed up the essence of hunting in the title of a *Saturday Evening Post* article: "Hunting Is Dirty Business."[7]

In all fairness to the contemporary scene, I do not want to leave out my own field, the arts. While innumerable examples of enormous brutality appear in every area of the arts from that of the mass medium of television to that of the more esoteric medium of painting, the art form of the cinema supplies sharp and sustained examples. The distinguished *New York Times* critic Bosley Crowthers summarized the *status quo* in two incisive articles entitled "Movies to Kill By" and "Another Smash at Violence":

> Movie makers and movie goers are agreeing that killing is fun. This is killing of a gross and bloody nature, often massive and excessive, done by characters whose murderous motivations are morbid, degenerate and cold . . . They can lead the halfway preconditioned general public to condone preposterous values and cruel deceits. By habituating the public to violence and brutality these films of excessive violence only deaden people's sensitivities and make slaughter seem like a meaningless cliche . . . I dread how widely such deliberate exploitation of the public's susceptibilities is poisoning and deadening our fiber and strength.[8]

Lately, even the arts, which should be man's expression of significant statements through disciplined form, have been devoted primarily to meaninglessness and to declarations of violence. Even when it is necessary for art to depict brutality and despair for the sake of intellectual honesty, art should do so in a manner bespeaking its disapproval and suggesting, by implication, a creative alternative. In its true sense, art, on the highest level, should manifest man's supreme refinement of mind, heart, and spirit rather than his utter defeat caused not only by bowing to the demands of man as animal but also by participating in acts of self-imposed degradation.

We should care about the so-called lower animals, out of enlightened self-interest, just as we should care about each other,

214

for people who engage in brutal activities ironically brutalize themselves. A brutal society is a degenerate one which is rotting from the inside out and which will perish. This inevitable result of brutalization is the prime lesson of history.

In almost every aspect of life that we have mentioned in which brutality is practiced, what masks as one activity is, in reality, another. So-called sports, for example, are actually forms of commerce in the sense of big business. Specifically, we are speaking of money, whether it is a demolition derby, rodeo, football game, or movie. One of the most crass examples of this materialistic philosophy in practice is the National Rifle Association's passionate protection of its own vested interests in maintaining the right to bear arms. (Actually, the constitutional right to bear arms refers not to individual citizens but to the state militia. The only arms we have a right to bear are the two connected to our shoulders!) Just think of the financial loss to the manufacturers of firearms should proper long-past-due legislation to control the possession and purchase of guns be enacted for the general welfare. I know exactly what it means in essence to combat brutality—specifically, it means to have the courage to challenge and to cope with individuals and organizations representing hundreds of millions of dollars.

Fortunately, throughout a part of man's recorded history, there have been a few wise, concerned, courageous human beings who have had the guts to advocate humaneness against all odds. Because in our society anyone involved in the humane ethics movement, especially women, are dismissed as hopeless sentimentalists, I have purposely chosen examples from the ranks of distinguished humane men. One of the individuals who comes to mind first in this noble assembly is the late genius Albert Schweitzer, whose humane philosophy and conduct gave rise to an entire school of thought known as "reverence for life." In an essay devoted to "The Sacredness of All That Lives," he wrote:

> It is the fate of every truth to be an object of ridicule when it is first acclaimed. Today it is considered an exaggeration to proclaim constant respect for every form of life as being the serious demand of a rational ethic. But the time is coming when people will be amazed that the human race was so long before it recognized that thoughtless injury to life is compatible with real ethics. Ethics is in its unqualified form, extended responsibility with regard to everything that has life.

215

There slowly grew up in me an unshakable conviction that we have no right to inflict suffering and death on another living creature unless there is some unavoidable necessity for it, and that we ought all of us to feel what a horrible thing it is to cause suffering and death out of mere thoughtlessness . . . I have grown more and more certain that at the bottom of our heart we all think this, and that we fail to acknowledge it and to carry our belief into practice chiefly because we are afraid of being laughed at by other people as sentimentalists, though partly also because we allow our best feelings to get blunted.

. . . the universal ethic of reverence for life shows the sympathy with animals, which is so often represented as sentimentality, to be a duty which no thinking man can escape.[9]

The eminent sociologist Lewis Mumford has defined Western man in the twentieth century aptly and succinctly as a "connoisseur of violence,"[10] while the renowned psychiatrist Erich Fromm has categorized modern men as either lovers of death known as necrophiles (human beings who are devoted to cruelty, brutality, and violence) or lovers of life called biophiles (human beings motivated by creative, constructive, unselfish, loving activities).[11]

In a lyrical book entitled *The Immense Journey,* the brilliant anthropologist Loren Eiseley summarized contemporary man's challenge in a brief, penetrating way when he wrote:

The need is not really for more brains, the need is now for a gentler, a more tolerant people than those who won for us against the ice, the tiger, and the bear. The hand that hefted the ax, out of some blind allegiance to the past fondles the machine gun as lovingly. It is a habit that man will have to break to survive, but the roots go very deep.

Perhaps no one in our time who has written about the desperate need for humane motivation in our society has surpassed the clear, persuasive statement made by Norman Cousins in a *Saturday Review* editorial entitled "Our Casual Approach to Violence":

We have not developed any substantial confidence in moral force or in the vitality of great ideas . . . our conditioning has made violence a seemingly normal part of our lives and we have a casual approach to it . . . The casualness with which violence is treated

216

and accepted may make it difficult for us to think today in totally different terms, even though our lives may depend on our ability to do so . . .[12]

By their very nature, human beings have a position of authority, which carries an inexorable challenge of responsibility so that they are never free of the necessity to ask themselves what and who they are—mineral, vegetable, animal, or man. Along with life itself, human beings have been endowed with free will, which, in practice, means the power to make any choice but not the ethical, moral right to make selfish ones. Some people have chosen to live out their lives in the form of stolid boulders, while others have decided merely to vegetate or to live an animal cycle of eating, sleeping, breeding, and dying. Fortunately, a few have chosen to be human and to carry the full load of responsibility this status implies. This rare, courageous group have decided to risk being sad so that they may also be joyful. To them big-game hunting does not mean stalking and killing the so-called lower creatures but rather tracking down the core of themselves in the hopes of becoming more compassionate and humane. Above all else, they know full well that it is truly a game for all the seasons of their lives.

The British author H. G. Wells once wrote that "human history becomes more and more a race between education and catastrophe."[13] Run, man, run in such a way that if you are asked who you are, you can answer with objectivity and intellectual honesty:

> I am not a mineral!
> I am not a vegetable!
> I am not an animal!
> I am, dear God, a man!

Because we humans are an infinitesimal part of the whole Divine Creation, we are consonantly connected to every mineral, vegetable, insect, fish, reptile, bird, animal and man, and because of the quality of our innate potential, ethically, our role as stewards is inescapable.

In the late Loren Eiseley's book, *The Unexpected Universe*, he reminds us in lyrical and persuasive ways of the need to complete the rainbow of existence by converting it into a full circle through compassion.[14]

We humans would be wise not just to run but also to "Race a Rainbow":

Find a star
Twirl it high
Race a rainbow
In the sky,
Never ever
Let them die.

Take a band
Of colored lights
Tie them into
Tails of kites,
Never let them
Out of sight.

If the circle's
Only half
Treat it with
A cosmic laugh,
Stretch it on
A lover's staff.

With compassion's
Tender hand
Make the circle
Something grand,
And cultivate the
Soul of man!

## NOTES

1. "Violence and History." *Time*, April 19, 1968.
2. *San Antonio Light*, March 14, 1966.
3. *San Antonio Evening News*, May 9, 1967.
4. York County Coast Star, Kennebunk, Maine, July 4, 1965.
5. March 10, 1966, *L'Osservatore*, Vatican City: "Along with live pigeon shooting all sports based on useless cruelty toward animals ought to be prohibited. One classic example is that of the bullfight, where there is a crescendo of cruelty to the bull with the banderillas, which tears its flesh, the pikes which prick it to bleed, spurring it to the highest degree of furor and danger."
6. Ashley Montagu, *Parade Magazine*, April 14, 1968, "Twentieth Century Violence and the Physician."
7. "Hunting Is a Dirty Business," *Saturday Evening Post*, October 21, 1967.
8. *New York Times*, July 1967.
9. Albert Schweitzer, *Albert Schweitzer, An Anthology* (New York: Harper & Bros., 1947).
10. Lewis Mumford, *The Myth of the Machine, The Pentagon of Power* (New York: Harcourt, Brace, Jovanovich, Inc. 1970).
11. Erich Fromm, *Saturday Review*, January 4, 1964, "Creators and Destroyers."
12. Norman Cousins, *Saturday Review*, August 31, 1957, "The Casual Approach to Violence."
13. H. G. Wells, *The Outline of History* (Somerset Publications, 1920).
14. Loren Eiseley, *The Unexpected Universe* (New York, Harcourt, Brace & World, 1964).

# What Future for Man and Earth? Toward a Biospiritual Ethic

# 12

Michael W. Fox

T HROUGHOUT THE UNITED STATES, communities and various corporate and social organizations celebrated the bicentennial year of 1976. But what of the future? A repetition of the last twenty decades? Americans are proud of their heritage and their traditional values of individualism and free enterprise. They have conquered the western frontiers and outer space and subdued nature for the betterment of humanity so that we have perhaps the highest standard of living in the world. Production, consumption, profit, agronomic expansion, technological growth—these are not the things we should celebrate. Rather, we should celebrate our awareness that this bicentennial must mark the end of such an era. It is like the end of a dream from which we are now being slowly awakened by the fact that growth is finite, nature's resources are nonrenewable, and, together with the countless species that we have made extinct or endangered, plus millions of square miles of once viable habitat, we too are endangered. We are endangered spiritually, socially, and economically because of the values, needs, and attitudes that form the very fabric of our culture as well as our national identity and heritage, and we are now beginning to question their worth and ultimate purpose in relation to human fulfillment in its deepest sense.

Perhaps having gone through this self-limiting and ultimately self-destructive mode of socio-economic growth and "progress," America may come to lead other nations and show them alternative values, needs, and attitudes that will benefit not only all people of one earth, but also all of earth, including all sentient beings and habitats, since all are interrelated and

219

interdependent. There is only one earth, and humanity must discover ways to accomplish unity of heart and mind between man and man, nation state and nation state, and man and nature.

This pledge of the American outdoorsman-sportsman-hunter (published originally "as a public service" in 1946 in *Outdoor Life*) aptly depicts the general attitude toward nature as a *resource:*

> I give my pledge as an American to save and faithfully to defend from waste the natural resources of my country—its air, soil and minerals, its forests, waters and wildlife.

A better pledge for today might be this one:

> I give my pledge as a world citizen to respect all of life as I respect my own kind, to cherish nature's creations and riches which I shall neither use thoughtlessly nor abuse willfully, since man and nature are of one earth and of one spirit.

This pledge is an improvement over the former one, which reflects nationalism, individualism, and a belief that nature is a resource; since there is no explicit reason why one should adhere to the first conservation pledge, it must be implicit in the notion that nature is a resource for man and little else.

The humane and conservation movements are part of a vital human imperative to evolve beyond the limited ego-states of individual, corporation, nation, and the like to a true sense of global community, an ecological awareness in which all men are of one earth and one mind, united in terms of the highest ethical values and rational conduct, as well as empathic compassion and reverence for all life.

## CONSCIOUSNESS AND VALUES

Can Western man survive without a radical change in attitudes and values toward compassion, humane action, and service to his fellows and to animals alike? What debt and obligation do we have to animals? The attitudes and values of man toward other life forms arise from the concepts that we hold of nature, of living beings, and of our relationships with others. If we change concepts and attitudes, then mankind will change—for better or for worse. As a man thinks, so he is.

The human brain is so evolved that we may change ourselves consciously—to exert free will over the predestined pattern of our field of existence. Thus it is not so much a question of genetic controls in man's evolution but self-control through self-awareness, through which we may essentially restructure our own minds (or reprogram our biocomputers). Man is clearly beyond direct control of genes and instincts provided he will utilize his rational and reflective mental abilities. He can choose, control, and direct what he thinks and does—and therefore what he is and will become. As genes carry information—biochemically encoded instructions—so concepts play an analogous role in influencing how we behave, create, act, and relate. While man cannot yet directly rearrange his genes *per se,* he does have the incredible capacity to change his "head" and his environment. The state of international and interpersonal relationships and of man's relationship with nature and other life forms indicates that the attitudes and values that influence the nature of these relationships need to be radically changed.

The world is not designed for man's exclusive pleasure and exploitation. As we multiply, we must create alternative resources that do not deplete existing resources, disrupt natural ecosystems, or destroy interdependent life systems (solar energy to replace fossil fuels is an example of such an alternative resource). Our physical and psychological as well as economic survival depends on this.

Our attitude toward the biosphere and other life forms may be changed because our survival depends on such a change. An optimistic view of mankind's contemporary crises—economic, environmental, political, social—is to see these crises as positive stimuli that will further the evolution of human consciousness. A conflict or crisis in conservation or environmental control may not automatically have beneficial consequences, however. Imagine a conflict between a rational altruist ($A$) and an egocentric materialist ($Z$): the conflict is often resolved in some social or economic policy without changing the consciousness of $Z$ one iota. $A$, for example, may wish to conserve wolves for their own intrinsic worth; $Z$ for his own self-interest. Without the insights of

*A*, *Z*'s shortsighted and self-serving interests could lead to extinction of the wolf. *Z* may see the value of "preserving" wolves only for their fur. Or *Z* may be a hunter and value the wolf solely as a vital element in keeping his "game" (deer, mountain sheep, caribou, and moose) in healthy population balance. Even if the wolf were protected for the ecologically sound reason that it would be a rational policy to maintain the balance of nature and to provide for the hunter's long-term interests, *Z*'s agreement would not guarantee a change in his awareness or values. The conceptual morality and ethical world view of *Z* does not change as a consequence of his interaction with *A*. *Z* may only "see" when his own survival is at stake. Or he may not see even then, since surely he would realize that his survival is at stake today if he could glimpse beyond his own immediate lifetime into the generation of his children's children. Witness the 1976 atrocity in Alaska, in which wolves were exterminated to maintain the moose population—not for the wolves but for the vested interest of "sportsmen."

Crises can unite humanity in a common bond of survival, and consciousness-raising can be a natural product of environmental crisis as well as an integral part of conservation and the humane movement (where, respectively, conservation is consciousness-raising in action and concern for animals can make us more humane). To be human means to harmonize with feeling—to emphathize with others, including animals. There is a fellowship of suffering and a respect for the need to survive and to maintain the continuity of the species. Such fellow-feeling, as emphasized by Prof. Northrop, should not be exclusive to one's family, race, nation, or species but should embrace all species: only then is man fully human in his humaneness. This is not an anthropomorphic state of sentimental projection with regard to other sentient beings but a state of pure being that transcends the egocentric, ethnocentric, and anthropocentric barriers of concept and attitude. We must think "zoöcentrically" and in a global perspective. The state of mind and the state of the world are one and we cannot hope to improve on the latter without regard for the former.

To empathize with fellow-feeling is to love. This is the essence of the teachings of all great religious masters. It is, as discussed by Prof. Morris, the key to freedom from suffering, fear, violence, greed, ignorance, and illusion. The struggle for survival was recognized by Buddha, who held that all of life is suffering; liberation was, as he saw it, through compassion, reverence, and understanding. Man upsets the cosmic equilibrium of ecology, society, and spirit when he thinks and acts without feeling and empathy for others, including plants and animals, oceans and forests. One must simply assist the process of creation, of birth, of living, and of dying. How different is this Zen Buddhist view of man's relationship with life from the Western interpretation via Darwin's evidence of the "survival of the fittest." Natural struggle and competition justified the competitive individualism of the industrial revolution. This biological interpretation lent support to the sociopolitical system of industrial growth, egocentricity, free enterprise, and so on. Freud contributed indirectly by proposing that the "animal" in man was the source of his baser "bestial" instinct and his destructive, selfish, and inhumane deeds. This negative regard for basic human nature justified man's alienation from and exploitation of nature. But worse, it took the spotlight away from the cause of humanity's problems—his ego-consciousness of selfish ethnocentric and anthropocentric values and attitudes. As I have stated elsewhere,[1] nothing is wrong with human nature; what is wrong is human nurture—the consciousness developed and acquired from the culture (and not from our genetic animal heritage), including the thoughts, values, attitudes, and related actions that lead to man's distorted world view (that is, that he is not an integral part of the world but has dominion over it to exploit it as he chooses).

Western philosophers have added little to understanding man's relationship and obligation (if any) to other sentient beings. The English philosophers Locke and Hobbes felt that our attitudes toward animals can transfer into attitudes toward other human beings; thus being humane toward animals would improve attitudes and relationships among people. This view does not imply that children should be taught to be kind to animals because it will make them better members of society when they grow up, but rather, our general regard for animals is inextricably related to our regard for humans. Furthermore, the dichotomy between self (ego) and other, and between species (animal and man) is more a conceptual separateness than a psychological, social, or ecological reality.

## MAN, NATURE, AND RELATIONSHIPS

Phenomenologically, man and the world are one, inseparable. Concepts of individuality must be broadened to a concept of interindividual relatedness. That is, a tree is more than a tree, but rather an intrinsic part of a whole nexus of interdependent and related centers of being that together constitute a pattern or field of relatedness. For domesticated animals, this field has been greatly modified and simplified by man, but for man in his role as planetary steward, the field is cosmic and almost incomprehensible in its ever-changing complexity. Man's consciousness must be broadened to an awareness of the enormity of this field, whose pattern and future he must not change without full knowledge of all consequences.

In relation to this theory field, according to Profs. Cobb & Hartshorne, both the Buddha and the philosopher Alfred North Whitehead saw reality composed not of "things," of individuals *per se*, but of actions, changing patterns of relationship, and unit events interrelated in the process of creation and actualization. Whitehead stated that "Everything that in any sense exists has two sides, namely its individual self and its signification in the universe," thus recognizing that all life forms share in the one reality and are significant elements in the total field of existence. For Western man, I regard the development of ego—of the individual—not as an end in itself but rather as a stage through which we must mature to a more ego-freed *transpersonal* stage of being and relatedness. Unfortunately, this complete sequence of development is arrested at various levels of ego-individuation, to the detriment of mankind and the world as a whole.

Man as a separate (even "superior") species is an erroneous, illusory humanocentric concept; it is a self-destructive trap, for when man destroys or demeans nature, he is also destroying or demeaning his own humanity as well as threatening his own survival.

The French philosopher Merleau-Ponty, according to Prof. Dallery, sees nature not as an object, nor as something to manipulate and exploit, but as an "interlocutor," giving meaning and ultimate significance to man as a consciously humane and empathic being. He states that man is not a natural species but a historical concept. We must therefore transcend our illusory egocentric species-boundaries, a'la Hartshorne, to discover our natural mind-potential in oneness with nature, a oneness for which we are genetically predisposed and predestined: one earth, one mind. We can perceive, project, and give meaning to life, and all life forces are equally significant and inseparable to the meaning (and reverence) for our own and all existence. Demean the latter and we demean and limit ourselves, since man is in and of the world, which is the only and ultimate reality beyond his humanocentric world view.

We do not always consciously demean and devalue others. The Cartesian view that animals are no more than unfeeling and unthinking machines discussed by Prof. Brumbaugh, for example, is extremely prevalent today: if it were not, then many biomedical researchers would not have the attitude or philosophical premise that allows them to perform countless unnecessary experiments and to use animals without much forethought as teaching aids in high school science and with graduate medical students.

Another view, in relation to the "sacrifice" of animals to science, is that it is justified simply on the grounds of knowledge for knowledge's sake. To finally know all, to have 100 percent objective, scientific proof, is impossible, since all of life is a dynamic, growing, ever-changing pattern of interrelated fields. Pure awareness, or coexistential knowledge of the "thing in itself" differs from objective (scientific) knowledge in that it includes such subjective qualities as empathy, identification (fellow-feeling), and understanding. We lose a part of the world in repressing this subjective mode of human consciousness by not seeing, relating, and being; egocentric needs, attitudes, skeptical empiricism, objectivism, and Cartesianism predominate. Objective knowledge is never absolute or final. Since the pattern of interrelated fields is always changing, there is no end to this mode of information-seeking. Objective knowledge is always historic, after the fact, which is of limited if any value except to monitor and predict repeated patterns of man/nature fields of interaction. (To use such knowledge to "control" such interactions is illusory and naive, since the very concept of control—control of nature or of man—separates the interrelated fields into controller and controlled.) At best, it merely feeds man's ego; at worst, it alienates him from the continuum. The point here is as stressed by Prof. Dallery, that man *is* his relations with the world and these are not wholly mechanical, causal, or conceptual; yet in believing that they are, man dehumanizes himself. In other words, the organism (in this case, man) *is* its environment, but the objectifying self or ego-consciousness separates man from nature.

This leads us to the topic of animal versus human rights and associated moral constraints.

### ANIMAL AND HUMAN RIGHTS

Kant held that only rational beings—that is, humans—have rights. But perhaps man has fewer rights because he is irrational. Animals have, I believe, by virtue of their existence, intrinsic value and thus rights within themselves in relation to ours. Their rights, like ours, are always relative and we must, if we are to be humane stewards, judge with caution and humility. All creatures, observes Hartshorne, contribute something in their mortal lives to the grand scheme of creation, from the primordial undifferentiated ocean of potential via the streams of life—species, phyla, and so on—returning to the eternal. Man is not the end, or the ultimate, but no more or less a part of creation than all the rest except that creation itself is beginning to express itself in him through consciousness.

Our failure to have reverence for *all* forms of life correlates with racism, prejudice, and alienation from God and from understanding nature and the meaning of life. We may, as Prof. Hartshorne suggests, be *inferior* to animals in that they more or less instinctively fulfill their being, while we, with free will and rational minds, fall short of self-fulfillment. Man is the conscious trustee of cosmic ends; animals fulfill these ends unconsciously; for example, wolves "husband" the moose as part of a balanced relatedness. But man is out of balance; we are an unbalanced species mentally and socially. Being alive fulfills others via eco-relationships, and only man is consciously aware of this and may choose to abdicate not his divine right to freedom and dominion but his divine obligation as trustee or steward of earth.

In a cosmological sense, living is a preparation for dying, and a growing of awareness for man throughout life. Within all existence and each individual field of relationship and experience is a center of pure essence or spirit. In Buddhism, this essence is expressed in pure being, as enlightened compassion and reverence for all life (since all life is of the same essence). The Nirvana state or principle represents this center as the eternal void of infinite potential beyond death and yet within the life-awareness of pure being. It is the essence of life fulfilled in and through consciousness and expressed in thought, feeling, and action. This Nirvana principle therefore penetrates the time-space continuum of mortal transience in all sentient beings, linking individuated species and patterned fields of relatedness with the aesthetic or cosmic continuum of undifferentiated potential.

It therefore follows, as Profs. Brumbaugh and Northrop have emphasized, that things identical in kind are identical in value, and this so-called formal "deontic" logic leads to a natural ethical obligation toward all forms of creation. Similarly, as Prof. Dallery has shown, the phenomenological approach, which involves no filtering or selective perception of what *is,* or fitting experiences to a preconceived set of concepts, values, or expectations, leads man objectively to a deeper understanding of his ethical obligations to all of life, since, like man, all life forms manifest the will to survive and have adopted patterns of structure and behavior to insure species continuation.

The ancient Indian Brihadaranyaka (Upanishad) cited by Prof. Morris states that "the inorganic is life that sleeps, the plant is life that feels, the animal is life that knows and man is life that knows that it knows." In other words, man differs qualitatively, but not absolutely—only in degree along an unbroken continuum. Our bodies contain the mineral elements of primordial rocks; our very cells share the same historically evolved components as those of grasses and trees;[2] our brains contain the basic neural core of reptile, bird, and fellow mammal.

I do not believe, however, that we should behave ethically and humanely toward animals simply because they feel pain, share in the same struggle for survival and continuation, and have

227

emotional reactions sometimes identical to ours. We should be humane to all sentient beings simply because we are *human;* otherwise we would base our ethics and morality on selfish anthropocentric judgments and evaluations. For example, to justify conservation of whales because they have complex brains (like ours) and wolves because they have a complex and affectionate extended family society (like ours) is anthropocentric valuation. It can distract us from revering all life in its own right and not in terms of similarities or affinities with our own species. Subjective aesthetics also operate insidiously in a similar way, some people having little or no concern for "ugly" or venomous species but showing obvious although selective concern for "defenseless" infantile or aesthetically pleasing species.

Thus a nonvaluing and nonjudgmental approach to animals is needed, one in which their own intrinsic rather than man-oriented worth is appreciated and reflected legally and morally in equality of rights. The humane movement thus becomes a potentiator of human moral and ethical development—of global consciousness— when animal rights are fought for. But what of human priorities, especially sociopolitical and socioeconomic ones that today seem to influence the lives and futures of all peoples of all nations? If the interests and priorities of men take precedence over those of animals, then man's interests and priorities must be re-evaluated: such is the consensus of the contributions to this volume. A re-evaluation is the first reflective step toward man's freedom from the mass hypnosis and egocentric blindness of anthropocentrism. Ask *why,* not in a short-term perspective of immediate gratification—to have now, to produce, consume, and profit—but in a long-term dimension of future generations. Awareness of others' (especially animals') rights and needs can make us more human, in terms of compassion, conscience, and reflective rational insight.

One who is respected has rights; animals, by virtue of their very existence and intrinsic worth, are to be respected and therefore have rights. If animals have no rights, then the people who do not respect them have no fair claim to their own egocentric rights. Animals should be given rights, not like those of people or objects, possessions or property, but more akin, as emphasized by Prof. Feinberg, to those of the special category already existing for mentally defective adults and pre-verbal

228

children who cannot "speak for themselves" but whose rights can be represented by legal counsel.[3]

The philosopher John Locke emphasized that man and animal share the same natural rights for life, liberty, and prosperity and the right not to suffer at the hands of others. The quality of "human rights" is basic to one's existence as a nondiscriminating element of society, and the same holds for animals, both wild and tame. Animal and human rights must not be degraded or exploited, although obviously in certain situations some rights of the individual must be forsaken for the general welfare. For example, leashing, neutering, and even debarking and declawing our pets may seem inhumane and a violation of their rights. But we must impose restraints on natural behaviors in certain contexts in our domesticated animals just as people must abide by certain rules and social constraints.

The humane movement must be politically involved, since socioeconomic factors are at the root of many forms of animal abuse. Abuse also has its roots in ignorance, indifference, blind tradition, and vanity, and the Humane Movement must focus even more on education to facilitate the consciousness-raising that will change society and its values from within. External restraints via legal injunctions, rescue operations (in the case of oiled sea birds), animal shelters, guerilla interventions (Operation Greenpeace) and the like are stopgaps, humane actions treating only the surface symptoms.

Animal rights will depend on man's assuming fully his role as steward* of the planet earth, and he must judge, regulate, and even destroy in order to maintain order, health, life, and harmony in the biosphere. Animals' rights must be addressed not from a zoöcentric standpoint, nor from an anthropocentric one, but on a biospiritual basis. There is no room or future for the romantic preservationist who would leave nature to itself, since nature *is* man, and we must monitor and regulate both with understanding and compassion.

### EVOLUTION AND MAN'S FUTURE

Man's attitude toward nature is a mirror of human consciousness, reflecting mankind's maturity of regard and

---

*Humane* steward as distinct from dominionistic exploiter.

attitude. The next stage in our evolution is toward eco- rather than ego-consciousness, and the crises of nature are crises in the development of human consciousness. We cannot therefore correct, control, or monitor nature without doing the same to ourselves, since man and nature are one. The lesson from nature that all is balance, harmony, and unity must be internalized in our thinking, feeling, and actions and not simply idealized as a utopian dream. Such a natural state can never exist until we reprogram or repattern human consciousness after the pattern manifest in its deepest significance in nature. For mankind, this would be the Natural Mind; it would represent the next great evolutionary advance for our species—eco-consciousness, being at one with nature: one earth, one mind.[4]

## NOTES

1. M.W. Fox, *Between Animal and Man* (New York: Coward, McCann, 1976).
2. L. Thomas, *The Lives of a Cell* (New York: Viking, 1974).
3. See P. Singer, *Animal Liberation* (New York: Random House, 1975); C. D. Stone, *Should Trees Have Standing?* (Los Altos, Calif.: Kaufmann, 1974). See also essays by Joel Feinberg and Charles Hartshorne in this volume.
4. See M. W. Fox, *One Earth, One Mind* (New York: Coward, McCann, forthcoming).

# Biographical Notes

**BRUMBAUGH, ROBERT S.** Professor of Philosophy, Yale University. Dr. Brumbaugh did his undergraduate and graduate work at the University of Chicago and completed his Ph.D. in 1942. Prior to accepting his appointment to Yale University (1952), he taught at Columbia University, Bowdoin College, and Indiana University. He served as a Research Fellow at the American School of Classical Studies, Athens, Greece (1962-1963). Dr. Brumbaugh is the author of *The Philosophers of Greece* (Thomas Y. Crowell, 1964) and *Plato and the Modern Age* (Crowell-Collier, 1962) among other works, and he is co-author (with Nathaniel N. Lawrence) of *Philosophers on Education: Six Essays on the Foundations of Western Thought* (Houghton Mifflin, 1963).

**CARAS, ROGER A.** Former Vice President and Director of The Humane Society of the United States. Adjunct professor of English, South Hampton College, and a graduate of the University of Southern California. He is a Joseph Wood Krutch Medalist, author of forty books largely on the subject of animals and natural history, a radio commentator ("Pets and Wildlife") for CBS-Radio, Special Correspondent for Animals and the Environment, ABC-TV Network News, Fellow of the Royal Society of Arts, London, and a Fellow of the Rochester Museum and Science Center. Has served on the boards of or as an officer of nearly two dozen national and international organizations concerned with the welfare of animals, man, and the planet.

**COBB, JOHN B., JR.** Ingraham Professor of Theology, the School of Theology at Claremont (California). Dr. Cobb received his Ph.D. in 1952 from the University of Chicago. In 1968 the University of Mainz, Germany, awarded him an honorary Doctor of Theology degree. He taught at Young Harris College (Georgia) and Emory University before joining the faculty at Claremont, and he was a Fulbright Lecturer at the University of Mainz (1965-1966). His special fields of study have been the relation of philosophy to theology, Protestant theology, and the philosophy of Whitehead. Among his publications are *Christian Natural Theology* (Westminister, 1965), *Living Options in Protestant Theology* (Westminster, 1962), and *Is It Too Late? A Theology of Ecology* (Bruce, div. of Benziger, Bruce and Glencoe, 1972). He edited (with James M. Robinson) *New Frontiers in Theology* (2 vols., Harper & Row, 1963-1964).

**DALLERY, CARLETON.** Assistant Professor of Philosophy, State University of New York at Stony Brook (Long Island). Dr. Dallery received his B.A., M.A., and Ph.D. degrees at Yale University and in 1960-1961 attended the University of Paris. From 1965 to 1968 he was an instructor of philosophy at Tufts University, Medford, Massachusetts. Dr. Dallery's principal areas of research are ancient philosophy, ethics, and phenomenology.

**FEINBERG, JOEL.** Professor of Philosophy, University of Arizona, Tucson. Dr. Feinberg completed his undergraduate and graduate work in philosophy at the University of Michigan. He taught at Brown University, Princeton University, the University of California at Los Angeles, and Rockefeller University before accepting his present position. He has been a visiting professor at the Universities of Colorado, Michigan, and Calgary (Alberta, Canada), as well as at Columbia and Princeton. His special fields of study have been ethics, social and legal philosophy, and the philosophy of mind. Among his many publications are *Reason and Responsibility: An Introduction to Philosophy* (Wadsworth, 1965), *Doing and Desiring: Essays in the Theory of Responsibility* (Princeton University Press, 1970), *Social Philosophy* (Prentice-Hall, 1973). He is co-editor (with Wesley Salmon) of *Contemporary Perspectives in Philosophy Series* (Prentice-Hall, 1964-1967). Dr.

Feinberg has served as a Fellow for the Center for Advanced Study in the Behavioral Sciences, Stanford University (1960-1961), and Liberal Arts Fellow, Harvard Law School (1963-1964).

**FOX, MICHAEL W.** Director, Institute for the Study of Animal Problems, a division of The Humane Society of the United States. Dr. Fox holds doctoral degrees in medicine, ethology (animal behavior), and veterinary medicine. Prior to joining The HSUS, he was Associate Professor at Washington University. He is the author of several scientific papers and technical and popular books, including *Understanding Your Dog* (Coward McCann, 1971), *Between Animal and Man* (Cowan McCann, 1976), *Behavior of Wolves, Dogs and Related Canids* (Harper & Row, 1972). Dr. Fox has also written a number of children's books, some of which are *The Wolf* (1974), *Ramu and Chennai* (1976), and *Wild Dogs Three* (1977), all published by Coward McCann, New York. A contributing editor to *McCall's* magazine, he also has a syndicated newspaper column, "Ask Your Vet," and is a member of the American Veterinary Medical Association, American Association for Laboratory Animal Science, and the Association of Animal Science.

**HARTSHORNE, CHARLES.** Ashbel Smith Professor of Philosophy, University of Texas, Austin. Dr. Hartshorne received his undergraduate and graduate degrees from Harvard University, did postdoctoral work at the Universities of Freiburg and Marburg (Germany), and holds an honorary L.H.D. from Haverford College. He taught at Harvard, the University of Chicago, and Emory University before accepting his present position in 1962. His awards and honors are many, including Fulbright visiting professorships at Melbourne University (Australia) and Kyoto University (Japan). He delivered the Terry Lecture at Yale in 1947 and has been a visiting professor or lecturer at the New School for Social Research, the University of Frankfurt (Germany), Union Theological Seminary, and Stanford University. He is noted for his work in metaphysics, the philosophy of religion, and the philosophies of Charles S. Peirce and Alfred N. Whitehead. Among his many publications are *Aquinas to Whitehead* (1976), *The Divine Reality* (2nd ed., Yale University Press, 1964), *The Logic* *of Perfection* (Open Court, 1962), *A Natural Theology for Our Time* (Open Court, 1964). He is editor (with P. Weiss) of *Collected Works of Charles Sanders Peirce* (Harvard University Press, 1931). Not least among his achievements is his reputation as an ornithologist and author of *Born to Sing: An Interpretation and World Survey of Bird Song* (Indiana University Press, 1973).

**LEE, AMY FREEMAN.** Lecturer in humane ethics, education, and painting. In a career spanning more than forty years, Ms. Lee has been active in painting, lecturing, writing, criticism, education, and the humane movement. She has been Founder/President of the Texas Watercolor Society, Chairman of the Board of Trustees of Incarnate Word College in San Antonio, Vice President and Executive Board Member of the San Antonio Blind Association, and National Secretary and National Board Member of The Humane Society of the United States. Since 1945 her paintings have been shown in more than 600 exhibitions, and she has had some 174 literary works published. Ms. Lee received an honorary Doctor of Letters degree from Incarnate Word College (1965), had a fellowship named in her honor by the San Antonio chapter of the Association of American University Women (1973), and was designated a "valuable human resource" by the American Bicentennial Research Institute of Human Resources.

**MONTAGU, ASHLEY.** Anthropologist, social biologist, and author. Educated at the Universities of London and Florence, Dr. Montagu received his Ph.D. from Columbia University. He holds an honorary D.Sc. degree from Grinnell College. He has served in many academic positions: lecturer at the New School for Social Research, assistant professor of anatomy and lecturer in physical anthropology at New York University, associate professor of anatomy at Hahnemann Medical College and Hospital (Philadelphia), and professor and chairman of anthropology at Rutgers University (1949-1955). He has been a research associate at the British Museum of Natural History and curator of anthropology for the Wellcome Historical Medical Museum (London), consultant on race to UNESCO, and the recipient of many prizes and awards. He has written more than forty books. Among the better known titles are *Man's Most Dangerous Myth: The Fallacy of Race* (4th ed., World Book, 1964), *Introduction to Physical Anthropology* (3rd ed., C. C. Thomas, 1960), *On Being Human* (Hawthorn, 1966), *The Natural Superiority of Women* (Macmillan, 1953), *Human Heredity* (2nd ed., World Book, 1964), *Statement on Race* (3rd ed., Oxford University Press, 1972). He is editor of *Man and Aggression* (rev. ed., Oxford University Press, 1973).

**MORRIS, RICHARD KNOWLES.** Professor of Education and Anthropology, *Emeritus,* Trinity College (Hartford, Connecticut). Dr. Morris finished his undergraduate work at Trinity College, studied law, and received his M.A. and Ph.D. degrees from Yale University. He was twice a summer visiting lecturer in the philosophy of education at the Johns Hopkins University. He did postdoctoral work at New York University and, as a Fulbright Research Scholar, at Osmania University (Hyderabad, A.P., India) during the summer of 1961. In 1964 he was an associate member of the Fourth East-West Philosophers' Conference in Honolulu. In 1967 he delivered the Fenian Centennial Address at University College, Galway, Ireland. Dr. Morris is the author of *John P. Holland: Inventor of the Modern Submarine* (U.S. Naval Institute, 1966) and author of numerous articles on history, education, and humane ethics. He is an adviser to the New England Regional Office, The Humane Society of the United States.

**NORTHROP, F. S. C.** Sterling Professor of Philosophy and Law, *Emeritus,* Yale University. Dr. Northrop was educated at Beloit College, 1915, received an M.A. in economics from Yale University in 1919 and in philosophy from Harvard University in 1922, and a Ph.D. in the philosophy of science from Harvard in 1924. In 1922-23 he was a graduate research fellow both at Trinity College, University of Cambridge, under McTaggart's direction in philosophy and at the Imperial College of Science and Technology, University of London, under Whitehead's direction in the philosophy of mathematical physics. He lived and studied Cantonese in South China, has traveled twice to India, Pakistan, and the Southeast Asian Buddhist nations. In 1939 he was one of five founding members of the East-West Philosophers' Conferences, Honolulu, Hawaii. In 1965 he was the keynote speaker at the National Leadership Conference of The Humane Society of the United States.

# Appendix

The Humane Society of the United States, which sponsored the project that resulted in this book, here provides the reader with a guide for building a humane ethic by beginning with the following principles adapted by the Society:

It is wrong to kill animals needlessly or for entertainment or to cause animals pain or torment.

It is wrong to fail to provide adequate food, shelter, and care for animals for which man has accepted the responsibility.

It is wrong to use animals for medical, educational, or commercial experimentation or research, unless absolute necessity can be demonstrated and unless such is done without causing the animals pain or torment.

It is wrong to maintain animals that are to be used for food in a manner that causes them discomfort or denies them an opportunity to develop and live in conditions that are reasonably natural for them.

It is wrong for those who eat animals to kill them in any manner that does not result in instantaneous unconsciousness. Methods employed should cause no more than minimum apprehension.

It is wrong to confine animals for display, impoundment, or as pets in conditions that are not comfortable and appropriate.

It is wrong to permit domestic animals to propagate to an extent that leads to overpopulation and misery.

# Subject Index

237

National Shooting Sports Foundation, 131
Natural history field theory, 194, 200
Natural resources, 73; alternative, 221
Natural sciences and humanities, 179
Natural selection, 119
Naturalism, biological, 189
Nature, 82; balance of, 113; human intervention in, 89; man's relation to, 104, 111-113, 221; mastering, 79; order of, 8; primitive relation to, 82; as a resource, 220
"Nature lore," 89
*Naturwissensschaften*, 176
Necrophile vs. biophile, 216
Neoplatonism, 10
Nervous system, 155
Nirvana, 198, 200
Nonviolence, 41

**O**

Oneness. *See* Unity
Original sin, doctrine of, 93, 98

**P**

Pain. *See* suffering
Perception, 74, 76, 78, 80; and values, 139
Pesticides (DDT), 78
Pet ownership. *See* Animals, as pets
Phenomenology, 22-24, 71-74, 77, 82, 84
Pigs, 29
Pleasure-pain dichotomy. *See* Utilitarianism
Pollution, 164
Population pressure, 171
Pragmatism, 37
Preadaptation. *See* Fitness
Predator-prey relationships, 112, 113, 222
Process Philosophy, 160
Psyche, 140-141, 201-202

**Q**

*Quale*, 199-200

**R**

Rationality, 15, 80, 166, 170; animal "reasoning," 17
Realism: biological, 181; naturalistic, 173, 194
Reason, Reasoning. *See* Rationality
Reflection, human, 123
Reincarnation, 10
Reverence for Life, *See* Schweitzer
Rights, animal. *See* Animals, rights of

Rights, human, 59, 60
Rodeo, 129-130, 210-211

**S**

Science: courses using animal subjects, 32; and humanities, 178; as prevailing modern philosophy, 32; specialization in, 168
Scientists, moral responsibility of, 34
Schweitzer, Albert, 30, 39, 215-216
Self-consciousness, 77, 121-123
Self-control, 221
Self-determination, 165
Self-enjoyment, 172
Self-fulfillment, 226
Self-interest, 166
Self-preservation, 156
Self-regulation; of systems, 112
Sheep, 29
Social Darwinism, 96
Soul, 7, 11, 12, 16, 140, 157, 171, 200; animal, question of, 15; rational, 140-141; relation to body, 15; vegetative, 12
Species, 157; boundaries of, 225; enhancement of, 156; extinction of, 147-148; metaphysics of, 202; preservation of, 67; rights of, 67, 147-148
Stewardship. *See* Animals, human responsibility toward
Struggle for existence, 82, 94, 95, 193
Suffering, 22, 179, 180, 192, 194, 195, 197, 222; animal, 2, 12, 22, 32, 56, 63, 171, 178; cure of, 192, 197; desensitization to, 21; pain, 19, 22, 57, 136, 174, 180, 194, 195
Survival: human, 221; of the fittest, 94, 150, 223

**T**

Taoism, 32
Technology, 72, 81, 164; industrial progress via, 95; problems created by, 34
Teleological anthropocentrism. *See* Anthropocentrism
Theology, God-is-dead, 195
Transcendental Ego, 176

**U**

Unity, 74, 112, 117, 123, 225; cosmological or cosmic, 31, 40, 42, 168; of living beings, 31, 104, 120
Utilitarianism, 18-19, 138-142, 143, 144, 145

**V**

Values, 145; aesthetic, 149; and consciousness, 220-222; instrumental,